ATI TEAS 6®

STUDY GUIDE 2020-2021

Academic Nursing Prep

Contents

Acknowledgements...1

About this Book 2

How to use this book 3

Exam Secrets!...4

Preparing for exams 5

About the ATI TEAS 8

Strategies 20

ATI TEAS English Language and Usage 37

ATI TEAS Math 57

ATI TEAS Reading.. 82

ATI TEAS Science 100

Practice test 190

Answers 257

Grading your ATI TEAS 301

Final Advice for ATI TEAS 302

Acknowledgements

There are many people to thank who helped me write this book, and I couldn't possibly thank them all. I feel it would be remiss not to thank one person out of the many, so I will instead, just thank every single one of you has helped along the way – you know who you are and I am eternally grateful.

About this Book

This book is a no-nonsense guide to acing your ATI TEAS. I will teach you about the different question types, how to study, how to prepare on the day, how to ace the exam on the day and get into the school of your dreams. Crucially, I will tell you all the secrets of the ATI TEAS exam that will help you to find shortcuts, answer questions quickly, and completely comprehend the nuances of the ATI TEAS.

A lot of books have excess detail and boring content, but not this one! I have cut the fluff and made a fast-paced guide ready to help you get the most out of every second. I have included all the key details you need to give you the key ingredients to acing your ATI TEAS.

I will not only teach you how to master each question type, but I will also show you how to maximize your efforts; both in studying, and in the exam room! So many students have the knowledge but underperform on the day, with my hints and tips you will get every point available to you for your knowledge.

It is best used as a study guide, read it, get the information that you need, and then study each section of questions independently. Use my useful hints and tips on effective studying (proven by research) and then, when you're ready, attempt the practice tests.

I wish you the best of luck in your studies, and hope that this book gets you into the school that you desire!

How to use this book

You can't underestimate the importance of doing well in the high-pressure high-stakes environment of test day. How well you do on the ATI TEAS will have a significant impact on your future- and I have the research and practical advice to help you execute on test day.

The book you're reading now is designed to help you avoid the most common errors test-takers frequently make.

It will show you tricks, tips and hints to answering the exam, not only having the bank of knowledge required but also managing the exam situation to your advantage, which questions to target and how to maximize your marks. It is crucial that you study this part of the book as closely as the content. It is these techniques that will change a good score into an excellent score!

I suggest going through it a number of times, as repetition is an important part of learning new information and concepts.

First, read through the study guide completely to get a feel for the content and organization. Read the general success strategies first, and then proceed to the content sections. Each tip has been carefully selected for its effectiveness.

Second, read through the study guide again, and take notes highlighting those sections where you may have a particular weakness. Then take the practice test and use it to see where you need to improve, then return to those areas.

Finally, bring the Study guide with you on test day and study it before the exam begins.

Exam Secrets!

This section is all about how best to prepare for any exam, before and after, it's worth reading: get all the details you need about preparing and how to score really well in an exam!

With any and all exams it is absolutely crucial that you prepare properly and that you have all the hints and tricks that you can have, available to you. The whole point of this book is to help you, not only learn about the ATI TEAS, about each question type and to practice the exams but also to help you get every extra mark that you can.

No time to hang about; let's look at how best to prepare for tests and exams.

Preparing for exams

I spoke to the experts and have all the details on how to prepare for exams (of any kind!). You should treat the ATI TEAS like any other normal exam and prepare for it in the ways that your teachers would have wanted you to prepare in high school! Prepare effectively in the build-up to it and you will get the score that you need. If you follow this advice you give yourself the best chance of acing your ATI TEAS, and any other exam for that matter so, as I teach you all about the rest of the exam, make sure you follow the good study habits all the way!

Without further ado, please check out my advice below.

Good Study Habits - what to do in the build-up to the exams.

1. Don't cram at the last second; try studying for 60-90 minutes per day for a week leading up to an exam. All-nighters simply don't work for most people, and students experience declining returns on their efforts when they attempt to study for four and five hours straight.

2. If you have any outstanding questions, go and get help at least three days before. You'll be able to go see somebody with an agenda if you've given yourself a mock test in advance.

3. Think about what written questions on the exam might be; outline potential essays as a form of pre-testing and practice.

4. Use the elimination process on multiple-choice questions. Cover the options first for multiple choice questions, and try answering the question on your own. Thus you will find the options for the answer less confusing. Make sure that you are aware of context, relationships and positionality between concepts, and multiple definitions of terms, as you prepare for multiple choice exams. A deep understanding of the vocabulary is a key to multiple-choice exam success.

5. Keep up with your work. If you attend class regularly, keep up with reading, and take notes conscientiously, studying can be a relatively pain-free process. Make sure to review and expand upon class notes regularly throughout the semester. Consider developing a

glossary or collection of note cards for vocabulary review in each class. Many students find that preparing for an individual class for 60-90 minutes per day, five or six days per week, will leave them well-prepared at exam time.

6. Find a group of other committed students to train with. A group study session is an ideal time for reviewing and comparing notes, asking each other questions, explaining ideas to each other, discussing the upcoming examination and difficult concepts, and delegating study tasks where appropriate. Set your group study session with an agenda and a specific timeframe, so that your work together is not off-topic.

7. Make sure you get lots of sleep. The time spent asleep is often the time when we synthesize information completely, especially the topics that are covered in the few hours before bedtime. Once you take the test you want to be as new as possible to be able to fully engage your working memory.

8. Find ways to apply class materials. Think about how course topics relate to your personal interests, societal issues and controversies, issues that have been raised in other classes, or different life experiences.

9. Develop a good routine 'morning-of' eat a good breakfast. Go ahead and play something upbeat if the music gets you going. Get some physical exercise, even if it's a brief walk or stretch. If you feel nervous, record your anxieties on paper or use mental imagery to imagine doing something you enjoy and then apply those feelings to the exam. Think of preparing for a performance like an athlete before a contest or a musician.

10. Create an assault plan. Write down the key terms or formulas you need before you continue. Think how you are going to use the allotted time.

11. If you have time at the end of the exam, go back and reread your work and look again at multiple-choice questions. Check to see that you answered every question before you take the exam. But remember, your first answer is usually the best one. Be extremely careful about changing the answers later on.

12. Do not do lots of different things while studying. Set time to study beforehand and follow through. This means leaving your room for most people and turning off visual/auditory distractions, including iPods, Facebook, and lyric music.

13. Reward yourself, please. If you've been studying conscientiously for a week or more, you should take a little time to relax before you start your studies again.

14. Carefully read out the directions.

15. Write a brief plan for the essay questions before beginning.

16. Leave to the end the most time-consuming problems, especially the ones with low point values.

17. Concentrate on the matter at hand. If you do the test one step at a time, you will find it far less likely to be overwhelming.

18. If you're stuck on a question, bypass that question. Mark the question off so at the end of the exam you can get back to it.

19. Take a moment to review your test preparation strategy. Take into account what has worked and what needs to be improved. In particular, take a moment to see if your study group was helpful.

20. Complete a mock test. Regularly answer questions on a paper without using your notes? If you complete a mock test 3-4 weeks before an exam, you'll then know where to focus your studying. Then do the same every week. You may also combat pre-test jitters by demonstrating to yourself what you know. A simple way to conduct a mock test is to ask a friend or classmate to give you an oral quiz based on concepts in the textbook or in either of your notes.

About the ATI TEAS

The TEAS is a multiple choice exam that contains four sections. The test contains 170 questions and has a three hour and 29 minute (219 minute) time limit. There are 170 total questions, but 20 of these questions are used for internal testing purposes and not scored. The TEAS subtest and time limits are:

Table 1 –TEAS subtests and time limits

Section	Time Limit	Number of Questions (Total)	Number of Questions (Scored)
Reading	64 minutes	53 questions	47 Questions
Mathematics	54 minutes	36 questions	32 Questions
Science	63 minutes	53 questions	47 Questions
English and Language Usage	28 minutes	28 questions	24 Questions
Totals	219 Minutes	170 Questions	150 Questions

I will go into much more detail for each section shortly, but before that let's discuss applying to nursing school.

Applying to Nursing School

Applying to Nursing School is not easy, over the last decade nursing school acceptance has become increasingly difficult. The call for individuals to join the ranks of registered nurses has been answered, in massive numbers.

For this reason, nursing schools have become incredibly competitive whereby perhaps in the past it was a bit simpler. Right now schools require very high GPAs, massive amounts of volunteer hours and it seems it is the hardest it has ever been to get into a Nursing School. So those of you wanting to get there need to know exactly what you should or shouldn't do to get in.

How to begin: you need to find the correct nursing program for you. There are many ways to get accepted into nursing School. First of all, you need to research multiple schools to find the school that is going to be the right fit for you. All sorts of schools now offer nursing programs including big public institutions to small private nursing schools, there are now so many options, as such, you need to find the right school for you.

So you need to find out a few things:

- Do you need lot of contact time with teachers to get help?

- Do you need to make the arrangements for your own clinical hours or does the school arrange them?

- Is it affordable?

- Can you get there?

- What learning environment is best for you?

Now, if during the research process many school are a good fit, by all means, apply to them all. There is nothing wrong with applying to multiple Nursing Schools. The more schools that you do submit an application to, then you have a greater chance of being accepted.

Another thing that you simply must do is to get lots and lots of volunteer hours or find some work within some sort of healthcare, something that will demonstrate your commitment to healthcare.

Pretty much all nursing schools now require volunteer hours. While there is no set amount required by colleges it can be anywhere from one hundred to multiple hundreds of volunteer hours.

Other things that you can do to improve your chances of becoming accepted are to become a CNA. Completing a Certified Nursing Assistant certificate and working as a CNA looks good on a resume. The certificate programs are normal just a few months and is a connection towards getting into Nursing. On top of this you need to make sure that you avoid an application or resume with grammatical or spelling errors, as these can disqualify an applicant immediately therefor the application that you submit to your chosen schools should be both accurate and complete.

The resume is the most important part of your application, it needs to be accurate, and without a lot of extra "fluff." – Like this book! Remove any track changes as this can lead the college to assume the applicant is not committed to nursing. Include any work history, volunteer hours, leadership activities and education.

Then of course, the reason that you bought this book - Take the TEAS!

The Test of Essential Academic Skill, or TEAS, is especially recommended for anyone hoping to get accepted into nursing school. While not every school may require it, a high score will make the applicant shine bright above the others. It is great opportunity for you to demonstrate your competency.

Ace the Entrance Interview

When you get to the interview, you want to demonstrate the best version of yourself, the one that fits the school, and also the nursing profession.

Make sure you have very strong nonverbal communication

It's about demonstrating confidence: standing straight, making eye contact and connecting with a firm handshake. That first nonverbal impression can be a great beginning—or quick ending—to your interview.

Dress appropriately

If you arrive and are dressed properly, looking professional, then your mindset will be in the correct place and you will give off the correct first impression.

Listen

From the very beginning of the interview, your interviewer is giving you information, either directly or indirectly. If you are not hearing it, you are missing a major opportunity. Good communication skills include listening and letting the person know you heard what was said. Observe your interviewer, and match that style and pace.

Don't talk too much

Telling the interviewer more than he needs to know could be a fatal mistake. When you have not prepared ahead of time, you may ramble when answering interview questions, sometimes talking yourself right out of the job. Prepare for the interview by reading through the job posting, matching your skills with the position's requirements and relating only that information.

Don't be too casual

The interview is a professional meeting to talk business. This is not about making a new friend. Your level of familiarity should mimic the interviewer's demeanor. It is important to bring energy and enthusiasm to the interview and to ask questions, but do not overstep your mark.

Use appropriate language

It's a given that you should use professional language during the interview. Be aware of any inappropriate slang words or references to age, race, religion, politics, or sexual orientation—these topics could send you out the door very quickly.

Don't be overconfident

Attitude plays a key role in your interview success. There is a fine balance between confidence, professionalism, and modesty. Even if you're putting on a performance to demonstrate your ability, overconfidence is as bad, if not worse, as being too reserved.

Take care to answer the actual questions you have been asked

When interviewers ask for an example of a time when you did something, they are asking behavioral interview questions, which are designed to elicit a sample of your past behavior. If you fail to relate a specific example, you not only don't answer the question, but you also miss an opportunity to prove your ability and talk about your skills. Therefore, have an answer lined up that you can use for expected questions.

Ask them some questions

When asked if they have any questions, most candidates answer, "No." Wrong answer. Part of knowing how to interview is being ready to ask questions that demonstrate an interest in what goes on in the company. Asking questions also gives you the opportunity to find out if this is the right place for you. The best questions come from listening to what you're asked during the interview and asking for additional information.

Don't appear needy

When you interview with the "please, please accept me" approach, you appear desperate and less confident. Reflect the three Cs during the interview: cool, calm, and confident.

Work on your answers

You know you can do well as a nurse, and throughout school; make sure the interviewer believes you can, too. One way to do this is by preparing well-thought-out answers to questions they're most likely to ask. Need some help with that?

Interview Questions for a Nursing Applicant May Include:

- Why do you want to be a nurse?
- How much time are you able to dedicate to studying and clinical hours?
- Describe a situation where you felt challenged
- What was your favorite prerequisite class and why?
- Can you discuss some hot nursing topics?

While getting accepted into nursing school can be difficult the rewards you get from doing so and from working hard in the process will inevitably be worth it. Even if it takes a few tries, continually improving the nursing school application and being persistent will eventually help you gain acceptance into nursing school.

How to register for the exam

1. Registration for a TEAS test closes when the test is full or 24 hours before the scheduled test start time. Don't wait until the last minute. Make sure you book your test well in advance. If a test is full, it will either disappear from the test options on the ATI website, or it will be marked "Sold Out".

2. Go to www.atitesting.com.

3. Create an account if you don't already have one.

    a. Click "Create an Account" in the box on the right of the screen. You will need an email address to create an account. Creating an account is free and is necessary to search test dates and register. You will also use this account when using ATI materials throughout your nursing program.

    b. Follow the directions to create your account with ATI.

    c. Select your Institution.

4. Write down your username and password that you create. They are needed to login to take the test.

5. You may register for a test immediately after creating your account or log back in later to register for a test.

6. If you are registering later, you must log in first to see the available test dates. Click "Online Store" at the top, then "Register for TEAS" in the sidebar to the left.

7. From the drop-down menu you will choose the Program Type, (TEAS for Nursing Students) the Country, State, then City, then "Next". Click on "Learn More" for specific information on that test. Click "Register" when you are ready to register for the test.

Note: "3 TEAS test attempts per year" means per admission cycle, NOT per calendar-year. In other words, a student may not test 3 times in a fall semester, then another 3 times in the spring semester of the same school year. Even though the calendar year changes, that still adds up to six test attempts in one admission cycle! Prepare well and plan to meet your goal the first time.

8. You will need a credit (or debit) card to pay for the test online. If you do not have a card, you may purchase a pre-paid credit card at any store that sells gift cards. The fee for the test is $71. Some students have reported being charged tax.

9. If you register for one test date and site, but change your mind before paying, remember to delete the one you decided against or your credit card will be charged for both.

10. The site does not automatically charge your card. You must select "Check Out". You will receive a confirmation email that your payment was received.

11. Your government-issued photo ID is required when you sign-in to take the test.

Is nursing the right move for you?

Before you begin down this route of studying and working hard for the TEAS, you need to be certain that the TEAS is for you. I have some key thoughts from qualified nurses to offer their thoughts as to what they wish they were told beforehand, and here they are:

1. How much critical thinking nurses do

This skill is so important that Department of Labor lists both inductive and deductive reasoning in the top five abilities RNs need for the job.

2. You can find day shifts—even as a new nurse

Though specific hiring situations will vary depending on location, there is no rule against new nurses finding their ideal shifts.

3. Hospital jobs are competitive

While some nurses might find work immediately in a hospital setting, others will need to broaden their searches.

When you are a brand new graduate, keep your mind open to all kinds of jobs to gain the experience that will give you more opportunity.

4. Witnessing patient suffering is never easy

Even if you've never felt squeamish at the sight of blood or injuries, seeing people in pain can be much less clinical than you think.

Consider your specialty with care, and give some thought to how you will react when your patients are hurting or dealing with grief. Certain types of nurses will deal with more severe health issues on their shifts than others.

5. How busy your shifts will get

Though you might have shifts where even wolfing down a granola bar feels like a luxury, the intrinsic value in caring for people makes the chaos worth it.

6. How attached you'll get to your patients

Despite all the dashing about, nurses still find time to grow fond of the people they care for.

7. How to save your legs

Nurses spend so much time on their feet that it's vital to make smart clothing choices.

It may seem like a small thing, but take it to heart and make comfort a priority when choosing footwear—your body will thank you.

8. That nurses can be mean to other nurses

Make sure you understand your rights as a professional, and don't put up with workplace abuse. New nurses naturally want to make a good impression and get along in their first jobs, but certain behaviors are never okay.

9. How easy it is to forget yourself

This sacrificial attitude is one of the greatest strengths of the nursing profession, but it can also be a detriment.

10. How many ways there are to be a nurse

As you begin your career, you might envision one path for yourself, but your skills and desires can lead you in different directions as you go. Nurses work in many different industries and settings.

Are you ready to become a Nurse?

Now that you know more about what becoming a Nurse is really like, do you think it's the job for you?

Not everyone has what it takes to be a nurse. But if you can handle it, you'll be rewarded by a career that truly makes a difference.

TEAS– Detailed Subtest Breakdown

TEAS Reading

The TEAS Reading subtest consists of 53 total questions (47 scored) and has a 64-minute time limit. The Reading subtest is intended to assess a candidate's reading comprehension.The test questions typically consist of a paragraph and multiparagraph passage and accompanying questions. You will be asked to interpret charts, graphs, maps, labels, measuring tools, and directions. The following objectives may be tested:

- Identify author's intent
- Identify themes, main ideas, and supporting details
- Differentiate opinion from fact
- Draw conclusions and make inferences
- Identify structure and text features
- Define Vocabulary
- Follow a set of directions
- Interpret graphic representations of information

- Determine where information may be found from an index of table of contents

TEAS Math

The TEAS Math subtest consists of 36 total questions (32 scored) and has a 54-minute time limit. A candidate's knowledge of algebra, data interpretation, numbers and operations, and measurement are assessed. The TEAS test will assess some of the following objectives:

- Convert between decimals, fractions and percentages
- Add and divide fractions and mixed numbers
- Solve math problems containing ratios, proportions and rate of change
- Convert between Roman and Arabic numbers
- Solve equations with one unknown variable
- Solve equations and inequalities containing absolute values
- Organize and interpret data from tables, graphs and charts
- Convert measurements
- Estimate metric quantities
- Measure the dimensions, weight and volume of objects

TEAS Science

The TEAS Science subtest consists of 53 total questions (47 scored) and has a 63-minute time limit. Candidates often find this section to be one of the most challenging. The TEAS Science subtest assesses a student's knowledge of scientific reasoning, life science, the human body, and physical and earth science. Candidates will be expected to demonstrate the following skills:

- Describe the functions of the following systems: circulatory, nervous, digestive, respiratory and immune systems.
- Describe general anatomy and physiology concepts

- Understand natural selection and adaptation

- Interpret the biological classification system

- Understand the parts of a cell and its corresponding functions

- Understand DNA and RNA

- Contrast respiration and photosynthesis

- Contrast meiosis and mitosis

- Utilize taxonomy

- Use Mendel's laws of genetics and the Punnett square

- Apply the periodic table of elements

- Describe the properties of atoms

- Determine the properties of matter

- Calculate diffusion rates and molarity

- Interpret pH scale values

- Determine force and motion

- Describe the parts of an experiment

- Interpret scientific arguments

TEAS English and Language Usage

The TEAS English and Language Usage subtest consists of 28 total questions (24 scored) and has a 28-minute time limit. This subtest covers the areas of grammar, sentence structure, punctuation, spelling and contextual words. The TEAS English test will assess a student's ability to perform the following skills:

- Interpret subject verb agreement rules

- Determine the meaning of words form their context in a sentence

- Identify and use various parts of speech including: possessives, pronouns, verbs, adverbs, and adjectives

- Use verb tenses accurately

- Determine the correct spelling of: irregular plurals, compound or hyphenated words, and frequently misspelled words

- Identify the correct capitalizations of names, titles, and addresses

- Differentiate between simple, compound, and complex sentences

- Identify the correct punctuation of sentences

- Change from passive to active voice

- General English ability

It is super important that if you think that you can walk in and be successful on the TEAS exam without studying and working hard, you cannot! The ATI recommends giving yourself six weeks to study for this important test.

Strategies

I will go through each subsection independently but there are some general strategies you should apply throughout preparation for your ATI TEAS.

General ATI TEAS Testing Strategies

The following are the general strategies for making sure that your overall performance on the ATI TEAS is good. These tips and strategies can be applied to all sections in the ATI TEAS.

Don't cram - The ATI TEAS tests you on knowledge you've accumulated over the course of your high school career, so there's no point in cramming. The day before the test, take it easy, watch a movie and then get a good night's sleep. Staying up the night before the test and studying will only stress you out and cause you to be tired the next day hence having a negative impact on performance.

Familiarize yourself with the test - Become familiar with the layout and format of the ATI TEAS before the actual day on which you sit it. During your test prep, learn and review the directions for each of the sections on the test. When you arrive, be prepared for what will arise in each section of the ATI TEAS. This will save valuable time during the test which can be spent working on questions.

Answer as many easy questions as you can; First - Answer the questions you're sure you know the correct answer to first. Go through the exam book, put a mark next to each question you skip so you can quickly find them later. After you've done the easy ones, go back and take on the more difficult questions.

Write in your test booklet; The ATI TEAS test booklet is yours. After the test it will be thrown in the trash. This means you should not worry about making sure it remains in mint condition. Use it. Write in it, cross out wrong answers and use it to do scratch work. Work out issues and jot down key information you'll need to answer certain questions, this is really useful for when you're struggling.

Don't, however, write on your answer sheet - your ATI TEAS answer sheet is scored by a computer. This computer is not able to tell the difference between a correct answer, a stray mark, or a sketch in the margin. Make sure that your answer sheet is marked correctly, neatly and free of any stray marks. Follow the directions given carefully as you mark correct answers on your answer sheet.

There is only one correct answer. On the ATI TEAS, there is only one correct answer to each question. Even if it appears as if there are two correct answers, you can only choose one answer – so select the best answer to each question. With this in mind, be wary of red herrings, sent to catch you out.

Easy questions tend to come before hard ones. This means that the ATI TEAS gets harder as you go. Keep this in mind as you move through the test answering easy questions first and then return to answer more difficult questions.

Guess. If you're faced with a hard question and you don't know the correct answer, just make an educated guess. Try to delete as many answer choices as you can, particularly if they're obviously incorrect and then select the answer that makes the most sense. There are no marks lost for wrong answers therefore it is always worth putting an answer down.

Be careful with your time. You must make sure that you do not spend lots of time on any one question. There is a time limit for completing the test, and it is easy to get held up in one question and therefore not even be able to access some easy questions. It is best to limit yourself to a set amount of time per question, with a small addition for harder questions, and a subtraction for easier ones. If you run out of this time on the question, skip it. There are easy marks on the paper and you don't want to miss them through being stuck in one question. The ATI TEAS consists of 4-5 small mini-tests that are timed. Pay close attention to how much time remains in each section, so you will not have to rush at the last minute to complete each test. Bring a watch or stopwatch that you can use for this on the test day, and use the same device when practicing.

Read each question very carefully. Until you have read a question in its entirety do not assume you know what it is asking. Sometimes students will give an answer they recall from a similar question from a practice test. Read the words to each question carefully.

Don't change your answers unless you're sure you made an error. Most of the time you would be better off sticking with your first choice.

Finally, do lots of practice. With any exam; practice is key!

English Section Strategies

The English section has passages which are followed by a selection of multiple-choice questions. These questions are designed to test your reading comprehension and may ask about specific content (sentences, phrases, concepts, etc.) covered in each passage. Several questions will test Usage and Mechanics (including grammar, sentence structure, punctuation and usage). Other questions will test Rhetorical Skills (organization, strategy, and style). You'll receive a score for your performance in each of these two categories.

Punctuation (10-15%) which will test your understanding of internal and end-of sentence grammatical conventions. Grammar and Usage (15-20%) tests your understanding of basic grammar rules. Sentence Structure (20-25%) tests your understanding of the relationship between clauses in order to link clauses and form sentences. The Strategy section (15-20%) is designed to test your ability to choose correct words and phrases within the context of an essay or passage. Organization questions (10-15%) test your ability to organize ideas and choose correct sentence structures within the context of a passage or essay. Style questions (15-20%) will test your ability to select the most appropriate words and sentence structures to maintain or support the style and tone of an essay.

On Punctuation questions you should read, review and consider the entire sentence, even if the question is asking you to focus on just a subset of the sentence. When answering ATI TEAS English questions, never focus on just part of the sentence. You must make sure your answer makes sense within the context of the entire sentence and passage.

When answering Grammar questions, read each question, and read it very carefully to be sure that you don't make mistakes. It's easy to select the wrong answer, even when you understand the concept, if you don't read the question carefully and understand what is being requested.

For Organization questions, find the choice that makes the most sense when put in front the first sentence of the passage.

For Strategy questions think about the whole thing and decide whether a suggested change makes it clearer or not.

When answering Sentence Structure questions, look at the sentence as a complete sentence and then decide if an answer choice offers the most natural and clear relationship.

To answer Style questions correctly you need to understand the meaning and tone.

Pay attention to the style of the writing. The correct answer will suit the individual author's style than other choices.

Carefully examine each answer option to see how they differ from one another.

If "No change" is a possible answer, only choose it if other options are wrong. This can be a dangerous choice if you aren't familiar with obscure grammar rules. Double check all other answers before selecting "no change". (Note: The "no change" answer is the correct answer about 25-30% of the time so please don't ignore it, it is a genuine choice that should be taken into account).

When given a selection of answers to choose from, try and insert each of the options into the sentence to see which one fits the best.

In questions with underlined text, check all the sentences around it to figure out how these sentences relate to the underlined section. Then, compare the answer you've selected with the underlined text.

Reading Section Strategies

Prose Fiction and Literary Narrative passages contain excerpts from literary and fiction texts. This section will ask you questions about the main theme of the passage, the narrator's tone and intent, the message of the passage, and which questions are or are not answered in the passage.

Social Science passages typically offer a straightforward discussion of social science topics, including sociology, education, and psychology, among others. You'll get questions about the main point of the passage, the author's view, and how information presented supports the subject of the passage.

Humanities passages often come from personal essays and memoirs, and address subjects such as literature, art, philosophy, or media. You'll likely be asked questions about the tone of the passage and point of view of the narrator.

Natural Science passages are nonfiction passages about science. They will cover all sorts of subjects, including biology, chemistry, technology, physics, or medicine. Questions often focus on specifics which must be supported by the text. This seems like a lot of content and enough to strike fear into students, but worry not; with the correct strategies you will be fine.

You need to focus on crucial information to answer each question as you read the passage. To do so: read the question first! - before you read the text.

Be very careful when you read the text. Focus on the main points of the passage and try not to get distracted by the details - as you may not need the detail that distracts you, when you come to the final answer.

Eliminate incorrect answer choices. All incorrect answers have incorrect options that you could choose. If you can pick out and remove all of the incorrect options, you will be left with the correct option. Which sounds simple!

Employ a 3-stage method (previewing, reading and reviewing) to improve your comprehension and understanding of each passage. As you read each passage, focus on the big ideas.

Take short notes as you read each paragraph focusing on the purpose of the passage. Keep track of the various people and opinions within the text, and refer to your notes when answering.

Frequently check back with the passage when determining correct answers. Make sure your answer is supported by the text.

Mathematics Sections Strategies

The mathematics section of the ATI TEAS is designed to test the math skills and knowledge you've acquired over your time in high school. There are eight content categories covered in the ATI TEAS mathematics test. These include Number & Quantity, Algebra, Functions, Geometry and Statistics & Probability.

It is advisable in this section to work out the answer before looking at the answers available to you. If none of the answer options match yours, redo the problem.

Calculators are usually only useful to compute figures. Do not rely too heavily on a calculator during the math section since you will have to work problems out to effectively solve them. If you don't understand how to approach a problem or use formulas a calculator won't be much help.

When possible, make a prediction as to what you believe the answer will be. If the final answer is completely different from your prediction, redo the problem, you may have made an error.

Once you have gotten to the answer, move on to the next problem. You have less than 60 seconds to answer each question. Always double check your calculations. When you rush it is easy to make mistakes.

The general instructions are fairly long. Read these instructions and become familiar with them the day before the test. Don't waste time reading these instructions on the day of the test.

Use the same method to approach every ATI TEAS math question. (1) Read the question. (2) Review the information provided in the question and the answer options. (3) Solve the question by back solving, picking numbers, using traditional math, or strategically guessing. (4) Make sure you answered the specific question being asked. To save time, back solve when you can. Back solving problems works when you see integers in the answer choices.

As you reach each question, translate the words into math and make notes as you go. It is much easier to see it written in math than in lots of wordy problems. This way you can more easily identify and solve the problem. Don't forget that "of" indicates multiplication is required.

Go back through your high school math and study number properties (odd, even, prime, and order of operation), triangles (30-60-90 and 45-45-90 rules, Pythagorean triplets 3:4:5, 5:12:13 and their multiples), common shapes and math relationships (values, ratios, and percent).

Watch out for "trap" answers. These include answers that are way off the mark, and clearly incorrect. Identifying trap answers will help you narrow your selection of answer options, if you can remove a few from a question your chances of getting it correct have vastly improved.

Science Section Strategies

The Science section will be made from seven passages that cover various scientific topics. Passages often contain charts, graphs, scientific opinions, or experiment summaries. Each of the seven passages is followed by up to seven questions. The key to doing well on the Science section of the ATI TEAS is being able to quickly and accurately read and comprehend scientific findings, postulates and data.

While the Science section of the ATI TEAS will test your knowledge, it is designed specifically to test science skills. These skills are the sort of skills you learn in high school. Hopefully you will already have a high school understanding of biology, physical science and earth science. The important thing is that by the time you graduate you understand how to apply the scientific method, collect and analyze data, and evaluate and test a hypothesis. These are the general areas that the science section will test you on, so make sure you are confident with them.

Since science problems are usually complicated, write notes in the booklet's margins while reading a passage. Then you can refer back to these when you need to do so.

Don't get distracted by unnecessary details. Some students find it easier to cross out unnecessary details when reading a passage. You can get put off by technical details and terminology. Even if these details or terms are confusing, you can still figure out the right answer. In most cases, technical terms and details won't have an impact on the final answer but have been put there to form a distraction.

Keep an eye out for contradicting details in science passages. Doing so can help you locate the correct answer. The science section is tough, often thought of as the hardest. There is a lot of required knowledge, you will find that the science section of this book is therefore quite content heavy in comparison to the rest.

Psychology in examinations

This section will help you prepare for all exams, how to manage stress levels and not freak out in the exam hall.

If you're one of the many people who gets stressed out when it comes to taking exams, then I have a few tips for you that will help you to overcome this and really concentrate on achieving good grades.

Stress Management

Firstly, look after your health. It's too easy to cram so much information into your brain and also try to get on with the rest of your life. You'll end up burning the candle at both ends, so to speak, and this can seriously damage your health.

Looking after your health means that you should be getting adequate rest. Eat and drink sensibly and in moderation, exercise your body and spend quality time on yourself.

Studying at every available opportunity can lead to information overload. Make yourself a program and stick to it as much as possible. Studying for 20 minutes at a time, followed by a 'reflection period' on what you have learned and then a 10-minute break - is ideal for optimum learning. We all have a shorter attention span than we think, so use this logic to maximize the attention that you have.

Make your learning fun. If you have someone to study with then use the opportunity to test each other on what you've learned so far, when you're away from your books. Forming a study group can really help with this.

If you find your mind begins to wander during your work, then there's no point in continuing at this time with your learning because your brain won't absorb the information as easily as it would if you were at your peak. Take a break, then return.

Practice relaxation exercises. Meditation is an excellent way to control your mindset in an exam. There are lots of free apps that can help you with some basic relaxation techniques if you find that you get stressed.

Do one thing at a time. Decide which topic you're going to study and don't change it. If you get interrupted, put the interruption to one side until you're ready to deal with it.

Day of the exam

It's always useful to have a routine and fall backs for the day of the exam, if you're well prepared and feeling comfortable then you are in the right place to do well!

Physical Strategies

Sleep: Get enough sleep the night before the exam. If you're foggy because of a lack of sleep, you will not be able to perform at your best. Sleep a few extra hours instead of studying a few extra hours.

Food: Eat moderately before your exams; avoid a heavy meal. If you eat too much, your brain will spend energy on the digestion of the food. On the other hand, if you skip a meal altogether, your brain will have inadequate fuel to function well. Aim for nutritional balance and moderation, if you practice this in advance, for practice tests and the like, then you will be prepared.

Alcohol: An easy mistake to make, but obvious, don't drink the night before your exam. Alcohol upsets the chemical balance in your body and affects the way your brain functions. It could also give you a hangover, which would be a real nuisance on exam day!

Drinks: With this in mind also avoid drinking diuretics that contain caffeine such as coffee, tea or cola, which could make you need to use the washroom more often, you want to make the most of all the time you have.

Water: Your body and your brain need water. Research has proven that your brain performs more efficiently when well-hydrated. Drink enough water, but not so much that you need to use the bathroom.

Temperature: The aim is to be as comfortable as possible during your exam so that you are not distracted. Take a sweater or jacket along in case of excessive air-conditioning or lack of sufficient heating. Choose a seat near a window for fresh air, if possible, but also avoid the window if there is a lot of noise outside. Arriving early may allow you to select the seat you feel most comfortable in.

Breathing: Deep breathing involves breathing slowly and deeply. Start by inhaling through your nose. You will find this to be relaxing. Try to make sure your chest isn't rising and falling, rather; expand your belly with each breath, while your chest remains still. Try to reach a count of 6 on each in breath, and 6 on each out breath. When you have mastered this process, you can add a pause of 6 seconds between the inhaling and exhaling breath.

Brain Gym techniques are worth looking at: This program of simple exercises can enhance learning and performance by improving the brain's neural pathways. Students of all ages have achieved higher test scores after engaging in a short brain gym session. Learn more about these simple techniques and give yourself an edge.

Psychological Techniques

Positive Visualization: This is a powerful psychological technique that can be used to enhance your positive feelings and diminish the negative ones. It is based on the fact that the mind and body are powerfully interconnected. You can create changes in your heart rate, skin temperature, and brainwave patterns by the thoughts you have. You can use this information to your advantage before and during your ATI TEAS. Imagine yourself doing really well; see yourself getting the score you need for your college, recalling the information easily and remaining calm and in control.

Handling Anxiety: Practice deep breathing techniques if you find yourself becoming nervous or overwhelmed. By breathing correctly, you can give your brain fuel to help it perform better.

Arrive early: This will help you avoid unnecessary stress in the immediate period before your exam. Allow for traffic, check the weather reports for exam day, or even travel to an external exam location in advance to get an idea of how long it will take you to travel there on the day of the exam.

Avoid other nervous test takers: While waiting for the exam to begin, avoid speaking to any nervous students and taking on their negative energy. If you can: remain confident and focused on doing well on the exam.

Bring necessary materials: Keep extra materials such as pens, pencils, calculators, rulers, or compasses packed and ready the night before the exam so you have time to locate or even purchase any misplaced or lost items. Knowing you have everything you need will make you feel calmer and well-prepared.

Mental Strategies for the day of the exam

Review output: If you have some time before the exam, use it to review material and practice your output. Don't try to learn new material at this stage.

Stay for the entire exam: Stay for the full length of the exam. Even if you feel you cannot recall any more, by relaxing or waiting in the exam hall, information and details might come to mind and enable you to score additional points. On exams, every point counts.

Make sure you focus on reading the instructions really carefully, preferably in advance. This is the most common avoidable mistake made by students. Don't let it happen to you. It's also worth knowing what the instructions for each section will be, in advance, that way you don't need to read them in detail and waste time on the exam day.

Read each question: Really read what you are being asked to do on each question. Don't presume it's the angle you're familiar with. Go back through it to see what you're actually being asked and remember that exams change all the time, so questions that appeared in the past may differ from those given in the present.

Focus on you: Don't look around at how other students are doing. For one thing it may appear that you're trying to cheat. If nothing else, it will distract you from your main task which is to do as well as possible on your exams.

Budget your time: Check how much each question counts towards your final mark and spend time on each answer accordingly. If you have a choice to write your answers in any order, do the easy ones first to build up your confidence.

How to take the ATI TEAS?

The following section is a summary of how to perform at your very best on the at of the ATI TEAS.

Much like any sporting event, an exam is a single day's performance that can vary, depending on a multitude of factors. As such the following will help you maximize your performance on the day.

Your ATI TEAS test day should be viewed in four sections:

- Before you leave your house

- At the test center

- During the test

- After the test

Before you leave your house on ATI TEAS test day

1. First of all, be sure to finish your studying for the test the night before you take it.

When you wake up in the morning, you don't want to have to worry about something you don't understand. Get all of your studying done in plenty of time, if you aren't sure about something on the day, leave it. The stress of panicking to study last minute will outweigh the gain. If there are any formulas or last minute tips that you want to be sure you're able to remember, write these down on a piece of paper that you can bring with you and look at on your way to the testing center—but remember, you cannot use this piece of paper during the exam.

2. Be sure to get plenty of sleep the night before you take the ATI TEAS.

Try to get at least eight hours of sleep, and be sure to factor in the time that it might take you to fall asleep and the time you might lose as a result of nervousness over the exam. Nobody performs at their best when they are exhausted, so do what you can to avoid being in that exact situation.

3. If you're particularly worried about being well-rested enough for the exam, it can help to plan out how early you will need to wake up and then count your sleep-cycles backwards so that you will wake up feeling refreshed. There are plenty of apps that will help you with this if you want to. Google is your friend here. Make sure, if you do decide to plot your sleep schedule: that you get started with it weeks if not months before the ATI TEAS so you are familiar with the app, and with the whole process.

4. Plan out your clothes the night before the exam.

It should be something comfortable. It should also be something professional. Showing up in a professional outfit will make you feel more prepared to take the test. Get it ready the night before the exam so that you can just wake up and get dressed first thing in the morning. Take a shower if you usually do or if it helps you get started with your day. Also be sure to pack a bag filled with everything that you need. This way in the morning, you have much less distractions.

5. With this in mind: Make sure that you stick to your morning routine the morning of the test so that your brain isn't busy making decisions. You should be walking into the testing center with a fresh mind. It also might be helpful to read something light and easy beforehand to get your brain warmed up a little bit. It is important to stress the light and easy bit. You wouldn't sprint 100 yards before running a marathon race, but you may go for a short jog to get the blood flowing - it's the same logic here.

6. For some students, it is helpful to have a ritual.

Before a big test, you might want to think of something specific that you could do for good luck, such as wearing a favorite pair of socks to the testing center, listening to your favorite song, or saying a special mantra before taking the exam. While this "good luck charm" doesn't have anything to do with the actual test, it can be nice to do something special that will make you feel comfortable and boost your confidence. Many athletes and successful business people follow this exact routine, so why not you!

At the testing center

7. Arrive at the testing center early and go to the bathroom, even if you don't think you need to!

You don't want to have to rush to the testing center in case there is traffic, and you also don't want to be distracted while taking the exam because you need to use the bathroom. It will be helpful to use the bathroom before the exam, so if you do need to go during a break, you will know where it is and the fastest way to get to it.

8. If you have last-minute questions, consult your sheet on which you wrote down last minute tips.

Don't strain yourself too much trying to memorize, you already know your stuff, and if you don't, now is not the time, all you will achieve is getting more stressed. Rather than scrambling to take in information at the last minute, it is more important that you get in the right mindset to take the test and remain calm and composed. This will be far more beneficial than the alternative.

During the test

9. Stay Calm. Practice the breathing techniques discussed earlier.

10. Bring a cold bottle of water with you—while you can't actually eat or drink anything while you're taking the exam, you can drink and snack during breaks.

Staying hydrated will avoid tiredness which is often a result of dehydration. Don't drink too much water, though, because you don't want to have to use the bathroom in the middle of the exam!

11. Utilize your breaks during the exam efficiently.

Move around so that your body and mind can sustain themselves for the next section of the exam, stretch, go to the bathroom, look out the window, or eat a snack!

After the test

12. When you are done taking the ATI TEAS, write down any areas of difficulty that you encountered.

Even though you will get a detailed score report that will tell you the areas on which you did well on and which ones you might need to improve, it's also useful to go through a stage of reflection. You can later compare this to your actual scores. This will also be helpful in case you want to study for the test again before you even get your score report back.

13. Once you finish the exam, go outside and do something fun.

Relax and forget about the test. Take the rest of the day off. Do something that you enjoy doing. You'll certainly have time to think more about it later (especially when you receive your score report). For now, it is most important that you have fun, remain balanced, and congratulate yourself on getting through a long, hard testing day.

Guessing/Process of elimination

Although content mastery is the best way to get a great ATI TEAS score, there are key testing strategies that perfect-scorers use to tilt the odds in their favor. Some of these strategies are secret, and others are well-known. But, one of the oldest and most dependable testing strategies of all time, is the process of elimination.

The process of elimination is a classic strategy that should and will be used on standardized tests and multiple-choice quizzes for the rest of time.

On the ATI TEAS, proper use of the process of elimination starts before you start crossing answers off.

By which, I mean that you should answer the question before you begin using elimination, for maximum effectiveness. Otherwise you'll just be eliminating answer choices based on your "feelings." Experience proves that this is risky, and will cost you points on the ATI TEAS.

So, before you attempt to eliminate, start by answering the question don't forget to write it down, too.

Now, as you move onto the elimination phase, it's important to ignore your gut instinct. What you should do is to find the errors that mean that you can eliminate an answer choice.

If you just eliminate an answer choice because you "don't feel like it's this one," then you might as well be guessing. The process of elimination is not guesswork; it is removal of known incorrect answers.

Remember that any error, no matter how minor, makes the whole answer choice wrong! As you develop your skills of elimination, you will learn to notice the errors hidden in each answer choice. Once you start noticing these, you really won't be able stop noticing them!

It takes practice and time to reach this point where you can spot the errors easily. The key is in being accurate but still finishing on time.

Note: As a strategy, the process of elimination is less effective on Math questions. Although there is a use for elimination on Math, it's better to just do the question. Techniques you learn from your math teacher or tutor would be the most effective, and the fastest.

So, instead of trying to forcibly eliminate your way to correct Math answers, study your ATI TEAS Math skills. Save the heavy-duty usage of the process of elimination for the other sections.

The process of elimination works well on the ATI TEAS because they are designed to trick you. This is most true in the verbal sections, particularly the Reading sections of the ATI TEAS

In the Verbal sections, the ATI TEAS deliberately uses words to trick and deceive you. Fake answer choices are carefully crafted with deceptive keywords. Many times, the wrong answer is actually true - it's just irrelevant.

As I said in the beginning of this book, the ATI TEAS is different to most other tests you take in high school. Most of your teachers in high school classes don't want to trick you, they just want to test you. But, the ATI TEAS does want to do exactly this!

Mistakes that you can make with the process of elimination:

- Trying to eliminate before you Pre-Answer.

- Not writing down your final answer.

- Finding that your final answer seems flawed but sticking with it regardless.

- Not eliminating all choices going with a gut instinct before the process of elimination is completely finished.

- Spending unnecessary time using Elimination due to lack of practice.

- Using the process of elimination too much in math sections - it's much better to just know how the math problem is supposed to work.

- Elimination is a fantastic strategy for higher ATI TEAS scores, but it has downsides as well. You must understand the strengths and weaknesses of the elimination strategy through hours of practice.

- Every powerful technique has corresponding limitations. The only way to confidently work past those barriers is to gain experience through mindful practice. Understand this as you practice elimination on the ATI TEAS tests.

Summary

Of course, the above strategies really help you in the ATI TEAS. They will improve the score that you will get. However, it is also incredibly important that you prepare for each section of the ATI TEAS properly as well. The above strategies will only support a detailed study program, not replace it.

ATI TEAS English Language and Usage

ATI TEAS English - An overview of the ATI TEAS English section

The ATI TEAS English has 28 questions that must be answered within the 28-minute time limit. In this chapter I will give you an overview of the content you will face, alongside some very useful hints and tips.

Vocabulary Acquisition

We've all encountered vocabulary words at some point during our education. Because of this, I know that you'll comprehend what is important about vocabulary acquisition: being able to recognize words and define them accurately. How you will conclude the right definitions will vary from question to question. Sometimes you will have to rely on your knowledge of root words, prefixes, and suffixes in order to figure out a definition. Other times, you will have to discern the definition based on how the word is used within the work. Regardless, the format of these questions is a bit different from what you may have come to expect from your standard vocabulary question.

First, you must recognize and comprehend that memorization is not the objective for this category. Simply cramming a list of words into your head won't ensure your success. Instead, you will have to read critically to come to the best possible answer. While some outside knowledge of vocabulary will help, especially in the realm of using root words to figure out a definition, there are other ways you can prepare that will prove just as useful. You'll want to be sure to brush up on your critical reading skills, particularly when it comes to analyzing the definitions of words.

Knowledge of Language

Knowing how to compose and organize your thoughts is a major part of communication and the English language. As such, the Knowledge of Language category of the English and Language Usage subtest assesses you on your ability to recognize and analyze how different pieces of writing are structured and framed in order to deliver their points. You will have to utilize multiple skills to do this. Some questions will require you to read a paragraph and discern how to best add onto or edit it in order to improve its development and organization. Others will ask you to draw from your knowledge of the most rudimentary aspects of writing, decide whether a work's tone is casual or formal, or tweak a sentence to improve its clearness. The Knowledge of Language category spans for approximately nine questions.

Answering questions under this category will again involve close and careful reading. As you read various selections and passages during your study periods, be sure to think about how the authors across use language. What is their tone? What about its structure? Does it make sense? How could it be improved? Were there any parts that confused you and how could they be reworked so they're easier to understand? This is the best mindset to have as you approach Knowledge of Language questions.

Conventions of Standard English

The third and final knowledge category of the English and Language Usage subtest, Conventions of Standard English, is just as long as the Knowledge of Language category: nine questions. It deals with the grammatical aspects of English and, as such, will assess your knowledge of the multiple ways to organize a sentence as well as punctuation and spelling.

The trick to doing well on questions under this category is to pay close and careful attention to every question. It can be incredibly easy to miss an error if you don't take the time to slow down and read carefully, which could cause you to miss out on valuable points. Whether grammar and spelling is your best subject or not one of your strong suits, it also won't hurt you to brush up on the conventions of either.

ATI TEAS English Test Question Types

Table 1- English language questions

Skills/Content Tested	Examples
Punctuation	commas, apostrophes, colons, semicolons, dashes, periods, question marks, and exclamation points

Grammar & Usage	subject-verb agreement, pronoun agreement, pronoun forms and cases, adjectives, adverbs, verb forms, comparative and superlative modifiers, and idioms
Sentence Structure	subordinate or dependent clauses, run-on or fused sentences, comma splices, sentence fragments, misplaced modifiers, shifts in verb tense or voice, and shifts in pronoun person or number
Strategy	adding, revising, or deleting sentences; how a sentence fits with the purpose, audience, and focus of a paragraph or the essay as a whole
Organization	opening, transitional, and closing phrases or statements; order and focus of sentences or paragraphs
Style	writing style, tone, clarity, and effectiveness; eliminating ambiguity, wordiness, and redundant material; clarifying vague or awkward material

The ATI TEAS English tests a variety of writing skills from fundamental grammar to effective written communication. This test section involves five passages which will all contain some mistakes, and lots of them. The ATI TEAS English test asks the person taking the test to edit the documents, as appropriate.

The ATI TEAS English test covers the full range of editorial skills in a multiple-choice format, but does not require students to know technical grammatical terms, instead ATI TEAS uses Reporting Categories to provide a more granular analysis of performance. ATI TEAS English Reporting Categories detail what students are tested on in this section:

Conventions of Standard English questions measure understanding of the conventions of Standard English grammar, usage, and mechanics. This reporting category focuses on Usage, Punctuation, and Sentence Structure and Formation.

Production of Writing questions measure understanding of the purpose and focus of a piece of writing. This reporting category focuses on Topic Development and Organization, Unity, and Cohesion.

Knowledge of Language questions focus on the use of word choice to make a passage more precise or concise, or to improve syntax, style, or tone.

Because this section is timed, the ATI TEAS English section also tests your ability to read quickly and general test taking skills as mentioned earlier in the book.

Sample ATI TEAS English Test Questions

To give you a better feel for the format and content of the ATI TEAS English test, below there are some sample test questions that you may face:

Determine which answer choice is the best version of the underlined portion of the sentence. If the original is the best version, select "NO CHANGE."

Fitzgerald attended <u>St. Paul Academy; his first</u> published story ran in his school newspaper.

   A. NO CHANGE

   B. St. Paul Academy; his first

   C. St. Paul Academy, his first

   D. St. Paul Academy, but his first

Answer: This question tests a student's knowledge of run-on sentences and punctuation rules. The original sentence fuses two independent clauses without proper punctuation. Due to the fact that there is an error in the original version of the underlined portion of the sentence, we can eliminate choice A. Choice C creates a new error: a comma splice. Two independent clauses cannot be connected by just a comma. Though choice D corrects the run-on sentence error, the addition of the conjunction "but," which implies a contrast, does not fit within the context of the sentence. Choice B, which connects the two independent clauses with a semicolon, correctly fixes the run-on sentence error without creating new errors. Thus, choice B is the correct answer.

Rhetorical Skills Question

Though many high-ranking government and military officials anticipated the possibility of war with Japan, the attack on Pearl Harbor came as a shock to the general population of Oahu, Hawaii.

On the morning of December 7th, two Army operators at a radar station picked up the signal of Japanese fighter planes approaching Pearl Harbor. Finally, a low-ranking officer dismissed their report, assuming that the signal must have come from American planes off the west coast of the United States.

Which of the following, if inserted to replace the underlined portion ("Finally,"), would provide the most effective transition between the previous sentence ("On the morning of...") and this one ("Finally, a low-ranking officer...")?

  A. NO CHANGE

  B. And,

  C. However,

  D. But,

Answer: When we consider the possible answer choices and the paragraph as a whole, we see that choices A, B, and D do not create an effective transition between the two sentences. We need a transitional word that shows that though there were warning signs of the Pearl Harbor attack, those warnings were not heeded, which is one of the reasons why the attack was such a shock to the general population. Choice C ("However,") would provide the most effective transition. Therefore, choice C is the correct answer.

General Strategies

The ATI TEAS English section will test grammatical and rhetorical concepts in ways that are designed to trip you up. As you can see above, It's not enough to simply choose the answer that "sounds right." In fact, many of the answers that "sound right" are included in order to trip you (as discussed in the early sections of this book).

1.   Punctuation.

Punctuation is by far the most important ATI TEAS grammar rule.

- Punctuation (commas, apostrophes, dashes, etc.)
- Subject/Verb agreement and Pronoun/Number agreement
- Idioms
- Wrong words (affect/effect, their/they're, etc.)
- Parallel construction
- Verb tenses and conjugations
- Run-on sentences and sentence fragments
- Misplaced modifiers
- Pronoun choice
- Sentence organization
- Tone/Mood
- Author's intent
- Relevance of sentences
- Word choice

2. Avoid Redundancy and Wordiness.

Redundancy questions are very common on the ATI TEAS English test. Redundancy means words or phrases that are unnecessary and can be eliminated without affecting the sentence's meaning. The ATI TEAS typically includes two different types that you should be aware of: two synonyms used to describe something and implied phrases that don't add anything to the sentence. The best thing to do in these situations is to remember to keep it short and simple and get rid of words that do not add value.

For *example*:

"Joanne is an outgoing and sociable person."

This sentence uses "outgoing" and "sociable" to describe Joanne, but these words are synonyms so one of them can be removed to avoid redundancy.

Similarly, another example of redundancy could look like this:

"The campers were terrified to come across a giant bear that towered over them."

Again, avoiding redundancy, we can take out the phrase "towered over them" since it is implied by the adjective "giant":

"The campers were terrified to come across a giant bear."

Just remember: keep sentences short and grammatically correct to avoid redundancy.

3. Don't choose the "NO CHANGE" too easily.

In ATI TEAS English, you should choose the "NO CHANGE" answer option if you can't detect anything wrong with the sentence. But this comes with a warning, "NO CHANGE" can be an easy option if you can't see anything immediately wrong with the grammar or syntax. But you need to be more careful than that. Make sure you're evaluating the grammar of the sentence and not just listening to how it sounds in your head. If you really think it's "NO CHANGE," double-check the answer choices to be sure. It can be the correct answer, but only one in four times, on average; don't over use it!

4. As I said in the earlier sections, practice is key. Do as much as you can.

It's not enough to just study grammar rules and read tips and strategies from a review book like this! It's also important to take practice tests:

- Get you used to the format of the test

- Show you the types of questions you can expect to see

- Get you familiar with the instructions

5.   Find Your Weaknesses.

In order to do really well, you need to find your weakest area, and focus on that. There's no point doing questions that you find the easiest over and over again. You need to improve on the questions you find hard. To do this, keep a note of all the questions that you either guess on, or get wrong. These are the questions on which you are weakest. Then, when you have the list. Use it to study. Go through the questions, search out similar questions, and seek support!

6.   Make Grammar a Part of Your Everyday Life.

Don't think of grammar as requirement of exams only, think of it as an essential life skill. To do this, you need to make grammar a part of your everyday life.

For example, you can:

- Look out for grammar mistakes in brochures, posters, grocery store signs, etc.

- Proofread your friends' essays and let them know that you're going to be brutal.

- Start posting, tweeting, texting, and messaging with a higher standard of grammar and punctuation.

- Read novels, formal publications, reports, anything of a high standard, so that you are witnessing good grammar, often.

- Look through some of your old essays and improve them.

- Follow grammar-related social media (there are plenty - google it)

7.   Pace Yourself and Leave Extra Time to Check Your Work.

This is no different to the advice given earlier, but it is equally important here.

If you have time, go back and check on a third time. Ignore the questions you're 100% sure about and focus on the questions you're still struggling with. In the last two minutes before the test is over, quickly go through and make sure you answered every question and filled them out correctly on the bubble sheet.

8. Know the Four Most Common Question Types.

The ATI TEAS may be difficult, but it's repeatable. You should know the following common questions:

I. Using correct punctuation: Identify which punctuation mark should be used (comma, apostrophe, semicolon, colon, dash, parenthesis, etc.) and where it should go in the sentence.

II. Choosing the correct form or word: Identify the best word to use in the sentence. Some questions might ask you to find the right form of the word, such as correct verb tense, singular or plural, correct pronoun, correct preposition, or correct idiom.

III. Logic questions: Choose the answer that expresses the correct relationship between two parts of the sentence, paragraph, or passage (conjunction, where a sentence should go, the relevance of a sentence, etc.)

IV. Finding the main idea and interpreting a passage: Identify the main purpose or point of the passage, sentence, or paragraph.

Grammar rules

While you read through the essays, you don't need to remember every grammar rule. Instead, think about the common grammar rules that are likely to come up on the exam.By focusing on what you know you'll see, you can increase your score while reducing the amount of time and energy you spend on each question. These are likely to be:

1. Run ons & Fragments

A complete sentence contains a subject, a predicate verb, and a complete thought. If any of the three is lacking, the sentence is called a fragment. A run-on contains too much information, usually because two independent clauses (two complete thoughts) are being improperly combined.

2. Verbs: Subject-verb agreement and Verb Tenses

The ATI TEAS English section often includes long sentences in which the main subject and the verb are separated by many words or clauses. If you identify the subject of each sentence and make sure the verb matches it, you can ace this grammar rule. In addition, the ATI TEAS tests your knowledge of past, present, future, past perfect, present perfect, and future perfect tenses.

3. Punctuation

Commas, apostrophes, colons, semicolons, dashes, periods, question marks, and exclamation points are all tested on the ATI TEAS. Know how to tackle them to grab some quick points on this test.

4. Idioms

Idioms are expressions native to the English language. Two-part idioms are commonly tested such as "neither...nor" and "not only...but also" as well as prepositional idioms like "opposed TO" and "participate IN." The ATI TEAS will also test verb and preposition idioms. Both of these types can be tricky because there is not a list of rules. Instead of trying to memorize each one, you should practice to get a sense of which idioms come up frequently.

5. Wordiness

As long as there are no new grammar errors introduced, the shortest answer choice is often correct. Redundancy is a type of wordiness where the same thing is said twice such as "happy and joyful." Keep it simple and to the point.

6. Parallel Structure

Parallelism is tested on the ATI TEAS English test in the context of phrases or items in a list. In parallel construction, the phrases or items must be in the same form. This can be tested with a number of parts of speech: nouns, verbs, prepositions, etc.

7. Pronouns

The most common error associated with pronouns is pronoun-antecedent agreement.The antecedent is the word the pronoun is replacing. A pronoun *must* have a clear antecedent in the sentence. A less common error is the ambiguous pronoun in which a pronoun could represent more than one noun. For example, "The president and his adviser spoke for hours before he reached a decision." The pronoun 'he' could be referring to the president or the adviser, so it is incorrect.

8. Modifiers: Adjectives/Adverbs & Modifying phrases.

Modifiers are words and phrases that describe nouns. Adjectives modify nouns, and adverbs modify verbs, adjectives, or other adverbs. Be on the lookout for suspicious adverb-noun and adjective-verb pairings. Also be aware that many sentences will begin with a modifying phrase and a comma. The subject after the comma must be the person or thing doing the action of the modifying phrase.

9. Word Choice: Transitions & Diction

Pay attention to transition words and phrases to make sure they reflect the author's purpose. Transitions can demonstrate continuation, contrast, or cause-and-effect. In addition, the ATI TEAS may try to fool you by using words that sounds similar to the intended words, but do not make sense in context (for example, replacing "could have" with "could of").

10. Organization and Strategy

The ATI TEAS English section will ask you to determine the order and focus of sentences or paragraphs. You will also be asked about adding, revising, or deleting sentences as well as how a sentence fits with the purpose, audience, and focus of a paragraph or the essay as a whole.

English Example Question

Technology is rapidly expanding the scope of capabilities for both professional and personal use; such is the case with smart phones. Professionals now have devices available to them capable of digital media, internet access, phone communication, multi-person scheduling and office tools for documents and presentations. Businesspeople that are often mobile may maximize the use of these critical features on smartphones. Individuals who simply enjoy the luxury of multi-function devices often use these devices for frivolous pursuits such as downloading catchy ringtones, instant messaging about the latest gossip and looking up the world record for most cans crushed on one's head during the Super bowl. This fusion of capabilities and increased availability of such devices could be a sign of a growing blend in society between work and personal life, or individuals could simply be taking a luxurious approach to their connectivity in personal lives.

1. The term "frivolous" implies that the author:

    A. Is fascinated by the endless capabilities on smart phones.

    B. Hopes that technology ceases to expand its scope.

    C. Believes that the average individual does not need a smartphone.

    D. Has a smartphone.

Answer: Believes that the average individual does not need a smartphone.

Based on the contextual description of trivial uses and knowledge, "frivolous" means useless or unnecessary. So if the author believes that individuals not involved in business are unnecessarily using smartphones that the author would think that these people do not need smartphones (choice C). The author makes no mention of their specific hopes for how the technology will turn out in the future, so choice B can be eliminated. The authors matter-of-fact tone allows you to rule out "fascination" (choice A), and there is no evidence to support whether or not the author has a smartphone (choice D). Choice C is the best option.

2. What is the purpose of the conclusion sentence?

    A. Draw a conclusion about what we know smartphones can do

    B. Assume where technology is headed and how it will affect society

    C. Comment on human connectivity through the use of smartphones

    D. Present two possible explanations for the growing popularity of smartphones

Answer: Present two possible explanations for the growing popularity of smartphones

The conclusion sentence states two possible paths that could explain the arrival of a growth in smartphone popularity. These two suppositions are guesses at what is causing this trend. Because the author injects minimal bias and leaves the answer to the reader's interpretation, the author is simply presenting explanations as choice D indicates. The other choices are either irrelevant or insufficiently supported by text evidence.

English Exercise

Now try this exercise question, and see how you can do.

More than Light Itself

On hot and humid summer evenings, almost everyone has witnessed fireflies, also called lightning bugs, flitting around **your yard or landing on a windowsill** (2) and occasionally emitting a soft glow. Flashing on and off like flashlights or twinkling holiday lights, a firefly is just one of the many organisms that can produce **it's** (3) own **light** (4). This feature, known as bioluminescence or cold light, **appears in nature quite often** (5).

All forms of light occur through a similar process. To understand this process, you must first know a little bit about atoms. Atoms are the **smaller** (6) parts of elements, such as iron and sodium, **which have the same chemical properties** (7). The center of an atom is called the nucleus and is composed of particles called protons and neutrons. Other particles, called electrons, orbit the nucleus of **an atom; just** (8) like the earth orbits the sun. The electrons' orbit does not change unless the electrons are excited or energized in some way. **QUESTION 9** Then, when they fall back to their normal energy level, they fall back to a lower orbit and release packets of energy called photons, **which produce light. Light from** (10) a lamp or streetlight is produced when electrons are excited by heat from electricity.

In bioluminescent organisms, electrons are excited by a chemical reaction, not heat, which is why the phenomenon is often referred to as cold light. The chemicals that various organisms use to create light are luciferin and luciferase. Luciferin is the substance that produces **light luciferase** (11) is the enzyme that causes the chemical reaction to begin. In the simplest terms, luciferase makes luciferin react with oxygen, which produces light.

QUESTION 12 1 Many organisms, **from bacteria and mushrooms to certain sea creatures, insects, and others are** (13) capable of producing their own light. 2 Certain fungi, such as the jack-o'-lantern mushroom, can also create light. 3 The orange jack-o'-lantern mushrooms are often found growing on trees in the fall. 4 Among the terrestrial creatures are fireflies, glowworms, and some centipedes and millipedes. 5 Fox fire is another type of glowing fungus, usually found growing on dead or decaying trees. 6 At night, the gills of the mushroom, found beneath the cap and partway down the stalk, emit a greenish light.

ATI TEAS English Exercise Questions

1. The writer is considering deleting "On hot and humid summer evenings" from the first sentence (adjusting the capitalization as needed). If the writer were to make this change, the paragraph would primarily lose:

    A. an indication of the tone that will be used in the rest of the passage.

    B. details that emphasize the time of year bioluminescence must occur.

    C. an example of the kinds of weather imperative for bioluminescence to occur.

    D. nothing, because it is irrelevant to the paragraph.

2.

    A. NO CHANGE

    B. their yard or landing on a windowsill

    C. his or her yard or landing on a windowsill

    D. your yard or landing on a windowsill

3.

    A. NO CHANGE

    B. its

    C. its'

D. them

4. Which of the following is NOT an acceptable alternative for the bold portion?

    A. light, this feature

    B. light; this feature

    C. light, and this feature

    D. light. This dramatic feature

5. The writer would like to indicate here the surprising frequency of bioluminescence. Which choice does this most effectively while maintaining the tone of the passage and the meaning of the sentence?

    A. Actually appears in nature at a higher frequency than one might come to expect.

    B. Actually appears in nature more often than you might think.

    C. Actually appears in nature more often than it does not.

    D. Actually shows up in nature more than you could ever even believe.

6.

    A. NO CHANGE

    B. most small

    C. smallest

    D. more small

7.

    A. NO CHANGE

    B. despite having the same chemical properties as the elements.

    C. that has the same chemical properties as the elements that contain them.

    D. and have the same chemical properties as the elements that contain them.

8.

    A. NO CHANGE

    B. atom just like

    C. atom, just like

    D. atom: just like

9. Given that all the following choices are true; which choice provides the most effective transition from the preceding sentence in the paragraph to the following one?

    A. When electrons absorb energy; they move to a higher orbit.

    B. When electrons take in energy, they resume their normal energy level and move to the highest orbit.

    C. After they are energized, they move into a lower orbit.

    D. After they are energized, they resume their normal energy level.

10. Which of the following is NOT an acceptable alternative to the bold portion?

    A. which produce light; light from

    B. which produce light. Light such as that from

    C. that produce light. Light from

    D. that produce light from

11.

    A. NO CHANGE

    B. light. Luciferase

    C. light, but luciferase

    D. light; and luciferase

12. Which of the following sentence orders makes the paragraph the most logical?

A. NO CHANGE

B. 1, 4, 6, 5, 2, 3

C. 1, 4, 2, 6, 5, 3

D. 1, 4, 2, 3, 6, 5

13.

A. NO CHANGE

B. from bacteria and mushrooms to certain sea creatures, insects, and others is

C. from bacteria and mushrooms to certain sea creatures and insects are

D. from bacteria, mushrooms, and certain sea creatures are

Questions 14 and 15 relate to the passage as a whole

14. The writer is considering adding a statement to the beginning of the passage, clarifying the purpose for writing. Which statement LEAST emphasizes the writer's purpose?

A. Reading this passage will inform you of instances of bioluminescence in nature and the science behind this phenomenon.

B. Although the primary cause of bioluminescence is unclear, after reading this passage, you'll know a little more about the science surrounding this magical feature of nature, a few examples of it in the wild, and the chemical reactions that cause it to occur.

C. After you finish reading this passage, you'll be able to explain scientific data about bioluminescence and provide a few examples of this wonder in the natural world around us.

D. When you've finished reading this information about bioluminescence, you'll be persuaded to study the complexities of the science behind this phenomenon, and the different forms of nature preserving themselves with a bioluminescent feature.

15. The writer would like to add a paragraph to the end of the passage challenging readers to donate money to fund research on bioluminescence in habitats around the world. Should this paragraph be added?

A. Yes, because the passage is left without a conclusion, and adding a challenge to the end of this piece is a great way to create a conclusion without repeating too much information.

B. Yes, because it would tie the whole point of the passage together while offering a way for readers to connect to the scientific data presented.

C. No, because although the passage is left without an appropriate conclusion, adding a paragraph about donating money changes the purpose of the essay.

D. No, because the paragraph that is currently at the end sums up the passage enough for the reader to be left with information about bioluminescence that he or she didn't know prior to reading.

Answers

1. **Correct Answer: A**

Although this phrase mentions weather, the rest of the essay never indicates that bioluminescence has anything to do with the weather, which gets rid of choices B and C. D is obviously incorrect. If you completed this question second, answering all of the easy questions first and coming back to this later, you'd know that!

2. **Correct Answer: C**

Here, the antecedent is everyone, which is singular. It requires the singular his or her, although we can all agree that you'd probably use the word their in spoken English.

3. **Correct Answer: B**

Here, we need the possessive pronoun for firefly, so it is appropriate. It's is a contraction of it is. Its' is not a word, and there, Choice D, changes the pronoun to plural when it must be singular.

4. **Correct Answer: A**

This one is tricky, because you have to figure out which one is NOT acceptable. Choice A creates a comma splice sentence, but every other choice is structurally sound.

5. **Correct Answer: B**

Choice A is too formal, choice C is inaccurate, and Choice D is too informal. Choice B maintains the casual tone the best.

6. **Correct Answer: C**

Here, the superlative form should've been used, which would make it smallest, which rules out choice A. Choices B and D are never appropriate.

7. **Correct Answer: D**

This is a matter of an ambiguous pronoun reference. We're not sure if the pronoun refers back to atoms or the elements. Choice A is incorrect because it doesn't fix the ambiguity. Choice B creates a different meaning and doesn't fix the ambiguity. Choice C actually creates a new error by using the singular pronoun has.

8. **Correct Answer: C**

Remember that a semicolon must follow the same rules as an end mark by joining independent clauses. Here, the second clause is not independent, so a better usage is a comma and the conjunction.

9. **Correct Answer: A**

This sentence must join the previous and following sentences together. Since the following sentence mentions the lower orbit in the comparative sense, we have to assume that higher is what it's being compared to.

10. **Correct Answer: D**

This is one of those NOT questions, which means you simply have to cross off the stuff that does work. Here, you're looking to form a correct sentence, so check each one by plugging in. Choice D changes the meaning of the sentences altogether, so it doesn't work.

11. Correct Answer: B

In the passage, the sentence is a run-on. So, choice A is out. Choice C creates faulty meaning, and Choice D uses the semicolon improperly.

12. Correct Answer: D

The easiest way to figure this out is by underlining the topic of each sentence, and paying close attention to transitions. That way, you'll logically figure out which should come next.

13. Correct Answer: C

Choice B creates another error: subject verb agreement. Choice D leaves out some information (insects), so it has to go. Choice A is wrong because the sentence isn't parallel in context.

14. Correct Answer: D

Here, you'll greatly benefit from having read the entire passage. If you skimmed, you'll miss out on what the author was clearly trying to do, which is to inform you about something. Since choice D says the author was trying to persuade you, it is wrong.

15. Correct Answer: C

Although Choices A and B indicate that the essay is missing a conclusion and it is, the reason for adding it is incorrect. That kind of a conclusion would neither tie anything together, nor would it keep the tone of the piece. Choice C indicates this.

ATI TEAS Math

The ATI TEAS Math consists of 36 questions in 54 minutes, 32 of these will be scored. A calculator is permitted but it is a limited operation calculator. There is no guessing penalty so it is always advisable to take a guess even if you have no idea what the answer is.

Some of the ATI TEAS math questions will be on algebra. Make sure that you can solve systems of linear equations, factor quadratics and understand functions. Brush up on exponents and radicals as well.

A good amount of the questions will be on intermediate algebra and coordinate geometry. Study the equations of conic sections, quadratic formula, inequalities and intersections of the graphs of functions. It may be worth getting some math help on these if it's been some time since you covered them in high school math.

The remaining percent of the ATI TEAS math section is geometry and a small number of trigonometry questions. Have a look at formulas for finding area, circumference and perimeter. Also know how to set up equations involving trig functions and the sides of a right triangle. This is all high school math, and you will be able to do it, but you may need to refresh.

If you don't know how to solve a problem, use your calculator to guess and check the answer choices. If the choices are numbers, plug them back into the problem to see which one works. This is a really useful tactic that helps a lot, often, not all of the options will work using this back solving technique. If the choices are equations, plug numbers into the equations to see which one gives you an answer that makes sense according to the problem.

If you get stuck on a question, mark it and come back to it later. Spend your time wisely on the problems that are easiest for you to do. All the problems are worth the same marks so don't waste valuable time on ones you can't solve. When time is almost up, go back and fill in any bubbles you missed, even if you have to guess, remember that you are not punished for incorrect answers (other than scoring zero for it) so make sure that you guess.

There is obviously a basic amount of pre elementary algebra that is expected from the ATI Teas, below is a breakdown of the math content you can expect to find on the ATI Teas Test.

Elementary Algebra

- Properties of exponents and square roots
- Evaluation of algebraic expressions through substitution
- Using variables to express functional relationships
- Understanding algebraic operations
- The solution of quadratic equations by factoring

Intermediate Algebra

- The quadratic formula
- Rational and radical expressions
- Absolute value equations and inequalities
- Sequences and patterns
- Systems of equations
- Quadratic inequalities
- Functions and modeling
- Matrices
- Roots of polynomials
- Complex numbers

Coordinate Geometry

- Graphing and the relations between equations and graphs, including points, lines, polynomials, circles, and other curves
- Graphing inequalities
- Slope
- Parallel and perpendicular lines

- Distance

- Midpoints

- Conics

Plane Geometry

- Properties and relations of plane figures, including angles and relations among perpendicular and parallel lines

- Properties of circles, triangles, rectangles, parallelograms, and trapezoids

- Transformations

- The concept of proof and proof techniques

- Volume

Trigonometry

- Trigonometric relations in right triangles

- Values and properties of trigonometric functions

- Graphing trigonometric functions

- Modeling using trigonometric functions

- Use of trigonometric identities

- Solving trigonometric equations

Example ATI TEAS Math Test Questions

To give you a better feel for the format and content of the ATI TEAS Math test, let's take a look at a few sample ATI TEAS Math questions.

Pre-Algebra Question: Mean, Median, and Mode

70, 80, 50, 20, 80, 30, 80

Seven students took an art history exam. Their scores are listed above. Which of the following statements regarding the scores is true?

I. The average (arithmetic mean) is Greater than 70.

II. The mode is Greater than 70.

III. The median is Greater than 70.

    A. None

    B. II only

    C. I and II only

    D. II and III only

Answer: First, find the average (arithmetic mean) of the test scores. Mean = (70 + 80 + 50 + 20 + 80 + 30 + 80)/7 = 58.57. 58.57 is not Greater than 70. Therefore, item I. is not true, and we can eliminate choice C. Second, find the median of the test scores. To do so, put the test scores in ascending or descending order: 20, 30, 50, 70, 80, 80, 80. The median (the number in the middle) is 70. Therefore, item III. is not true, and we can eliminate choice D. Third, find the mode of the test scores (the number that appears most frequently): 80. Therefore, item II. is true. Choice B is the correct answer.

Geometry Question: Plane Figures and Angles

If line m intersects the square as shown, what must the value of $x + y$ be?

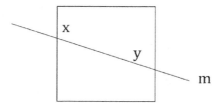

    A. 45

    B. 75

    C. 85

D. 180

Answer: The sides of a square are parallel, so line m is a transversal to the sides of the square. That means that the angle next to (to the right of) angle *y* is equal to angle *x* by alternate interior angles. That also means that angle *x* is supplementary to angle *y*. Thus, *x* + *y* = 180. Choice D is the correct answer.

Math Hints and tips

Timing: You are given 54 minutes to answer 36 questions. That's pretty easy to remember, but don't think that you should allot the same amount of time for each question. Like most math standardized tests, the difficulty range on the ATI TEAS math is relatively wide: practice answering the easier questions quickly so you'll have adequate time to answer the tougher ones.

Directions: The instructions on the math portion are relatively long and detailed. Don't waste time reading them on the day of the test. Read them before and know exactly what they will be.

Choose the correct solution to each question and fill in the corresponding bubble on your answer sheet.

Do not continue to spend time on questions if you get stuck. Solve as many questions as you can before be returning to any of the remaining questions if time permits. Use a watch or stopwatch to make sure that you don't spend more time than is necessary on any particular question.

You may use a calculator on this test for any question you choose. However, sometimes it's worth not using a calculator - you may be fast without it.

It's worth remembering that unless otherwise stated, you can assume:

- Figures are NOT necessarily drawn to scale.

- Geometric figures are two dimensional.

- The term line indicates a straight line.

- The term average indicates arithmetic mean.

- It's always a good idea to approach each math question using the same tactics each time.

1. Read the question

2. Look at the information provided in the question and the answer choices

3. Solve:

    a. Back solve

    b. Pick Numbers

    c. Use Traditional Math

    d. Strategically Guess

4. Check to make sure that you answered the specific question that was asked.

5. Avoid using Algebra if you can - it's often much faster to put the numbers in. I know this may not be how you were taught math in class, but this is not a standard math exam. It is a high pressure, high speed math test, so picking numbers is a good move as it speeds up your progress. This is especially helpful for number properties questions. Pick numbers that follow the rules of the question and are small and easy to work with. Avoid picking 0 or 1 because they have special properties.

6. You can back solve when you see integers in the answer choices.

7. Translate the words in the question into math so that you can solve more easily. Take it one word or phrase at a time.

8. Recognizing number properties will save you time on test day. Number properties rules include odds and evens, prime numbers, and the order of operations.

9. Know the difference between values, ratios, and percentage. A ratio is a relationship between numbers. You need to be able to convert between percentage, fractions, and decimals very quickly.

10. You should understand key information about triangles. You must know the 30-60-90 and 45-45-90 rules.

11. Find common shapes on the ATI TEAS to help you break complex figures into simple polygons. Look in particular for triangles and squares.

12. Be on the lookout for trap answers on the ATI TEAS. Watch out for answers to steps along the way to the final answer and be careful when you see a negative sign.

Math Examples and explanations

1. Angles A and B are complementary and the measure of angle A is twice the measure of angle B. Find the measures of angles A and B.

Answer

Let A be the measure of angle A and B be the measure of angle B. Hence

A = 2B

Angles A and B are complementary; hence

A + B = 90°

But A = 2B; hence

2B + B = 90

3B = 90

B = 90 / 3 = 30°

A = 2B = 60°

2. ABCD is a parallelogram such that AB is parallel to DC and DA parallel to CB. The length of side AB is 20 cm. E is a point between A and B such that the length of AE is 3 cm. F is a point between points D and C. Find the length of DF such that the segment EF divide the parallelogram in two regions with equal areas.

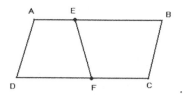

Answer

Let A1 be the area of the trapezoid AEFD. Hence

A1 = (1/2) h (AE + DF) = (1/2) h (3 + DF), h is the height of the parallelogram.

Now let A2 be the area of the trapezoid EBCF. Hence

A2 = (1/2) h (EB + FC)

We also have

EB = 20 - AE = 17, FC = 20 - DF

We now substitute EB and FC in A2 = (1/2) h (EB + FC)

A2 = (1/2) h (17 + 20 - DF) = (1/2) h (37 - DF)

For EF to divide the parallelogram into two regions of equal areas, we need to have area A1 and area A2 equal

(1/2) h (3 + DF) = (1/2) h (37 - DF)

Multiply both sides by 2 and divide them by h to simplify to

3 + DF = 37 - DF

Solve for DF

2DF = 37 - 3

2DF = 34

DF = 17 cm

3. Find the measure of angle A in the figure below.

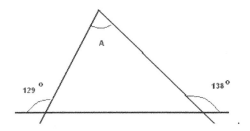

Answer

A first interior angle of the triangle is supplementary to the angle whose measure is 129° and is equal to 180 - 129 = 51°

A second interior angle of the triangle is supplementary to the angle whose measure is 138° and is equal to 180 - 138 = 42°

The sum of all three angles of the triangle is equal to 180°. Hence A + 51 + 42 = 180

A = 180 - 51 - 42 = 87°

4. ABC is a right triangle. AM is perpendicular to BC. The size of angle ABC is equal to 55 degrees. Find the size of angle MAC.

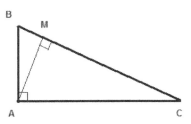

Answer

The sum of all angles in triangle ABC is equal to 180°. Hence angle ABC + angle ACM + 90° = 180°

Substitute angle ABC by 55 and solve for angle ACM angle ACM = 180 - 90 - 55 = 35°

The sum of all angles in triangle AMC is equal to 180°. Hence angle MAC + angle ACM + 90° = 180°

Substitute angle ACM by 35 and Solve for angle MAC angle MAC = 180 - 90 - angle ACM = 180 - 90 - 35 = 55°

5. Find the size of angle MBD in the figure below.

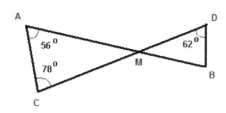

Answer

The sum of all angles in triangle AMC is equal to 180°. Hence 56 + 78 + angle AMC = 180 angle AMC = 180 - 56 - 78 = 46°

Angles AMC and DMB are vertical angles and therefore equal in measures. Hence angle DMB = 46°

The sum of angles of triangle DMB is equal to 180°. Hence angle MBD + angle DMB + 62 = 180

Substitute angle DMB by 46 and solve for angle MBD. angle MBD + 46 + 62 = 180 angle MBD = 180 - 46 - 62 = 72°

6. The size of angle AOB is equal to 132 degrees and the size of angle COD is equal to 141 degrees. Find the size of angle DOB.

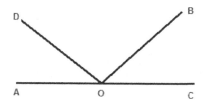

Answer

angle AOB = 132 and is also the sum of angles AOD and DOB. Hence angle AOD + angle DOB = 132°(I)

angle COD = 141 and is also the sum of angles COB and BOD. Hence

angle COB + angle DOB = 141° (II)

We now add the left sides together and the right sides together to obtain a new equation.

angle AOD + angle DOB + angle COB + angle DOB = 132 + 141 (III)

Note that:

angle AOD + angle DOB + angle COB = 180°

Substitute angle AOD + angle DOB + angle COB in (III) by 180 and solve for angle DOB.

180 + angle DOB = 132 + 141

angle DOB = 273 - 180 = 93°

7. Find the size of angle x in the figure.

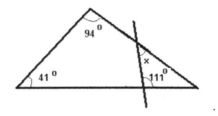

Answer

The interior angle of the quadrilateral on the left that is supplementary to x is equal to 180 – x

The interior angle of the quadrilateral on the left that is supplementary to the angle of measure 111° is equal to 180 - 111 = 69°

The sum of all interior angles of the quadrilateral is equal to 360°. Hence 41 + 94 + 180 - x + 69 = 360

Solve for x

41 + 94 + 180 - x + 69 = 360

384 - x = 360

x = 384 - 360 = 24°

8. The rectangle below is made up of 12 congruent (same size) squares. Find the perimeter of the rectangle if the area of the rectangle is equal to 432 square cm.

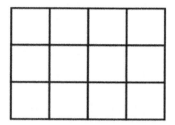

Answer

If the total area of the rectangle is 432 square cm, the area of one square is equal to =

432 / 12 = 36 square cm

Let x be the side of one small square. Hence the area of one small circle equal to 36 gives x^2 = 36

Solve for x

x = 6 cm

The length L of the perimeter is equal to 4x and the width W is equal to 3x. Hence L = 4 × 6 = 24 cm and W = 3 × 6 = 18 cm

The perimeter P of the rectangle is given by:

P = 2 (L + W) = 2(24 + 18) = 84 cm

9. ABC is a right triangle with the size of angle ACB equal to 74 degrees. The lengths of the sides AM, MQ and QP are all equal. Find the measure of angle QPB.

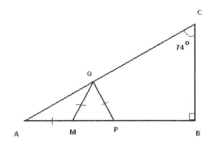

Answer

Angle CAB in the right triangle ACB is given by 90 - 74 = 16°

Sides AM and MQ in size and therefore triangle AMQ is isosceles and therefore angle AQM = angle QAM = 16°

The sum of all interior angles in triangle AMQ is equal to 180°. Hence 16 + 16 + angle AMQ = 180

Solve for angle AMQ angle AMQ = 180 - 32 = 148°

Angle QMP is supplementary to angle AMQ.

Hence angle QMP = 180 - angle AMQ = 180 - 148 = 32°

Lengths of QM and QP are equal; hence triangle QMP is isosceles and therefore angle QPM is equal in size to angle QMP. Hence angle QPM = 32°

Angle QPB is supplementary to angle QPM. Hence angle QPM = 180 - angle QPM = 180 - 32 = 148°

10. Find the area of the shaded region.

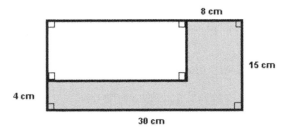

Answer

The area of the given shape may be found by subtracting the area of the rectangle at the top left from the area of the large rectangle.

Dimensions of the rectangle at top left length = 30 - 8 = 22 cm, width = 15 - 4 = 11 cm

Area of given shape = 30 × 15 - 22 × 11 = 208 cm²

11. Find the area of the given shape.

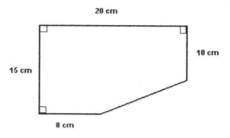

Answer

The area of the given shape may be found by subtracting the area of the right triangle (red) from the area of the large rectangle (see figure below).

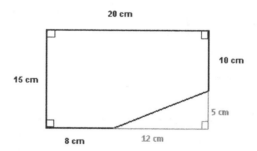

Sides of the right triangle (red) are given by 15 - 10 = 5 cm and 20 - 8 = 12 cm

Area of given shape = 20 × 15 - (1/2) × 12 × 5 = 270 cm²

12. The vertices of the inscribed (inside) square bisect the sides of the second (outside) square. Find the ratio of the area of the outside square to the area of the inscribed square.

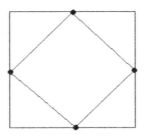

Answer

Let 2 x be the size of the side of the large square (see figure below).

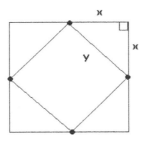

The area of the large square is $(2x) \times (2x) = 4x^2$

The area of the inscribed square is $y \times y = y^2$

Use of Pythagoras theorem gives $y^2 = x^2 + x^2 = 2x^2$

Ratio R of the area of the outside square to the area of the inside square is given by $R = 4x^2 / y^2 = 4x^2 / 2x^2 = 4/2 = 2/1$

13. The art teacher at Hill Side High School is decorating her classroom by reproducing famous Art work on her walls. She has a piece that is 8 inches wide and 10 inches tall that she wants to replicate to scale on the wall. If the painting on the wall will be 6 feet tall, then approximately how wide will the painting be, in feet?

A. 5

B. 7

C. 9

D. 11

Correct Answer: A

Notice that the dimensions of the picture are given in inches, and the question asks for the dimensions of the finished painting in feet. Start by converting the dimensions of the original picture from inches to feet. To make the conversion, divide each measurement by 12. The width is 8/12 = 0.67 feet, and the height is 10/12 = 0.83 feet. Next, set up a proportion of the original measurements to the finished measurements: 0.67/0.83 = x/6. To solve for x, which is the width of the finished painting, first cross-multiply: 0.83x = (0.67) (6), or 0.83x = 4.02. Then, divide both sides by 0.83: x = 4.02 ÷ 0.83 = 4.84. The question asks for the *approximate* width of the finished painting, so round 4.84 to 5.

14. The formula for line *l* in standard form is 5x - y = 2. Which of the following gives the formula for line *l* in slope-intercept form?

A. $y = 5x + 2$

B. $y = 5x - 2$

C. $y = 2x - 5$

D. $y = -5x - 2$

Correct Answer: B

Slope-intercept form is $y = mx + b$, where m is the slope of the line, and b is its y-intercept. To put the given equation in that form, first subtract 5x from both sides: -y = -5x + 2. Next, divide both sides by -1, making sure to divide all three terms: y = 5x -2. If you picked a different answer choice, you may have made a mistake with the negatives.

15. The expression |2-14| - |-25| is equal to:

A. 41

B. 37

C. 13

D. -13

Correct Answer: D

Remember order of operations on this problem. First, do the subtraction within the first absolute value sign to get $|-12| - |-25|$. Next, apply the absolute value to each term to get 12 -25, and do the subtraction: 12 -25 = -13.

16. In $\triangle JKL$ the measure of $\angle J$ is exactly 37°, and the measure of $\angle K$ is less than or equal to 63°. Which of the following phrases best describes the measure of $\angle L$?

A. Exactly 120°

B. Exactly 100°

C. Exactly 80°

D. Greater than or equal to 80°

Correct Answer: D

All the angles in a triangle add up to 180°. Because the problem gives a range of possible values for the measure of $\angle K$, plug in a number that is less than 63°, such as 60°, then solve for $\angle L$:

$37° + 60° + \angle L = 180°$

$97° + \angle L = 180°$

$\angle L = 83°$

Only D. describes this result.

17. If 3x - 1 > 26, then which of the following is the smallest possible integer value of x?

A. 6

B. 7

C. 8

D. 10

Correct Answer: D

First, simplify the given inequality. Start by adding 1 to both sides: 3x > 27. Next, divide both sides by 3: x > 9. Because x must be greater than 9, its smallest possible integer value is 10.

18. Paul is tying red and white ribbons around a gift box. He begins by tying the white ribbon and one red ribbon around the box. These two ribbons intersect on one face of the box at a 62° angle, as shown in the figure below. Now Paul wants to tie a second red ribbon onto the box so that the two red ribbons are parallel. What is the degree measure of the angle, indicated below, between the white ribbon and the bottom red ribbon?

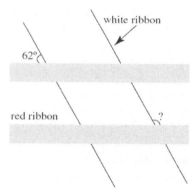

A. 62°

B. 76°

C. 90°

D. 118°

Correct Answer: D

This diagram of ribbons is essentially just parallel lines intersecting. The question states that the second red ribbon will be parallel to the first, and the two sides of the white ribbon are parallel to each other. The rule with intersecting parallel lines is that all big angles are equal, all small angles are equal, and any big angle plus any small angle equals 180°. The angle in question is a big angle, so to find its measurement, subtract the given small angle measurement from 180°: 180° - 62° = 118°.

19. In right triangle ΔPRS shown below, Q is the midpoint of PR. What is the length of QR, to the nearest inch?

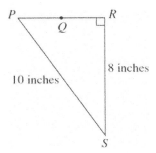

A. 2

B. 3

C. 4

D. 6

Correct Answer: B

Begin by finding the measurement of *PR*. If you recognize the side lengths of the triangle as a Pythagorean triple, you know that *PR* = 6.
Otherwise, use the Pythagorean Theorem, $a^2 + b^2 = c^2$, where *c* is the hypotenuse.
Make *PR* side a:

$a^2 + 8^2 = 10^2$

$a^2 + 64 = 100$

$a^2 = 36$

$a = 6$

Since the midpoint is the exact center of a line, *QR* is half the length of *PR*: *QR* = 6 ÷ 2 = 3.

20. Josie notices that the textbooks for her past 3 math courses have the same length and width, but each year's textbook has more pages and weighs more than the previous year's textbook. Josie weighs the textbooks, to the nearest 0.1 ounce, for her past 3 math courses and wonders about the relationship between the number of pages in math textbooks and the weights of those textbooks. She graphs the number of pages and corresponding weights of her 3 math textbooks in the standard (x,y) coordinate plane, as shown below, and discovers a linear relationship among these 3 points. She concludes that the equation of the line that passes through these 3 points is $y = 0.1x + 2.2$.

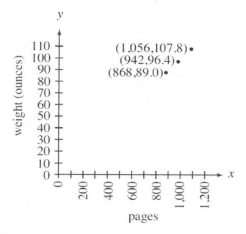

How much more, in ounces, does a math textbook with 1,056 pages weight than one with 868 pages?

    A. 18.8

    B. 19.8

    C. 54.1

    D. 77.3

Correct Answer: A

The three marked points on the graph show the weight (which is the given x-coordinate) for books of three different lengths (the y-coordinate gives the number of pages). The weight of a book with 1,056 pages is 107.8 ounces, and the weight of a book with 868 pages is 89.0

ounces. To find how much more the longer book weighs, subtract the two weights: 107.8 -89 = 18.8.

21. Josie notices that the textbooks for her past 3 math courses have the same length and width, but each year's textbook has more pages and weighs more than the previous year's textbook. Josie weighs the textbooks, to the nearest 0.1 ounce, for her past 3 math courses and wonders about the relationship between the number of pages in math textbooks and the weights of those textbooks. She graphs the number of pages and corresponding weights of her 3 math textbooks in the standard (x,y) coordinate plane, as shown below, and discovers a linear relationship among these 3 points. She concludes that the equation of the line that passes through these 3 points is $y = 0.1x + 2.2$.

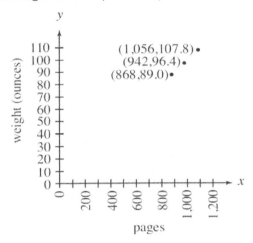

According to Josie's equation, how much would a math textbook with 1,338 pages weight, in pounds? (Note: 16 ounces = 1 pound)

    A. 7.4

    B. 8.5

    C. 10.2

    D. 13.6

Correct Answer: B

Josie's equation, $y = 0.1x + 2.2$, is given in the description of the graph. The number of pages is shown on the x-axis of the graph, so substitute 1,338 for x in the equation: $y = 0.1(1,338) + 2.2 = 133.8 + 2.2 = 136$. This gives you the weight of the book in ounces, but the question asks for its weight in pounds. Notice that the question tells you, in the note, how many ounces are in a pound, in case you don't know. To find the weight of the book in pounds, divide its weight in ounces by 16: $136 / 16 = 8.5$.

22. All line segments that intersect in the polygon below do so at right angles. If the dimensions given are in centimeters, then what is the area of the polygon, in square centimeters?

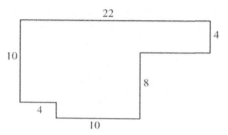

A. 168

B. 176

C. 184

D. 192

E. 200

Correct Answer: D

First, divide the shape into smaller rectangles:

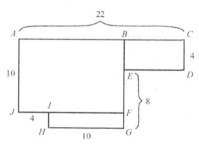

In this diagram, the points have been labeled for reference. Use the formula for the area of a rectangle, $A = lw$, to find the area of each smaller rectangle. Rectangle *BCDE* has a length of 4. To find its width, note that *AC*, which is equal to 22, will have the same measurement as *JI* + *HG* + *ED*. The measurements of two of those segments are given, so solve for *ED*:

$4 + 10 + ED = 22$

$4 + ED = 22$

$ED = 8$

The area of *BCDE* = 4 × 8 = 32. Next, find the area of *IFGH*. The width is given, but you need to find the length. *AJ* plus *IH* must equal *CD* plus *EG*, so fill in the values you know and solve for *IH*:

$10 + IH = 4 + 8$

$10 + IH = 12$

$IH = 2$

The area of *IFGH* = 2 × 10 = 20. Now find the area of *ABFJ*. Its length is given, and the width is *JI* + *IF*. Since *IF* = *HG*, the width is 4 + 10 = 14, and the area is 10 x 14 = 140. Finally, add up all the individual areas to find the area of the entire figure: 32 + 20 + 140 = 192.

23. Mr. Jones spent 6 days grading 996 essays. He averaged 178 essays per day for the first 3 days. Which of the following is closest to his average speed, in essays graded per day, for the final 3 days?

    A. 154

    B. 157

    C. 160

    D. 163

Correct Answer: A

To find the average speed of essay grading, divide the total essays graded by the number of days it took to grade them. This can be written as an equation, (total essays/Number of days).

If Mr. Jones averaged 178 essays per day for the first 3 days, you can find the total number of essays he graded in those three days:

178 = Total / 3

Total = 178 × 3 = 534

In his last 3 days, he then had 996 -534 = 462 essays left to grade. Use the equation to find the average speed for the last 3 days: Average = 462/3 = 154.

24. For all values of y, which of the following is equivalent to $(y + 1)(y^2 - 3y + 2)$?

    A. $y^3 + y^2 - y - 2$

    B. $y^3 + y^2 + 2y + 2$

    C. $y^3 - 2y^2 - y + 2$

    D. $y^3 - 2y^2 + y - 2$

Correct Answer: C

To correctly multiply, each term in the second set of parentheses must be multiplied by both terms in the first set of parentheses. To ensure you don't miss something, write out all six terms, then combine like terms. Multiply each term in the second set of parentheses first by y, then by 1: $(y + 1)(y^2 -3y + 2) = y^3 + y^2 -3y^2 -3y + 2y + 2$. Count to be sure you have six terms before proceeding! Combine like terms to get $y^3 -2y^2 -y + 2$. If you picked another answer, you may have either forgotten a term or made a mistake with your negatives.

25. For ∠D in ΔDEF below, which of the following trigonometric expressions has value 4/5?

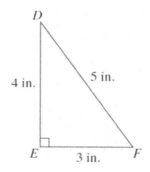

A. sin D

B. tan D

C. cos D

D. sec D

Correct Answer: C

Use *SOHCAHTOA* to solve this problem. Because 5, the number in the denominator, is the hypotenuse of the triangle, the answer to the question must be one of the trig functions that has H in the denominator (that is, sine or cosine), so you can eliminate (B), (D). 4, the number in the numerator, is the side adjacent to $\angle D$. Since $\cos \theta$ =adj/hyp, (C) is correct.

26. Over the weekend, Charlie bought 22 songs from an online music store. He spent a total of $17.90 on contemporary and classical songs. If contemporary songs cost $0.95 each and classical songs cost $0.75 each, then how many contemporary songs did Charlie buy? (**Note:** There is no sales tax charged on these songs because they were purchased online.)

A. 7

B. 9

C. 10

D. 13

Correct Answer: A

Plug in the Answers! If Charlie bought 7 contemporary songs, he must have bought 15 classical songs because he bought 22 in all. This means that Charlie spent 7($0.95) + 15($0.75) on songs altogether. These numbers add up to $17.90, which is the number we want, making A. the correct answers.

ATI TEAS Reading

The English test and the Reading test are very different to each other and cover very different material. ATI TEAS English tests your knowledge of English grammar and usage conventions whereas, ATI TEAS Reading tests your reading comprehension skills.

Timing on ATI TEAS Reading

Unlike the Math section, where you take each problem as it comes, there is instead a way you should be reading passages for ATI TEAS Reading. You need to think about the time it takes to read the passages when it comes to approaching ATI TEAS Reading.

It's a good idea to save most of your time for reading the passages. This feels counter-intuitive, I know, but the longer you spend on each passage, the quicker you'll be able to answer each question correctly and you'll be more accurate while you do it.

A target would be 6 minutes reading and annotating each passage, and then 3 or 4 minutes on each set of questions. Although this sounds odd, if you practice it, you will do well.

Every now and then, it is entirely plausible that you will get a question on ATI TEAS Reading that just you don't know how to do. Maybe you're reading it incorrectly; maybe there's just something about the question. With good preparation, you can reduce the risk of this happening.

Your school's English classes will have prepared you for this section, so you will be reasonably well prepared through this.

Some ATI TEAS tests (like Science) are more abstract and people occasionally question why they are on the ATI TEAS, the presence of the Reading test on the ATI TEAS makes sense. When you get to nursing school, you'll find that you're reading *a lot*.

But don't worry: even if you don't read much outside of your required schoolwork, it's not too late to start! Picking up some extracurricular reading is the best thing you can do to start boosting your ATI TEAS Reading scores. Because the ATI TEAS Reading test covers four subject areas, make sure to read in a variety of areas. General interest publications like *The New Yorker* and *The Atlantic* are very good for this kind of reading, while *The Economist* and *Scientific American* are good sources for social science and hard science reading practice.

Any reading you're currently doing for fun can be turned into study, as long as you treat it like an ATI TEAS passage (and that means reading it like an ATI TEAS passage).

When you start studying for ATI TEAS Reading, it can feel like every question is completely different to the rest. You can do one question then the next one is completely different.

But, if you pay attention as you work through the questions; you'll start to see a pattern emerging. Noticing these types of questions is an effective way to improve your score, because there's a particular approach that works best for solving each one.

Knowing what to expect on test day is not makes the test day much calmer, but it's also just good practice. As you encounter different types of reading passages and questions, various techniques can help you get to the right answers—if you know how to approach them.

ATI TEAS Reading Passages

Here's what to specifically hone in on as you read each one:

Literary Narrative Passages

Literary Narrative passages will include a story of events and revelation of character. You should be looking for the passage's mood or tone, the relationship of the characters, and the emotions and perspective meant by what the characters say and how they say it. Fiction passages often ask questions about how an author often uses dialogue to both describe a situation to a reader and demonstrate a character.

Social Science Passages

Social Science passages show information gathered by research. As you are reading, focus on names, dates, concepts and particular details. Pay attention to which name goes with which concept in a discussion and write down who says what. Keep an eye out for cause-effect relationships, comparisons, and sequences of events.

Humanities Passages

Passages in humanities define or examine concepts or artworks. Some passages of humanities from memoirs or personal essays may seem like fiction passages, but here they are treated as fact. Pay close attention to the speaker and perspective. A question may ask students to determine the likely response of the narrator to a hypothetical argument or circumstance. In these passages, students are asked to infer or distinguish the kinds of relationships between things, ideas, individuals, patterns or thinking styles.

Natural Science Passages

Natural Science passages usually present a science subject and explain the meaning of the topic. In a passage of natural sciences, the speaker is generally concerned with connections between natural events. As with social science passages, specific consideration should be given to cause-effect interactions, parallels, and occurrence chains. You always need to keep track of any specific laws, regulations and hypotheses as you go!

Approaching All Types of ATI TEAS Science Passages

Many non-fiction passages, notably natural science passages, will include some specific or technical language. However, don't fear, the article should provide clues to the meaning of the word (if it doesn't, you'll still find a reference with a definition; it doesn't explicitly check complicated vocabulary).

As with every subject on the ATI TEAS, remember you can do the passages in any order. Some students are not fans of fiction and prefer to leave the literary narrative passage for last. Work with your preferences and strengths and complete the four passages in that order!

ATI TEAS Reading Question Types

In addition to learning how to read effectively, familiarizing yourself with the problem forms on the ATI TEAS Reading Test may help you learn how to tackle other questions, which questions you may want to bypass or save last, or which questions have certain tricks or traps. By learning how the test works, you'll get more questions right.

There are 8 basic question types on the ATI TEAS Reading test:

- Detail

- Main Idea

- Comparative Relationships

- Cause-Effect Relationships and Sequence of Events

- Inferences/Generalizations

- Meaning of Words

- Author's Voice

- Author's Method/Purpose

Here's what you need to know about each of them:

Detail Questions

Detail questions ask you to, as the name suggests find details in the passage. Most of the time, they involve nothing more than simply locating a word or phrase in the text. These are the easiest questions. The trick, though, is that ATI TEAS Reading passages are long, and detailed questions often don't give line numbers or paragraph references. As such don't get trapped in a long search of the passage as you attempt to find out tiny details.

Example: The passage states that, on average, students in 2015 applied to how many more nursing schools than students in 2005?

Main Idea Questions

Main idea questions ask you to determine the primary message of a paragraph, section, or an entire passage. You will see a main idea question on just about every single ATI TEAS Reading passage so you should always be prepared for one. After you finish reading the passage, summarize for yourself the main idea of the passage so you have it straight in your mind and won't be tempted by distracting answer choices that misstate what the passage says or pick up on only one part of the passage. For questions that ask you about a specific paragraph or section, remember that the first and last sentences of paragraphs are often key.

Example: The main purpose of the third paragraph is to demonstrate the author's:

Comparative Relationships

Comparative relationship questions ask you to evaluate how two or more people, viewpoints, events, theories, or so on compare. They require a higher level of thinking than the aforementioned detailed questions.

Example: According to the author, the significant difference between the director's opinion and the star actor's opinion was:

And another example: According to the passage, high school students today are different from teenagers in the past because:

Cause-Effect Relationships and Sequence of Events

Cause-effect and sequence of event questions are fairly similar; they both require you to understand what happened before something else or what happened to cause something else. They are like detailed questions in that the answer will be directly stated in the passage. The only thing you need to be careful about is realizing that the order events are discussed in the passage is not necessarily the order in which they happened.

Example: The narrator conveys that her dismissal from her first job directly resulted in:

Inferences/Generalizations

Inference and generalization questions are typically the hardest questions on the ATI TEAS because the answer won't be directly stated in the passage but will need you to take a lot of information and summarize. It is important to remember that with these questions, do not assume too much. You will only ever have to make a small leap beyond what the passage states. So if you find yourself rationalizing how an answer choice could be true, then you may have missed something. It should be more obvious.

Example: It would be reasonable to infer that the boy was not surprised by the arrival of his mother because:

Meaning of Words

Meaning of words questions are also known as word-in-context questions. You're not usually asked around complicated words here. The paragraph usually picks a term that may have multiple meanings depending on the context and asks you to pick the right one. There are two key approaches to answer these questions. First, place a blank where the word is in the passage and fill it with your own word. Then go to the answer choices and see which one best matches your choice. The other strategy is to read each answer choice back into the passage and see which one makes the most sense in the passage context (even if it doesn't make sense grammatically).

Example: As it is used in line 58, *combed* most nearly means:

Author's Voice

Author's voice questions ask you to infer how a speaker (or writer) feels about his subject. These can be difficult questions, but you should know that half of ATI TEAS Reading passages will ask you a question like this, so you should prepare for them as you read. Really hard to go back and evaluate without re-reading (which you really don't have time for). Look for clues as you read that show how an author or narrator feels about something: often these are strong adjectives, adverbs, or verbs. Sound or voice questions are often particularly important in writing.

Example: The narrator recalls her childhood in a remote area of Canada with a feeling of:

Author's Method/Purpose

Author's method or author's purpose questions challenge you to draw conclusions about what an author wants to do with a passage or why he or she has created the passage in some way. These are not incredibly common questions, but you should be prepared. The best way to prepare for these types of questions is to pay close attention to passage form when you read, and how each sentence expands on the previous one.

Example: In the context of the whole passage, the author most likely chose to include the examples of the extinction of certain bird species in order to:

Hints and Tips: ATI TEAS Reading

Now that you have seen the types of questions you are likely to see, have a look at my tips for the reading section:

Questions First

The most important things on the ATI TEAS Reading Test aren't the passages. The most important things are the questions; despite the fact they take the most time. When you start a new passage, closely read the questions. Why? They contain the keywords you will need to discover in the passages. Underline/mark any proper nouns the questions mention and mark any line numbers mentioned in a question. These will be easy to spot later and will be good for saving time.

It's good to have a general idea of what the passage is about. Take a moment and read the first few sentences. then start searching for keywords. This is also known as skim reading. Before taking any practice tests, get to know the question types already discussed. Though the question types on the ATI TEAS Reading Test normally go from easiest to most difficult, but that's not for certain, so make sure you know all the question types.

Save the Last Question for Last

Generally, the last question will focus on the passage as a whole. So save it for the end. You will have invested a lot of information by the time you get to it and therefore will be more likely to understand it.

The ATI TEAS Reading Test (and to an equal extent the Science Test) relies on your ability to actively read. Fortunately for you, active reading on the ATI TEAS is a lot easier than it might seem at first glance.

Active reading means reading with a target in mind. This is why I suggest to look at the questions first. As you read the passage, consistently ask yourself questions: does that answer a question? How does it answer the question? Do I need more information before I mark an answer?

If you're never tried Active reading, this can seem daunting, but with practice, it will become an unconscious part of your study schedule.

Timing ATI TEAS Reading

The time isn't as tough as it is on ATI TEAS Math. But, that doesn't mean it's easy. Mastering speed is the first thing you can do to make ATI TEAS Reading more manageable.

Time yourself as you practice

If you are spending more than 3 minutes reading and marking passages, you are risking not being able to finish all of the questions on test day. As you become more and more confident with your accuracy, try to get as precise as possible with the timing of your note-taking.

When you do a practice test for reading, do so with a timer. You may want to set the timer to go off every 9-10 minutes. Don't rush, but make sure you can move confidently from one passage to the next and answer all of the questions in the time you are given. Then, after 9 minutes, move on to the next passage.

Do the passages in any order, you will have 4 passages and you must always answer all 40 questions, but that doesn't mean you have to answer them in the order in which they are presented on the test. As you practice, you will start to realize which passages are easier and which are more challenging for you.

But, when you do this, be extra careful to write your answers in the correct place on your answer sheet. It sounds simple, but many students have fallen foul of this.

How to Deal with "Except," "Not," or "Least" Questions on the ATI TEAS

Some of the ATI TEAS Reading passages contain test questions with words like "Except," "Not," or "Least" in them. To start, rephrase the question in easier language.

Try to figure out what it's really asking. This will really help you get to the bottom of one of the trickiest types of questions on the ATI TEAS.

It is useful to determine what your job is to do, then to write it down. If a question asks, "Which of the following does NOT match the tone of the passage?" your task may be to "eliminate choices that fit the tone." This will give you a better idea of how to approach the answer choices.

Whilst questions such as this are open-ended, go back to the passage and make a prediction whenever possible. Even for a question like, "All of the following is true about Hamlet except:" you can still refer back to the passage and locate the paragraph that provides details about Hamlet.

You'll need to examine these answer choices more slowly and critically than other Reading questions. Don't rush through them. Carefully eliminate choices based on information from the passage. If you realize during the ATI TEAS Reading section that you won't have time to finish all of the questions, go to the passages with which you have had the most success in the past.

The ATI TEAS Reading Example

Stem cells have recently become an important focus for scientific research around the world. They have two important characteristics that distinguish them from other types of cells. First, they are unspecialized cells that renew themselves for long periods through cell division. Also, under certain physiologic or experimental conditions, they can be induced to become cells with special functions such as the beating cells of the heart muscle or the insulin-producing cells of the pancreas.

Scientists primarily work with two kinds of stem cells from animals and humans: embryonic stem cells and adult stem cells, which each have different functions and characteristics. Scientists discovered ways to obtain or derive stem cells from early mouse embryos more than 20 years ago. Many years of detailed study of the biology of mouse stem cells led to the discovery, in 1998, of a means to isolate stem cells from human embryos and grow the cells in the laboratory.

These are called human embryonic stem cells. The embryos used in these studies were created for infertility purposes through in vitro fertilization procedures, and when they were no longer needed for that purpose, they were donated for research with the informed consent of the donor.

Stem cells are important for living organisms for many reasons. In the 3- to 5-day-old embryo, called a blastocyst, a small group of about 30 cells called the inner cell mass gives rise to the hundreds of highly specialized cells needed to make up an adult organism. In the developing fetus, stem cells in developing tissues give rise to the multiple specialized cell types that make up the heart, lung, skin, and other tissues. In some adult tissues, such as bone marrow, muscle, and brain, discrete populations of adult stem cells generate replacements for cells that are lost through normal wear and tear, injury, or disease. It has even been hypothesized that stem cells may someday become the basis for treating diseases such as Parkinson's disease, diabetes, and heart disease.

Scientists want to study stem cells in the laboratory so they can learn about their essential properties and what makes them different from specialized cell types. As scientists learn more about stem cells, it may become possible to use the cells not just in cell-based therapies but also for screening new drugs and toxins and understanding birth defects. Current research goals include both determining precisely how stem cells remain unspecialized and self-renewing for so long and identifying the signals that cause stem cells to become specialized cells.

1. The author's primary purpose in writing this passage was to:

    A. argue the necessity for an effective diabetes treatment and oppose the use of mouse embryonic stem cell research

    B. aggressively defend the ethicality of gathering embryonic stem cells from human embryos

    C. hesitantly debate the role stem cells will most certainly play in future medicine

    D. explain stem cell research in relatively basic terms and point out its greatly untapped potential

Correct answer: D.

The primary purpose of the passage is to introduce and describe stem cells. Additionally, the passage emphasizes the potential importance of stem cell research to our society.

2. According to the passage, the hypothesis, given in the end of the third paragraph, that stem cells hold the key to treating some of the most troublesome diseases of our time would suggest which of the following?

   A. Stem cell research will provide the means for several preventive therapies, which could be put in place in a developing fetus.

   B. Research in the field of stem cells is rapidly nearing its limit of applicability.

   C. Cells that have already become specialized are of little use when it comes to disease treatment.

   D. Stem cell research could prove more important in the medical world than anyone could have possibly anticipated.

Correct answer: D.

The importance of the research is unknown, but the potential that stem cells hold may be greater than anyone can imagine based on the small amount of research that has been conducted.

3. Which one of the following statements is best supported by the properties of stem cells listed by the author?

   A. A single cell may originate as a stem cell, but it could still live the majority of its life span as a muscle tissue cell.

   B. Stem cells embody the peak of evolutionary achievement.

   C. Embryo donors are vastly decreasing in numbers as legislation is passed against these sorts of infertility procedures.

   D. Birth defects are most often caused by improper differentiation of cells from stem cells.

Correct answer: A.

This answer is correct because stem cells can originate in undifferentiated form and then turn into a specific type of cell.

4. Which one of the following statements, if true, lends the most support to the author's argument that stem cell treatments will become a valuable staple in the medical world in years to come?

   A. Currently, stem cells are considered relative mysteries of science, but many researchers still believe in their promise.

   B. Stem cells multiply without any contact inhibition, much like cancer cells.

   C. Though stem cells have much potential as a new form of medical treatment, there is doubt whether we will ever be able to efficiently manipulate them.

   D. By inducing stem cells to differentiate into the tissue of choice, doctors can use healthy new cells to replace an afflicted patient's damaged or diseased cells.

Correct answer: D.

If this statement were true, then stem cells could potentially cure any disease. This potential would certainly cause them to become a valuable staple of the medical community.

5. Which one of the following can replace the word essential in line 54 without significantly changing the author's intended meaning?

   A. auxiliary

   B. fundamental

   C. necessary

   D. superfluous

Correct answer: B.

Scientists want to learn the basics about stem cells, which is why they want to understand their essential or fundamental properties.

6. Which one of the following best describes the organization of the passage?

A. A topical theory is offered, the author supports the theory with mundane evidence, and then he or she concludes by calling the reader to action using emotional persuasion.

B. Clashing hypotheses are produced, the merits of each side are debated, and then the hypotheses are merged into a single, more accurate theory.

C. A topic is introduced, its known features and its mystery are discussed, and then future goals and applications are proposed.

D. A scientific enigma is explained, its history is chronicled, and then certain applications are attacked for their simplicity.

Correct answer: C.

The first paragraph introduces the topic of stem cells. The second and third paragraphs discuss the features and mysteries of stem cells. Finally, the fourth paragraph discusses the future goals of the research.

The ATI TEAS Reading Exercise

Directions: Each passage is followed by several questions. After reading a passage, choose the best answer to each question and fill in the corresponding oval on your answer document. You may refer to the passages as often as necessary.

Here they are, two North Americans, a man and a woman just over and just under forty, come to spend their lives in Mexico and already lost as they travel cross-country over the central plateau. The driver of the station wagon is Richard Everton, a blue-eyed, black-haired stubborn man. On the seat beside him is his wife, Sara. She pictures the adobe house where they intend to sleep tonight. It is a mile and a half high on the out-skirts of Ibarra, a declining village of one thousand souls. Tunneled into the mountain is the copper mine Richard's grandfather abandoned fifty years ago during the Revolution of 1910.

Dark is coming on and, unless they find a road, night trap at this desolate spot both the future operator of the Malaguefia mine and the fair-haired unsuspecting future mistress of the adobe house. Sara Everton is anticipating their arrival at a place curtained and warm, though she knows the house has neither electricity nor furniture and, least of all, kindling beside the hearth. There is some doubt about running water in the pipes. The Malaguefia mine, on the other hand, is flooded up to the second level.

"Let's stop and ask the way," says Sara. And they take a diagonal course across a cleared space of land. But the owner of this field is nowhere in sight.

"We won't get to Ibarra before dark," says Sara.

"Do you think we'll recognize the house?"

"Yes," he says, and without speaking they separately recall a faded photograph of a wide, low structure with a long veranda in front. On the veranda is a hammock, and in the hammock is Richard's grandmother, dressed in eyelet embroidery and holding a Fluted fan.

Five days ago the Evertons left San Francisco in order to extend the family's Mexican history and patch the present onto the past. To find out if there was still copper underground and how much of the rest of it was true, the width of the sky, the depth of the stars, and the air like new wine. To weave chance and hope into a fabric that would clothe them as long as they lived.

Even their closest friends have failed to understand. "Call us when you get there," they said. "Send a telegram." But Ibarra lacks these services. "What will you do for light?" they were asked. And, "How long since someone lived in the house?" But this question collapsed of its own weight before a reply could be composed.

Every day for a month Richard has reminded Sara, "We mustn't expect too much." And each time his wife answered, "no." But the Evertons expect too much. They have experienced the terrible persuasion of a great-aunt's recollections and adopted them as their own. They have not considered that memories are like corks left out of bottles. They swell. They no longer fit.

Now here, lost in the Mexican interior, Richard and Sara remember the rock pick Richard's grandfather gave him when he was six. His grandfather had used the pick himself to chip away copper ore from extrusions that coursed like exposed arteries down the slopes of the mountains. "What does he know about mining?" Richard's friends have asked one another. "What does she know about gasoline stoves? In case of burns, where will they find a doctor?" The friends learn that the Evertons are taking a first aid manual, antibiotics for dysentery, and a snakebite kit. There are other questions relating to symphony season tickets, Christmas, golf, sailing. To these, the answers are evasive.

A farmer, leading a burro, approaches the car from behind. He regards the two Americans. "You are not on the road to Ibarra," he says. "Permit me a moment." And he gazes first at his feet, then at the mountains, then at their luggage. "You must drive north on that dry arroyo for two kilometers and turn left when you reach a road. You will recognize it by the tire tracks of the morning bus unless rain has fallen. But this is the dry season."

"Without a tail wind we won't be bothered by the dust," says Richard, and turns north.

He is mistaken. The arroyo is smooth and soft with dust that, even in still air, spins from the car's wheels and sifts through sealed surfaces, the flooring, the dashboard, the factory-tested weather stripping. It etches black lines on their palms, sands their skin, powders their lashes, and deposits a bitter taste on their tongues.

"This must be the wrong way," says Sara, from under the sweater she has pulled over her head.

Richard says nothing. He knows it is the right way, as right as a way to Ibarra can be, as right as his decision to reopen an idle mine and bring his wife to a house built half of nostalgia and half of clay.

1. The passage is told from what point of view?

    A. First person, narrated by a minor character

    B. First person, narrated by a main character

    C. Third person, narrated by a voice outside the action of the story

    D. Third person, narrated through the perspective of one character

2. What does the passage suggest about how many, if any, preceding visits the Evertons have made to Ibarra?

A. They have visited Ibarra before, but not for several years.

B. They have been to Ibarra regularly to visit Richard's grandmother.

C. They visited Ibarra once before to examine the Malaguefia mine.

D. They have not been to Ibarra prior to this visit.

3. The main point made in the eighth paragraph is that:

A. when everything is carefully planned, there's no risk of disappointment

B. older relatives should not try to persuade family members to change lifestyles.

C. people cannot live on their own memories but should instead look to the future.

D. it's unwise to form expectations based on other people's enticing stories of another time.

4. Based on the passage, how does the house in Sara's thoughts most likely compare to the actual house where the Evertons plan to sleep?

A. Sara's imagined house is much more inviting than the actual house.

B. Sara pictured a house that's nearly a perfect copy of the actual house.

C. The actual house is much grander than Sara is imagining.

D. The actual house is just as uninviting as the house in Sara's imagination

5. It could most reasonably be considered ironic that while Richard and Sara's copper mine:

A. is located on the side of a mountain; they get lost traveling cross-country to Ibarra.

B. was abandoned in 1910; Sara still remembers the rock pick Richard was given when he was six.

C. is located near the village of Ibarra; no one has lived in the house for several years.

D. is flooded to the second level; the house is likely to be without running water.

6. Richard thinks he and Sara will recognize the house where they intend to sleep because:

   A. it's made of adobe

   B. Richard's grandmother described it to them

   C. they have seen an old photograph of it

   D. it's the only house with a veranda

7. As it is used in paragraph 5 the phrase "the rest of it" refers to the:

   A. amount of copper still left to be dug out of the mine

   B. stories that Richard and Sara have heard about the natural appeal of the region.

   C. town of Ibarra that Richard is anxious to find out more about

   D. close friends they left behind along with their old lives in San Francisco.

8. The services mentioned specifically refer to:

   A. symphony tickets and sailing excursions

   B. medical aid and antibiotics.

   C. electricity and running water

   D. telephone calls and telegrams

9. The list "symphony season tickets, Christmas, golf, sailing" is a reference to Richard and Sara's:

   A. unwillingness to spend money frivolously

   B. concerns about heading for Ibarra.

   C. recreational opportunities in Mexico

   D. former social lives in San Francisco.

10. According to the passage, the farmer tells the Evertons that it's the dry season to make the point that the:

A. tire tracks of the bus should still be visible on the road

B. drive to Ibarra will be hot and dusty.

C. Evertons should reach Ibarra before it begins to rain.

D. Evertons should have brought drinking water with them

Answers:

1. Correct Answer: C

2. Correct Answer: D

3. Correct Answer: D

4. Correct Answer: A

5. Correct Answer: D

6. Correct Answer: C

7. Correct Answer: B

8. Correct Answer: D

9. Correct Answer: D

10. Correct Answer: A

ATI TEAS Science

The TEAS Science subtest consists of 53 total questions (47 scored) and has a 63 minute time limit. The most recent version of the exam expanded the science subtest. Candidates often find this section to be one of the most challenging and hence this book will contain a bit of extra content when compared to the other sections in here. The TEAS Science subtest assesses a student's knowledge of scientific reasoning, life science, the human body, and physical and earth science.

A student is required to have quite a depth of knowledge in ATI TEAS Science, and this section will go into detail for each of the required knowledge statements. In this section you will find a lot of factual information that is provided for you to help you learn the required content. If that after all this you find you are not sure about certain topic areas, it would be wise to get some extra help.

You will be required to:

- Describe the functions of the following systems: circulatory, nervous, digestive, respiratory and immune systems.

- Describe general anatomy and physiology concepts

- Understand natural selection and adaptation

- Interpret the biological classification system

- Understand the parts of a cell and its corresponding functions

- Understand DNA and RNA

- Contrast respiration and photosynthesis

- Contrast meiosis and mitosis

- Utilize taxonomy

- Use Mendel's laws of genetics and the Punnett square

- Apply the periodic table of elements

- Describe the properties of atoms

- Determine the properties of matter

- Calculate diffusion rates and molarity

- Interpret pH scale values

- Determine force and motion

- Describe the parts of an experiment

- Interpret scientific arguments

Describe the functions of the circulatory, nervous, digestive and immune system

1. Circulatory System

The human circulatory system keeps blood, oxygen and nutrients flowing through the body. The circulatory system, also known as the cardiovascular system, is a vast network of organs and blood vessels that acts both as a delivery and waste removal system for the body. Nutrients, oxygen and hormones are delivered to every cell and as these necessities are provided, waste products such as carbon dioxide are removed.

Not only does the circulatory system keep our cells healthy, but it also keeps us alive. The heart constantly receives signals from the rest of the body that direct how hard it needs to pump to properly supply the body with what it needs. For example, when asleep, the body sends electrical signals to the heart that tell it to slow down. When participating in heavy exercise, the heart receives the message to pump harder to deliver extra oxygen to the muscles.

How the circulatory system works

The heart lies at the center of the circulatory system and pumps blood through the rest of the network. This hollow muscle is made up of four chambers: The left and right atriums make up the two chambers at the top and the left and right ventricles form the two chambers at the bottom. The chambers are separated by one-way valves to ensure that blood flows in the correct direction.

The rest of the circulatory system is made up of two independent networks that work together: The pulmonary and systemic systems.

The pulmonary system is responsible for providing fresh oxygen to the blood and removing carbon dioxide. Oxygen-poor blood arrives from veins leading to the right atrium of the heart. The blood is then pumped through the right ventricle, then through the pulmonary artery, which splits off into two and divides into increasingly smaller arteries and capillaries before entering the lungs. The tiny capillaries form a network within the lungs that facilitate the exchange of carbon dioxide and oxygen. From the lungs, the oxygen-rich blood flows back toward the heart.

Next, the systemic system of arteries, veins and capillaries takes over. Arteries and veins are not the same, although they are both types of blood vessels. Arteries carry oxygen-and nutrient-rich blood from the heart to all parts of your body, according to the National Cancer Institute. Veins carry the oxygen-and nutrient-poor blood back to the heart. The capillaries are the smallest type of blood vessel, and provide the bridge between the arteries and veins.

As the oxygen-rich blood arrives from the lungs, it enters the left atrium and then travels through to the left ventricle before being pumped throughout the body. The blood gets pumped through the aorta artery (the largest artery in the body) before entering the smaller arteries that carry the blood to every part of the body. As the blood delivers nutrients and oxygen to each cell, carbon dioxide and other waste products are picked up as the blood flows through the capillaries and into the veins.

The contraction and relaxation of the heart – the heartbeat – is controlled by the sinus node, which is a cluster of cells situated at the top of the right atrium. The sinus node sends electrical signals through the electrical conduction system of the heart that direct the muscle to contract or relax.

The heartbeat is divided into two phases: the systole and diastole phases. In the first, the ventricles contract and push blood out into the pulmonary artery or the aorta. At the same time, the valves separating the atria and ventricles snap shut to prevent blood from flowing backwards. In the diastole phase, the valves connecting to the atrium open, and the ventricles relax and fill with blood. The sinus node controls the pace of these two phases.

Adult humans have a total of about five to six quarts (a little less than five to six liters) of blood pumping through their bodies. On average, the heart pumps about 100,000 times per day, pushing about 2,000 gallons (7,570 liters) of blood through a total of 60,000 miles (96,560 kilometers) of blood vessels. It only takes about 20 seconds for blood to travel through the entire circulatory system.

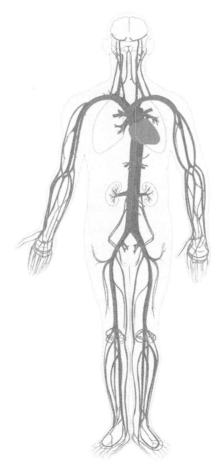

Figure 1: Circulatory system.

Circulatory system diseases

Heart disease is the leading cause of death for both men and women in the United States, claiming 610,000 people per year.

Heart disease is a broad term that covers a wide range of diseases and disorders, including stroke (the blockage of blood to the brain), heart attack (the flow of blood to the heart is blocked), hypertension (high blood pressure causing the heart to work harder), arteriosclerosis (the arteries become thick and stiff) and aneurysm (a damaged blood vessel that can lead to internal bleeding).

Risk factors for heart disease include age, sex, family history, poor diet, smoking and stress, as well as high blood pressure and elevated cholesterol levels, according to the Mayo Clinic. There are many ways that heart disease can be prevented, including keeping other health conditions under control, maintaining a healthy diet, participating in regular physical activity and keeping stress levels at a minimum.

2. Nervous System

The nervous system is a complex collection of nerves and specialized cells known as neurons that transmit signals between different parts of the body. It is essentially the body's electrical wiring. Structurally, the nervous system has two components: the central nervous system and the peripheral nervous system.

According to the National Institutes of Health, the central nervous system is made up of the brain, spinal cord and nerves. The peripheral nervous system consists of sensory neurons, ganglia (clusters of neurons) and nerves that connect to one another and to the central nervous system.

Functionally, the nervous system has two main subdivisions: the somatic, or voluntary, component; and the autonomic, or involuntary, component. The autonomic nervous system regulates certain body processes, such as blood pressure and the rate of breathing, that work without conscious effort. The somatic system consists of nerves that connect the brain and spinal cord with muscles and sensory receptors in the skin.

Description of the nervous system

Nerves are cylindrical bundles of fibers that start at the brain and central cord and branch out to every other part of the body.

Neurons send signals to other cells through thin fibers called axons, which cause chemicals known as neurotransmitters to be released at junctions called synapses. There are over 100 trillion neural connections in the average human brain, though the number and location can vary. For example, the brains of highly creative people have more connections among three specific regions of the brain than less creative thinkers.

A synapse gives a command to the cell and the entire communication process typically takes only a fraction of a millisecond. Signals travel along an alpha motor neuron in the spinal cord 268 mph (431 km/h); the fastest transmission in the human body.

Sensory neurons react to physical stimuli such as light, sound and touch and send feedback to the central nervous system about the body's surrounding environment, motor neurons, located in the central nervous system or in peripheral ganglia, transmit signals to activate the muscles or glands.

Glial cells, derived from the Greek word for "glue," are specialized cells that support, protect or nourish nerve cells.

Diagnosing nervous system conditions

There are a number of tests and procedures to diagnose conditions involving the nervous system. In addition to the traditional X-ray, a specialized X-ray called a fluoroscopy examines the body in motion, such as blood flowing through arteries. Other standard neurological exams include an MRI (magnetic resonance imaging), CT scan, and an electroencephalogram (EEG), which records the brain's continuous electrical activity. Positron emission tomography (PET) is a procedure that measures cell or tissue metabolism and brain activity to detect tumors or diseased tissue or tumors.

A spinal tap places a needle into the spinal canal to drain a small amount of cerebral spinal fluid that is tested for infection or other abnormalities.

Diseases of the nervous system

Of all the diseases of the nervous system, the most common difficulty that people have is pain, and much of that is nerve-related. There are 100 million people who live with chronic pain. Patients with nerve disorders experience functional difficulties, which result in conditions such as:

- Epilepsy, in which abnormal electrical discharges from brain cells cause seizures.

- Parkinson's disease, which is a progressive nerve disease that affects movement.

- Multiple sclerosis (MS), in which the protective lining of the nerves is attacked by the body's immune system. Amyotrophic lateral sclerosis (ALS), also known as Lou Gehrig's disease, is a motor neuron disease which weakens the muscles and progressively hampers physical function.

- Huntington's disease, which is an inherited condition that cause the nerve cells in the brain to degenerate.

- Alzheimer's disease, which covers a wide range of disorders that impacts mental functions, particularly memory.

The nervous system can also be affected by vascular disorders such as:

- Stroke, which occurs when there is bleeding on the brain or the blow flow to the brain is obstructed;

- Transient ischemic attack (TIA), which are mini-type strokes that last a shorter period of time but mimic stroke symptoms; and Subarachnoid hemorrhage, which is specifically bleeding in the space between your brain and the surrounding membrane that can be the result of a trauma or rupturing of a weak blood vessel;

- Infections such as meningitis, encephalitis, polio, and epidural abscess can also affect the nervous system.

Treatments vary from anti-inflammatory medications and pain medications such as opiates, to implanted nerve stimulators and wearable devices and many people also turn to herbal and holistic methods to reduce pain, such as "acupuncture".

The branch of medicine that studies and treats the nervous system is called neurology, and doctors who practice in this field of medicine are called neurologists. Once they have completed medical training, neurologists complete additional training for their specialty and are certified by the American Board of Psychiatry and Neurology (ABPN).

There are also physiatrists, who are physicians who work to rehabilitate patients who have experienced disease or injury to their nervous systems that impact their ability to function.

3. Digestive System

The Human digestive system, is the system used in the human body for the process of digestion. The human digestive system consists primarily of the digestive tract, or the series of structures and organs through which food and liquids pass during their processing into forms absorbable into the bloodstream. The system also consists of the structures through which wastes pass in the process of elimination and other organs that contribute juices necessary for the digestive process.

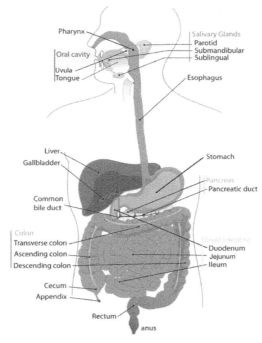

Figure 2: Digestive system

Structures And Functions Of The Human Digestive System

The digestive tract begins at the lips and ends at the anus. It consists of the mouth, or oral cavity, with its teeth, for grinding the food, and its tongue, which serves to knead food and mix it with saliva; the throat, or pharynx; the esophagus; the stomach; the small intestine, consisting of the duodenum, the jejunum, and the ileum; and the large intestine, consisting of the cecum, a closed-end sac connecting with the ileum, the ascending colon, the transverse colon, the descending colon, and the sigmoid colon, which terminates in the rectum. Glands contributing digestive juices include the salivary glands, the gastric glands in the stomach lining, the pancreas, and the liver and its adjuncts—the gallbladder and bile ducts. All of these organs and glands contribute to the physical and chemical breaking down of ingested food and to the eventual elimination of non-digestible wastes. Their structures and functions are described step by step in this section.

The abdominal organs are supported and protected by the bones of the pelvis and ribcage and are covered by the greater omentum, a fold of peritoneum that consists mainly of fat.

Mouth and oral structures

Little digestion of food actually takes place in the mouth. However, through the process of mastication, or chewing, food is prepared in the mouth for transport through the upper digestive tract into the stomach and small intestine, where the principal digestive processes take place. Chewing is the first mechanical process to which food is subjected. Movements of the lower jaw in chewing are brought about by the muscles of mastication (the masseter, the temporal, the medial and lateral pterygoids, and the buccinator). The sensitivity of the periodontal membrane that surrounds and supports the teeth, rather than the power of the muscles of mastication, determines the force of the bite.

Mastication is not essential for adequate digestion. Chewing does aid digestion, however, by reducing food to small particles and mixing it with the saliva secreted by the salivary glands. The saliva lubricates and moistens dry food, while chewing distributes the saliva throughout the food mass. The movement of the tongue against the hard palate and the cheeks helps to form a rounded mass, or bolus, of food.

The teeth are hard, white structures found in the mouth. Usually used for mastication, the teeth of different vertebrate species are sometimes specialized. The teeth of snakes, for example, are very thin and sharp and usually curve backward; they function in capturing prey but not in chewing, because snakes swallow their food whole. The teeth of carnivorous mammals, such as cats and dogs, are more pointed than those of primates, including humans; the canines are long, and the premolars lack flat grinding surfaces, being more adapted to cutting and shearing (often the more posterior molars are lost).

On the other hand, herbivores such as cows and horses have very large, flat premolars and molars with complex ridges and cusps; the canines are often totally absent. Sharp pointed teeth, poorly adapted for chewing, generally characterize meat eaters such as snakes, dogs, and cats; and broad, flat teeth, well adapted for chewing, characterize herbivores.

The differences in the shapes of teeth are functional adaptations. Few animals can digest cellulose, yet the plant cells used as food by herbivores are enclosed in cellulose cell walls that must be broken down before the cell contents can be exposed to the action of digestive enzymes. By contrast, the animal cells in meat are not encased in non-digestible matter and can be acted upon directly by digestive enzymes. Consequently, chewing is not so essential for carnivores as it is for herbivores. Humans, who are omnivores (eaters of plants and animal tissue), have teeth that belong, functionally and structurally, somewhere between the extremes of specialization attained by the teeth of carnivores and herbivores.

Each tooth consists of a crown and one or more roots. The crown is the functional part of the tooth that is visible above the gum. The root is the unseen portion that supports and fastens the tooth in the jawbone. The shapes of the crowns and the roots vary in different parts of the mouth and from one animal to another. The teeth on one side of the jaw are essentially a mirror image of those located on the opposite side. The upper teeth differ from the lower and are complementary to them. Humans normally have two sets of teeth during their lifetime. The first set, known as the deciduous, milk, or primary dentition, is acquired gradually between the ages of six months and two years. As the jaws grow and expand, these teeth are replaced one by one by the teeth of the secondary set. There are five deciduous teeth and eight permanent teeth in each quarter of the mouth, resulting in a total of 32 permanent teeth to succeed the 20 deciduous ones.

The lips and cheeks

The lips, two fleshy folds that surround the mouth, are composed externally of skin and internally of mucous membrane, or mucosa. The mucosa is rich in mucus-secreting glands, which together with saliva ensure adequate lubrication for the purposes of speech and mastication.

The cheeks, the sides of the mouth, are continuous with the lips and have a similar structure. A distinct fat pad is found in the subcutaneous tissue (the tissue beneath the skin) of the cheek; this pad is especially large in infants and is known as the sucking pad. On the inner surface of each cheek, opposite the second upper molar tooth, is a slight elevation that marks the opening of the parotid duct, leading from the parotid salivary gland, which is located in front of the ear. Just behind this gland are four to five mucus-secreting glands, the ducts of which open opposite the last molar tooth.

The roof of the mouth

The roof of the mouth is concave and is formed by the hard and soft palate. The hard palate is formed by the horizontal portions of the two palatine bones and the palatine portions of the maxillae, or upper jaws. The hard palate is covered by a thick, somewhat pale mucous membrane that is continuous with that of the gums and is bound to the upper jaw and palate bones by firm fibrous tissue. The soft palate is continuous with the hard palate in front.

Posteriorly it is continuous with the mucous membrane covering the floor of the nasal cavity. The soft palate is composed of a strong, thin, fibrous sheet, the palatine aponeurosis, and the glossopalatine and pharyngopalatine muscles. A small projection called the uvula hangs free from the posterior of the soft palate.

The floor of the mouth

The floor of the mouth can be seen only when the tongue is raised. In the midline is a prominent, elevated fold of mucous membrane (frenulum linguae) that binds each lip to the gums, and on each side of this is a slight fold called a sublingual papilla, from which the ducts of the submandibular salivary glands open.

Running outward and backward from each sublingual papilla is a ridge (the plica sublingualis) that marks the upper edge of the sublingual (under the tongue) salivary gland and onto which most of the ducts of that gland open.

The gums

The gums consist of mucous membranes connected by thick fibrous tissue to the membrane surrounding the bones of the jaw. The gum membrane rises to form a collar around the base of the crown (exposed portion) of each tooth.

Rich in blood vessels, the gum tissues receive branches from the alveolar arteries; these vessels, called alveolar because of their relationship to the alveoli dentales, or tooth sockets, also supply the teeth and the spongy bone of the upper and lower jaws, in which the teeth are lodged.

The tongue

The tongue, a muscular organ located on the floor of the mouth, is an extremely mobile structure and is an important accessory organ in such motor functions as speech, chewing, and swallowing. In conjunction with the cheeks, it is able to guide and maintain food between the upper and lower teeth until mastication is complete.

The motility of the tongue aids in creating a negative pressure within the oral cavity and thus enables infants to suckle. Especially important as a peripheral sense organ, the tongue contains groups of specialized epithelial cells, known as taste buds, that carry stimuli from the oral cavity to the central nervous system. Furthermore, the tongue's glands produce some of the saliva necessary for swallowing.

The tongue consists of a mass of interwoven striated (striped) muscles interspersed with fat. The mucous membrane that covers the tongue varies in different regions. The tongue is attached to the lower jaw, the hyoid bone (a U-shaped bone between the lower jaw and the larynx), the skull, the soft palate, and the pharynx by its extrinsic muscles. It is bound to the floor of the mouth and to the epiglottis (a plate of cartilage that serves as a lid for the larynx) by folds of mucous membrane.

Salivary glands

Food is tasted and mixed with saliva that is secreted by several sets of glands. Besides the many minute glands that secrete saliva, there are three major pairs of salivary glands: the parotid, the submandibular, and the sublingual glands. The parotid glands, the largest of the pairs, are located at the side of the face, below and in front of each ear. The parotid glands are enclosed in sheaths that limit the extent of their swelling when inflamed, as in mumps. The submandibular glands, which are rounded in shape, lie near the inner side of the lower jawbone, in front of the sternomastoid muscle (the prominent muscle of the jaw). The sublingual glands lie directly under the mucous membrane covering the floor of the mouth beneath the tongue.

The salivary glands are of the type called racemose, from the Latin racemosus ("full of clusters"), because of the cluster like arrangement of their secreting cells in rounded sacs, called acini, attached to freely branching systems of ducts. The walls of the acini surround a small central cavity known as an alveolus. In the walls of the acini are pyramidal secreting cells and some flat, star-shaped contract cells called myoepithelial, or basket, cells.

The latter cells are thought to contract , like the similar myoepithelial cells of the breast, which by their contraction expel milk from the milk ducts.

The secreting cells may be of the serous or the mucous type. The latter type secretes mucin, the chief constituent of mucus; the former, a watery fluid containing the enzyme amylase. The secreting cells of the parotid glands are of the serous type; those of the submandibular glands, of both serous and mucous types, with the serous cells outnumbering the mucous cells by four to one. The acini of the sublingual glands are composed primarily of mucous cells.

The salivary glands are controlled by the two divisions of the autonomic nervous system, the sympathetic and the parasympathetic. The parasympathetic nerve supply regulates secretion by the acinar cells and causes the blood vessels to dilate. Functions regulated by the sympathetic nerves include secretion by the acinar cells, constriction of blood vessels, and, presumably, contraction of the myoepithelial cells. Normally secretion of saliva is constant, regardless of the presence of food in the mouth. The amount of saliva secreted in 24 hours usually amounts to 1–1.5 liters.

When something touches the gums, the tongue, or some region of the mouth lining, or when chewing occurs, the amount of saliva secreted increases. The stimulating substance need not be food—dry sand in the mouth or even moving the jaws and tongue when the mouth is empty increases the salivary flow. This coupling of direct stimulation to the oral mucosa with increased salivation is known as the unconditioned salivary reflex. When an individual learns that a particular sight, sound, smell, or other stimulus is regularly associated with food, that stimulus alone may suffice to stimulate increased salivary flow. This response is known as the conditioned salivary reflex.

Saliva

Saliva dissolves some of the chewed food and acts as a lubricant, facilitating passage through the subsequent portions of the digestive tract . Saliva also contains a starch-digesting enzyme called amylase (ptyalin), which initiates the process of enzymatic hydrolysis; it splits starch (a polysaccharide containing many sugar molecules bound in a continuous chain) into molecules of the double sugar maltose. Many carnivores, such as dogs and cats, have no amylase in their saliva; therefore, their natural diet contains very little starch. Substances must be in solution for the taste buds to be stimulated; saliva provides the solvent for food materials.

The composition of saliva varies, but its principal components are water, inorganic ions similar to those commonly found in blood plasma, and a number of organic constituents, including salivary proteins, free amino acids, and the enzymes lysozyme and amylase. Although saliva is slightly acidic, the bicarbonates and phosphates contained within it serve as buffers and maintain the pH, or hydrogen ion concentration, of saliva relatively constant under ordinary conditions.

The concentrations of bicarbonate, chloride, potassium, and sodium in saliva are directly related to the rate of their flow. There is also a direct relation between bicarbonate concentration and the partial pressure of carbon dioxide in the blood. The concentration of chloride in the blood varies from 5 millimoles per litre at low flow rates to 70 millimoles per litre when the flow rate is high. The sodium concentrations in similar circumstances vary from 5 millimoles per litre to 100 millimoles per litre. The concentration of potassium in the blood is often higher than that in the blood plasma, up to 20 millimoles per litre, which accounts for the sharp and metallic taste of saliva when flow is brisk.

The constant flow of saliva keeps the oral cavity and teeth moist and comparatively free from food residues, sloughed epithelial cells, and foreign particles. By removing material that may serve as culture media, saliva inhibits the growth of bacteria. Saliva serves a protective function, for the enzyme lysozyme has the ability to lyse, or dissolve, certain bacteria. The secretion of saliva also provides a mechanism whereby certain organic and inorganic substances can be excreted from the body, including mercury, lead, potassium iodide, bromide, morphine, ethyl alcohol, and certain antibiotics such as penicillin, streptomycin, and chlortetracycline.

Although saliva is not essential to life, its absence results in a number of inconveniences, including dryness of the oral mucous membrane, poor oral hygiene because of bacterial overgrowth, a greatly diminished sense of taste, and difficulties with speech.

Pharynx

The pharynx, or throat, is the passageway leading from the mouth and nose to the esophagus and larynx. The pharynx permits the passage of swallowed solids and liquids into the esophagus, or gullet, and conducts air to and from the trachea, or windpipe, during respiration. The pharynx also connects on either side with the cavity of the middle ear by way of the Eustachian tube and provides for equalization of air pressure on the eardrum membrane, which separates the cavity of the middle ear from the external ear canal. The pharynx has roughly the form of a flattened funnel. It is attached to the surrounding structures but is loose enough to permit gliding of the pharyngeal wall against them in the movements of swallowing. The principal muscles of the pharynx, involved in the mechanics of swallowing, are the three pharyngeal constrictors, which overlap each other slightly and form the primary musculature of the side and rear pharyngeal walls.

4. Respiratory System

Breathing is the process that brings oxygen in the air into your lungs and moves oxygen and through your body. Our lungs remove the oxygen and pass it through our bloodstream, where it's carried off to the tissues and organs that allow us to walk, talk, and move. Our lungs also take carbon dioxide from our blood and release it into the air when we breathe out.

- The sinuses are hollow spaces in the bones of your head. Small openings connect them to the nasal cavity. The sinuses help to regulate the temperature and humidity of the air your breathe in, as well as to lighten the bone structure of the head and to give tone to your voice.

- The nasal cavity (nose) is the best entrance for outside air into your respiratory system. The hairs that line the inside wall are part of the air-cleansing system.

- Air can also enters through your oral cavity (mouth), especially if you have a mouth-breathing habit or your nasal passages may be temporarily blocked.

- The adenoids are overgrown lymph tissues at the top of the throat. When your adenoids interfere with your breathing, they are sometimes removed. The lymph system, consisting of nodes (knots of cells) and connecting vessels, carries fluid throughout the body. This system helps your body resist infection by filtering out foreign matter, including germs, and producing cells (lymphocytes) to fight them.

- The tonsils are lymph nodes in the wall of your pharynx. Tonsils are not an important part of the germ-fighting system of the body. If they become infected, they are sometimes removed.

- The pharynx (throat) collects incoming air from your nose and passes it downward to your trachea (windpipe).

- The epiglottis is a flap of tissue that guards the entrance to your trachea. It closes when anything is swallowed that should go into the esophagus and stomach.

- The larynx (voice box) contains your vocal cords. When moving air is breathed in and out, it creates voice sounds.

- The esophagaus is the passage leading from your mouth and throat to your stomach.

- The trachea (windpipe) is the passage leading from your pharynx to the lungs.

- The ribs are bones supporting and protecting your chest cavity. They move a small amount and help the lungs to expand and contract .

- The trachea divides into the two main bronchi (tubes), one for each lung. The bronchi, in turn, subdivide further into bronchioles.

- The right lung is divided into three lobes, or sections.

- The left lung is divided into two lobes.

- The pleura are the two membranes that surround each lobe of your lungs and separate the lungs from your chest wall.

- The bronchial tubes are lined with cilia (these are like very small hairs) that have a wave-like motion. This motion carries mucus (sticky phlegm or liquid) upward and out into the throat, where it is either coughed up or swallowed. The mucus catches and holds much of the dust, germs, and other unwanted matter that has invaded your lungs. Your lungs get rid of the mucus through coughing.

- The diaphragm is the strong wall of muscle that separates your chest cavity from your abdominal cavity. By moving downward, it creates suction to draw in air and expand the lungs.

- The smallest section of the bronchi are called bronchioles, at the end of which are the alveoli (plural of alveolus).

- The alveoli are the very small air sacs that are the destination of air that you breathe in. The capillaries are blood vessels that are imbedded in the walls of the alveoli. Blood passes through the capillaries, brought to them by the pulmonary artery and taken away by the pulmonary vein. While in the capillaries, the blood moves carbon dioxide into the alveoli and takes up oxygen from the air in the alveoli.

5. Immune System

The overall function of the immune system is to prevent or limit infection. An example of this principle is found in immune-compromised people, including those with genetic immune disorders, immune-debilitating infections like HIV, and even pregnant women, who are susceptible to a range of microbes that typically do not cause infection in healthy individuals.

The immune system can distinguish between normal, healthy cells and unhealthy cells by recognizing a variety of "danger" cues called danger-associated molecular patterns (DAMPs). Cells may be unhealthy because of infection or because of cellular damage caused by non-infectious agents like sunburn or cancer. Infectious microbes such as viruses and bacteria release another set of signals recognized by the immune system called pathogen-associated molecular patterns (PAMPs).

When the immune system first recognizes these signals, it responds to address the problem. If an immune response cannot be activated when there is sufficient need, problems arise, like an infection. On the other hand, when an immune response is activated without a real threat or is not turned off once the danger passes, different problems arise, such as allergic reactions and autoimmune disease.

The immune system is complex and pervasive. There are numerous cell types that either circulates throughout the body or reside in a particular tissue. Each cell type plays a unique role, with different ways of recognizing problems, communicating with other cells, and performing their functions. By understanding all the details behind this network, researchers may optimize immune responses to confront specific issues, ranging from infections to cancer.

Location

All immune cells come from precursors in the bone marrow and develop into mature cells through a series of changes that can occur in different parts of the body.

Skin: The skin is usually the first line of defense against microbes. Skin cells produce and secrete important antimicrobial proteins, and immune cells can be found in specific layers of skin.

Bone marrow: The bone marrow contains stem cells that can develop into a variety of cell types. The common myeloid progenitor stem cell in the bone marrow is the precursor to innate immune cells—neutrophils, eosinophils, basophils, mast cells, monocytes, dendritic cells, and macrophages—that are important first-line responders to infection.

Immune Cells: The common lymphoid progenitor stem cell leads to adaptive immune cells—B cells and T cells—that are responsible for mounting responses to specific microbes based on previous encounters (immunological memory). Natural killer (NK) cells also are derived from the common lymphoid progenitor and share features of both innate and adaptive immune cells, as they provide immediate defenses like innate cells but also may be retained as memory cells like adaptive cells. B, T, and NK cells also are called lymphocytes.

Bloodstream: Immune cells constantly circulate throughout the bloodstream, patrolling for problems. When blood tests are used to monitor white blood cells, another term for immune cells, a snapshot of the immune system is taken. If a cell type is either scarce or overabundant in the bloodstream, this may reflect a problem.

Thymus: T cells mature in the thymus, a small organ located in the upper chest.

Lymphatic system: The lymphatic system is a network of vessels and tissues composed of lymph, an extracellular fluid, and lymphoid organs, such as lymph nodes. The lymphatic system is a conduit for travel and communication between tissues and the bloodstream. Immune cells are carried through the lymphatic system and converge in lymph nodes, which are found throughout the body.

Lymph nodes are a communication hub where immune cells sample information brought in from the body. For instance, if adaptive immune cells in the lymph node recognize pieces of a microbe brought in from a distant area, they will activate , replicate, and leave the lymph node to circulate and address the pathogen. Thus, doctors may check patients for swollen lymph nodes, which may indicate an active immune response.

Spleen: The spleen is an organ located behind the stomach. While it is not directly connected to the lymphatic system, it is important for processing information from the bloodstream. Immune cells are enriched in specific areas of the spleen, and upon recognizing blood-borne pathogens, they will activate and respond accordingly.

Mucosal tissue: Mucosal surfaces are prime entry points for pathogens, and specialized immune hubs are strategically located in mucosal tissues like the respiratory tract and gut. For instance, Peyer's patches are important areas in the small intestine where immune cells can access samples from the gastrointestinal tract .

Anatomy and Physiology of the Human Body

Simply stated, human anatomy is the study of the parts of the human body. Human anatomy includes both gross anatomy and microscopic anatomy. Gross anatomy includes those human structures that can be seen with the naked eye.

Some key terms I will use are below:

Anatomy: The study of the parts and structures of the human body.

Physiology: The study of the functions of the human body.

Gross anatomy: The study of the parts and structures of the human body that can be seen with the naked eye and without the use of a microscope.

Microscopic anatomy: The study of the parts and structures of the human body that can NOT be seen with the naked eye and only seen with the use of a microscope.

The frontal plane: Also referred to as the coronal plane, separates the front from the back of the body.

Ventral surface: The front of the body.

Dorsal surface: The back of the body.

Transverse plane: Also referred to as the cross-sectional plane separates the top of the body at the waist from the bottom of the body.

Sagittal plane: Also referred to as the medial plane separates the right side of the body from the left side of the body.

Anterior: Closer to the front of the body than another bodily part.

Posterior: Further from the front of the body than another bodily part.

Superior: One bodily part is above another bodily part.

Inferior: One bodily part is below another bodily part.

Cytology: A subdivision of microscopic anatomy that is the study of the parts and structures of the body's cells.

Histology: A subdivision of microscopic anatomy that is the study of the parts and structures of the body's tissues.

Cell: The basic building blocks of the human body and the bodies of all other living species.

Prokaryotes: One of the two types of cells that don't have organelles or a nucleus.

Eukaryotes: One of the two types of cells that have a nucleus containing genetic material and organelles.

Cell wall: The area around the cell that protects the cell membrane and the cell from threats in its external environment.

Extracellular: The environment outside of a cell.

Intracellular: Inside the cell.

Permeability: The ability of the cell to let particles into the cells and to get particles out of the cell.

Cell nucleus: The place in the cell that contains chromosomes and the place where both DNA and RNA are synthesized and replicated.

Organelles: The "mini organs" in the cell that perform a specific role.

Mitochondria: This organelle produces and stores energy in the form of adenosine triphosphate (ATP) with a complex cycle of production known as the Krebs's cycle.

Lysosomes: The organelle that breaks down and disposes of cellular wastes.

Endoplasmic reticulum: The organelle that synthesizes proteins and lipids.

Golgi apparatus: The organelle that processes and stores the proteins and lipids that it receives from the endoplasmic reticulum.

Ribosomes: The organelle that synthesize protein with the linking of different amino acids as per the instructions of the messenger RNA molecules.

Passive transport: The movement of molecules across membranes that does NOT require the use of cellular energy to perform this transport.

Active transport: The movement of molecules across membranes that requires the use of cellular energy to perform this transport.

Diffusion: The movement of molecule from an area of higher concentration to the area or side of the membrane that has the lesser concentration.

Osmosis: A type of passive transport that does NOT require the use of cellular energy to move water and solute particles.

Meiosis: Cell division where the resulting cells have half of the original number of chromosomes.

Mitosis: Cell division where the nucleus of the cell replicates itself into two identical copies of itself.

Tissues: A group of cells with similar structure that join together to perform a specialized function.

Epithelial tissue: Also referred to as epithelium, it is the type of tissue that skin and glands are made of.

Connective tissue: The type of tissue that ligaments, tendons and bones are made of.

Skeletal muscle tissue: Striated muscle that enables voluntary bodily movement.

Smooth muscle tissue: Muscle that is not striated and not under voluntary control.

Cardiac muscle tissue: Striated, involuntary muscle that is found only in the heart. This tissue enables cardiac functioning.

Nervous tissue: Neural tissue in the central and peripheral nervous systems.

Organs: A self-contained group of tissues that serves at least one bodily function to maintain normal bodily functioning and the homeostasis, or balance, of the body.

Bodily systems: Groups of bodily tissues that group together to perform specific roles and functions in the body to maintain its homeostasis.

General Anatomy of the Human Body

Gross anatomy can be compared to the structure of a house as shown in a blueprint of a house or by looking at and inspecting a house in person with the naked eye. As you look at the house's interior and exterior you will see a foundation, a roof, doors, windows, floors, a plumbing system, an electrical system, ceilings, etc. Similarly, when you view the exterior and interior of the human body with the naked eye, you are able to see its gross anatomy. For example, as you look at the human body with the naked eye, you will see its interior when the inner parts of the body are exposed, and you will see the exterior of the intact body. You will see the human's skeletal foundation, you will see the head as its roof, you will see the doors and windows in terms of the body's openings such as the mouth, the floor as the feet, an internal plumbing system with the external and internal structures and organs of the urinary and digestive systems, and you will see the brain and the heart, when exposed, as the electrical system of the body.

Microscopic anatomy, as contrasted to gross anatomy, is the study of those parts of the human body that cannot be seen with the naked eye. Structures that are viewed only with a microscope are structures included in the study of microscopic anatomy.

Microscopic anatomy is further divided into the exploration of the histological and cytological studies.

Cytology is the branch of microscopic anatomy that studies the cells and histology is the branch of microscopic anatomy that studies tissues.

From the smallest to the largest part of the human anatomy, in that sequential order, are the:

- Cells

- Tissues

- Organs

- Systems

Whereby

Cells > Tissues > Organs > Systems

Below are some terms relating to anatomy, anatomical structures and anatomical directions that you must be familiar with.

Anatomical Position

The anatomical position, with terms of relative location noted.

The anatomical position is the frame of reference for many other terms relating to anatomy, anatomical structures and anatomical directions. The anatomical position consists of a standing upright person facing forward with the person's arms on their sides next to the body and the feet together. What makes the anatomical position different from a normal standing position is the fact that the palms of the hands are unnaturally facing forward rather than naturally facing the leg, as you can see in the picture above.

Anatomical Planes

Simply stated, the anatomical planes of the human body are imaginary lines going through the body that give us some point of reference when we are studying anatomy.

The frontal plane, also referred to as the coronal plane, which is shown in the picture above, is the imaginary line that separates the front from the back of the body. The term used for the front of the body is the ventral surface and the term used for the back of the body is the dorsal surface of the body.

The transverse plane, also referred to as the cross sectional plane, which is shown in the picture above, is the imaginary line that separates the top of the body at the waist from the bottom of the body.

The sagittal plane, also referred to as the medial plane, which is shown in the picture above, is the imaginary line that separates the right side of the body from the left side of the body.

Anterior and Posterior Relationships

The anatomical position, with terms of relative location noted.

The term anterior is a relative and comparative directional term that is used to describe that a bodily part or anatomical structure is closer to the front of the body than another bodily part or anatomical structure. For example, the sternum, or breast bone, is anterior to the heart.

The term posterior is a relative and comparative directional term that is used to describe that a bodily part or anatomical structure is further behind another bodily part or anatomical structure. For example, the lungs are posterior to the ribs.

Superior and Inferior Relationships

The term superior is a relative and comparative directional term that is used to describe that a bodily part or anatomical structure is above another bodily part or anatomical structure. For example, the knee is superior to the foot of the body when it is in the anatomical position.

Similarly, the term inferior is a relative and comparative directional term that is used to describe that a bodily part or anatomical structure is below another bodily part or anatomical structure. For example, the foot is inferior to the knee of the body when it is in the anatomical position.

Medial and Lateral Relationships

The term medial is a relative and comparative directional term that is used to describe that a bodily part or anatomical structure is more towards the center of the body in comparison to another bodily part or anatomical structure. For example, the nipple is medial to the shoulder.

The term lateral is a relative and comparative directional term that is used to describe that a bodily part or anatomical structure is more away from the center of the body in comparison to another bodily part or anatomical structure. For example, the shoulder is lateral to the nipple.

Proximal and Distal Relationships

The term proximal is a relative and comparative directional term that is used to describe that a bodily part or anatomical structure is closer to the body mass than another bodily part or anatomical structure. For example, the shoulder is proximal to the elbow.

The term distal is a relative and comparative directional term that is used to describe that a bodily part or anatomical structure is further away from the body mass than another bodily part or anatomical structure. For example, the knee is distal to the hip.

Deep vs Superficial Relationships

The term deep is a term to describe that a bodily part or anatomical structure is further away from the surface of the body than another bodily part or anatomical structure. For example, muscle is deeper than the skin.

Similarly, the term superficial is a term to describe that a bodily part or anatomical structure is closer to the surface of the body than another bodily part or anatomical structure. For example, skin is the most superficial organ of the body.

Cells of the Body

Cells are the basic building blocks of the human body and the bodies of all other living species, including other mammals and plant life. Some living organisms like the amoeba and the paramecium are one celled, or unicellular, living bodies, but, for the most part, living organisms are made up of trillions and trillions of cells.

There are two different types of cells. These are prokaryotes and eukaryotes. Prokaryotes are cells that don't have organelles or a nucleus. Bacteria are an example of a prokaryote cell. Eukaryotes are cells that have a nucleus containing genetic material and organelles, as described below. The cells of the human, animals and plants are examples of eukaryote cells.

The generalized structure and molecular components of a cell

Cells consist of a:

- Cell wall
- Cell membrane
- Cytoplasm
- Cytoskeleton

- Nucleus
- Organelles

The cell's cell wall protects the cell membrane and the cell from threats in its external environment; the external environment of the cell is referred to as extracellular. In contrast, the intracellular environment is the internal environment of the cell.

Cell membranes envelope cells and these membranes are somewhat like the gate keepers of the cell. The cell membrane performs this gate keeping function with its level of permeability. Permeability, simply defined, is the ability of the cell to let particles into the cells and to get particles out of the cell, as based on the concentration of these substances inside and outside of the cell.

Cytoplasm makes up the bulk of a living cell. The major components of the cytoplasm are things like calcium, for example, the organelles which are described immediately bellow and the cytosol which makes up the bulk of a living cell. Organelles are found in the cytoplasm of the cell.

The cytoskeleton, similar to the skeletal system of the body, is made of protein and it maintains the shape and form of the cell so that it does not collapse as parts of the cell move about and the cell itself moves about.

The nucleus of the cell, as found in eurkaryotic cells, is the informational depository of the cell. The nucleus is the place that contains chromosomes and the place where both DNA and RNA are synthesized and replicated.

Organelles, which the word connotes are "mini organs" that perform a specific role in the cell. Organelles include cellular structures like the Golgi apparatus and the mitochondria, among other things, which are in the cytosol of the cell.

In addition to the mitochondria, other organelles are the:

- Lysosomes
- Endoplasmic reticulum
- Golgi apparatus

- Ribosomes

The mitochondria, produce and store energy in the form of adenosine triphosphate (ATP) with a complex cycle of production known as the Krebs's cycle.

Essentially; the mitochondria are the energy power plants of the cell.

The lysosomes, break down and dispose of cellular wastes. In the most basic form the lysosomes are garbage recyclers and garbage disposal systems for the cells.

Endoplasmic reticulum connect the nucleus of the cell to the cell's cytoplasm. These smooth and rough tubes and the ribosomes within play a role in the synthesis or manufacture of protein and lipids. Again, simplified, the endoplasmic reticulum can be looked at as the manufacturing plants of the cells.

The Golgi apparatus connects to the endoplasmic reticulum and it gets lipids and proteins from it. The Golgi apparatus processes these products and readies them for transport to other areas of the cell, as needed. Again simplified, the Golgi apparatus can be viewed as the storage room for processed products.

Cell Processes

In addition to the functions and processes of the different parts of the human cell, cells also perform other processes that you should be familiar with.

These processes include:

1. Passive Transport (Diffusion and Osmosis)

2. Active Transport

3. Meiosis

4. Mitosis

1. Passive Transport

Passive transport is the movement of molecules across membranes that does not require the use of cellular energy to perform this transport. Diffusion and osmosis are two forms of passive transport.

A. Diffusion

Diffusion is a type of passive transport that does not require the use of cellular energy to move molecules, other than water molecules, from an area of higher concentration to the area of lesser concentration.

An example would be, if some particles are dissolved in a glass of water. At first, the particles are all near one corner of the glass. If the particles randomly move around ("diffuse") in the water, they eventually become distributed randomly and uniformly from an area of high concentration to an area of low concentration, and organized.

For example, molecules and ions can move across a cell's selective semipermeable membrane from an area of higher concentration to the area or side of the membrane that has the lesser concentration. In a sense, diffusion is the equalization of both sides of the semipermeable membrane. For example, if a substance or an electrolyte like sodium is scant in the environment outside of the cell, the semipermeable cell's membrane will release and move sodium outside of the cell to the areas of less concentration with diffusion.

Ions are electrically charged molecules such as electrolytes, in the human body. Electrolytes that have a negative electrical charge are called anions and electrolytes that have positive electrical charge are called cations. Electrolytes and the levels of electrolytes play roles that are essential to life. For example, these electrically charged ions are necessary to contract muscles, to move fluids within the body, they produce energy and they perform many other roles in the body and its physiology.

Electrolytes, similar to endocrine hormones, are produced and controlled with feedback mechanisms that control low and high levels of electrolytes.

The body's cations, or positively charged electrolytes, that move in and out of cells with diffusion, are listed below:

- Sodium which is abbreviated as Na^+
- Potassium which is abbreviated as K^+
- Calcium which is abbreviated as Ca^+

- Magnesium which is abbreviated as Mg^+

The body's anions, or negatively charged electrolytes, that move in and out of cells with diffusion, are listed below:

- Chloride which is abbreviated as Cl^-

- Hydrogen phosphate which is abbreviated as $(HPO_4)^-$

- Bicarbonate which is abbreviated as $(HCO_3)^-$

- Sulfate which is abbreviated as $(SO_4)^-$

B. Osmosis

Osmosis is a type of passive transport that does not require the use of cellular energy to move water and solute particles with the stored energy found in the cell's active transport proteins.

2. Active Transport

Active transport is the movement of molecules that does require the use of cellular energy to perform this transport.

3. Meiosis

In meiosis, the chromosome or chromosomes duplicate (during interphase) and homologous chromosomes exchange genetic information (chromosomal crossover) during the first division, called meiosis I. The daughter cells divide again in meiosis II, splitting up sister chromatids to form haploid gametes. Two gametes fuse during fertilization, creating a diploid cell with a complete set of paired chromosomes.

Meiosis and mitosis are two forms of cell division. When meiosis occurs, the parent or origin cell, half of the original number of chromosomes result.

Human cells have 23 types of chromosomes and each has its own set of genetic material. These 23 types of chromosomes are paired, so the human cell has a total of 46 chromosomes because 23 x 2 = 46 total chromosomes.

Meiosis consists of several phases, that include:

A. Interphase during which time the chromosomes share and retain genetic DNA material and duplicate to create homologous chromosomes

B. Meiosis I during which time the homologous chromosomes are paired up and then divided and split into two daughter nuclei

C. Meiosis II during which time the two daughter nuclei divide and split into four daughter nuclei

D. Meiosis is the process that occurs during the fertilization of the ovum with sperm.

4. Mitosis

Mitosis divides the chromosomes in a cell nucleus.Mitosis, a form of asexual replication, occurs when the nucleus of the cell replicates itself into two identical copies of itself. In other words, genetic twins result from mitosis. The stages of mitosis in the correct sequential order, are:

A. DNA replication

B. Prophase

C. Prometaphase

D. Metaphase

E. Telophase

Cells divide and reproduce in two ways, mitosis and meiosis. Mitosis results in two identical daughter cells, whereas meiosis results in four sex cells. Below I will highlight the keys differences and similarities between the two types of cell division.

Table 1: Differences between mitosis and meiosis

Differences	
Mitosis	Meiosis
Involves one cell division.	Involves two successive cell divisions.

Results in two daughter cells.	Results in four daughter cells.
Results in diploid daughter cells (chromosome number remains the same as parent cell).	Results in haploid daughter cells (chromosome number is halved from the parent cell).
Daughter cells are genetically identical.	Daughter cells are genetically different.
Occurs in all organisms except viruses.	Occurs only in animals, plants and fungi.
Creates all body cells (somatic) apart from the germ cells (eggs and sperm).	Creates germ cells (eggs and sperm) only.
Prophase is much shorter.	Prophase I takes much longer.
No recombination/crossing over occurs in prophase.	Involves recombination/crossing over of chromosomes in prophase I.
In metaphase individual chromosomes (pairs of chromatids) line up along the equator.	In metaphase I pairs of chromosomes line up along the equator.
During anaphase the sister chromatids are separated to opposite poles.	During anaphase I the sister chromatids move together to the same pole.

Table 2: Similarities between mitosis and meiosis

Similarities	
Mitosis	Meiosis
Diploid parent cell.	Diploid parent cell.
Consists of interphase, prophase, metaphase, anaphase and telophase.	Consists of interphase, prophase, metaphase, anaphase and telophase (but twice!).

In metaphase individual chromosomes (pairs of chromatids) line up along the equator.	In metaphase II individual chromosomes (pairs of chromatids) line up along the equator.
During anaphase the sister chromatids are separated to opposite poles.	During anaphase II the sister chromatids are separated to opposite poles.
Ends with cytokinesis.	Ends with cytokinesis.

Tissues of the Body

Tissues are a collection or group of cells with similar structures that join to form a tissue with a distinct purpose and function. Cells collect to form tissues and tissues collect to form organs.

The four types of tissue are:

1. Epithelial tissue

2. Connective tissue

3. Muscle tissue

4. Nervous tissue

1. Epithelial Tissue

The types of epithelial tissue are:

- Columnar and shaped like columns

- Cuboidal and shaped like cubes and

- Squamous types

These different types of epithelial tissue can have one layer or they can be stratified and have multiple layers.

Epithelial tissues form all glands and they play an important role and function in the body in terms of sensations, in terms of the protection of underlying structures and organs, in terms of secretion, and in terms of absorption. It covers the entire body in the skin and it also lines the inner surfaces of organs as well as the circulatory system vessels.

The lifespan of epithelial tissue is relatively short when compared to other types of tissues, but epithelial tissue is readily replaced with mitosis cell division, as discussed above.

2. Connective Tissue

The type of tissue that is surrounded with what is called its matrix. Connective tissue also has different types, as based on the matrix that surrounds its cells such as:

A. Loose Connective Tissue

Loose connective tissue lies in a soft matrix such as fluid and/or fibers. Fat, which is called adipose tissue, is an example of loose connective tissue.

B. Dense Connective Tissue

Dense connective tissue lies in a matrix of strong collagen fibers. Tendons and ligaments, as more fully described below in the section on the Muscular System, are comprised of dense connective tissue.

C. Supporting Connective Tissue

Supporting connective tissue lies in a highly firm matrix to support the body and bodily parts. Bones and cartilage are supporting connective tissues.

D. Fluid Connective Tissue

Fluid connective tissue lies in and is surrounded with a liquid matrix. An example of a fluid connective tissue is blood which is surrounded with plasma, the matrix for this type of connective tissue.

3. Muscle Tissue

As the name connotes, form the tissues of the muscles which serve to move the body. The body contains three types of muscle tissue: (a) skeletal muscle, (b) smooth muscle, and (c) cardiac muscle.

A. Skeletal Muscle

Skeletal muscle, which is also referred to striated muscle, is muscle that enables voluntary bodily movement. This tissue is composed of long muscle fibers and it is a part of all voluntary muscular movements including those used for range of motion exercises and those that serve as sphincters which control urination and defecation through the ends of the urinary and digestive systems, respectively.

Muscle fibers are stimulated or innervated by nerves to contract and relax under voluntary control.

B. Smooth Muscle

Smooth muscle, in sharp contrast to skeletal muscle, is not striated and it is not under voluntary control. Smooth muscle is found in the digestive system where it performs peristalsis and it is also found in other organs and systems such as the vascular system where it dilates and constricts blood vessels, all of which are involuntary muscular activities.

C. Cardiac Muscle

Cardiac muscle tissue, is similar to skeletal muscle because it too is striated; however, it is also different because cardiac muscle is not voluntary like skeletal muscle is and it is not widespread throughout the body like skeletal muscle is. Cardiac muscle is restricted to the heart and it contract s and relaxes the heart during the cardiac cycle according to the electrical signals and impulses sent by the parts of the heart.

4. Nervous Tissue

Nervous tissue consists of both neural tissue and cells which are referred to as neurons: Neurons consist of a cell body, a nucleus, an axon and dendrites that connect to other neurons.

Nervous tissue and neurons are found throughout the central nervous system and the peripheral nervous system. The central nervous system consists of the brain and the spinal cord, and the peripheral nervous system consists of all the other nerves and nervous tissue in the body.

The peripheral nervous system is divided into two major functional subsystems which are the autonomic nervous system and the somatic nervous system.

- The autonomic nervous system controls automatic and involuntary physiological functions of the body that are outside of our control. Some of the physiological functions under the control of the autonomic, or automatic, nervous system are the movements of smooth, involuntary muscles, in contrast to voluntary skeletal muscles, like those that create peristalsis in the digestive system and the constriction of the eye's pupil when it is exposed to light.

- The somatic nervous system, in sharp contrast to the autonomic nervous system, controls voluntary physiological bodily functions such as voluntary muscular movement with the skeletal muscles of the body. The somatic nervous system has efferent nerves which send and receive motor function related nerve signals and also efferent nerves which send and receive sensory function related nerve signals.

Natural selection and adaptation

Natural selection is a mechanism of evolution. Organisms that are more adapted to their environment are more likely to survive and pass on the genes that aided their success. This process causes species to change and diverge over time. Natural selection is one of the ways to account for the millions of species that have lived on Earth. Charles Darwin (1809-1882) and Alfred Russel Wallace (1823-1913) are jointly credited with coming up with the theory of evolution by natural selection, having co-published on it in 1858. Darwin has generally overshadowed Wallace since the publication of On the Origin of Species in 1859.

In Darwin and Wallace's time, most believed that organisms were too complex to have natural origins and must have been designed by a transcendent God. Natural selection, however, states that even the most complex organisms occur by totally natural processes.

In natural selection, genetic mutations that are beneficial to an individual's survival are passed on through reproduction. This results in a new generation of organisms that are more likely to survive to reproduce.

For example, evolving long necks has enabled giraffes to feed on leaves that others can't reach, giving them a competitive advantage. Thanks to a better food source, those with longer necks were able to survive to reproduce and so pass on the characteristic to the succeeding generation. Those with shorter necks and access to less food would be less likely to survive to pass on their genes. Adrian explains, 'If you took 1,000 giraffes and measured their necks, they're all going to be slightly different from one another. Those differences are at least in part determined by their genes.

'The ones with longer necks may leave proportionally more offspring, because they have fed better and have maybe been better in competing for mates because they are stronger. Then, if you were to measure the necks of the next generation, they're also going to vary, but the average will have shifted slightly towards the longer ones. The process carries on generation after generation.'

What is an adaptation?

An adaptation is a physical or behavioral characteristic that helps an organism to survive in its environment, but not all characteristics of an animal are adaptations. Adaptations for one purpose can be co-opted for another. For instance, feathers were an adaptation for thermoregulation - their use for flight only came later. This means that feathers are an exaptation for flight, rather than an adaptation.

Adaptations can also become outdated, such as the tough exterior of the calabash fruit (Crescentia cujete). This gourd is generally thought to have evolved to avoid being eaten by Gomphotheres, a family of elephant-like animals. But these animals went extinct around 10,000 years ago, so the fruit's adaptation no longer has a survival benefit. Selection for adaptation is not the only cause of evolution. Species change can also be caused by neutral mutations that have no detriment or benefit to an individual, genetic drift or gene flow.

Survival of the fittest

In terms of evolution, an animal that is 'fit' is one that is adapted to its environment. This concept is at the core of natural selection, although the term 'survival of the fittest' has often been misunderstood and may be best avoided.

There is also a degree of randomness to evolution, so the best-adapted animal won't always be the one to survive. Adrian explains, 'If you're going to get hit by a rock or something, it's just bad luck. But on average and over time, the ones that survive are the ones that are fittest - the ones that have the best adaptations.'

What are Darwin's finches?

Darwin collected many animal specimens during the voyage of HMS Beagle (1831-1836). Among his best-known are the finches, of which he collected around 14 species from the Galápagos Islands. The birds sit within the same taxonomic family and have a diverse array of beak sizes and shapes. These correspond to both their differing primary food sources and divergence due to isolation on different islands.

Darwin realized that differences between species of mockingbird on the islands were greater than between those he'd seen across the continent. He began contemplating while aboard HMS Beagle, but it took several years before he came up with his theory of evolution by natural selection. The finches - once they had been identified as different species by the British ornithologist John Gould - became one useful example among the many other animals he saw.

Darwin thought that natural selection progressed slowly and only occurred over a long period of time. This may often be true, but it has been shown that in some cases a new species can evolve within a lifetime.

Interpret the biological classification system

Biological classification is the scientific procedure that involves the arrangement of the organisms in a hierarchical series of groups and sub-groups on the basis of their similarities and dissimilarities.

Need for Classification

Right from the archaic times, several attempts have been made to classify the living organisms. The first man to attempt a scientific basis of classification was Aristotle. He used simple morphological characters to classify plants as trees, shrubs, and herbs. He classified the animals into two groups:

- Enaima (with red blood)

- Anaima (without red blood)

However it was obvious there was a need for a more detailed classification.

Types of Classification System

Based on the types of system of classification, organisms are classified into the following kingdoms.

A. Two Kingdom Classification System

In the year 1758 Linnaeus (the father of taxonomy system) divided all the living organisms into two kingdoms. These are Plantae and Animalia.

Features of Kingdom Plantae

The significant features of the kingdom Plantae are:

- They have a cell wall.

- Autotrophic mode of nutrition is followed. The reserve food is starch.

- A big central vacuole is present.

- There aren't any excretory organs, nervous system, sense organs and muscular system.

- No locomotion is seen except in some lower algae.

- Plantae absorbs inorganic nutrients from outside.

- They experience unlimited growth but have well-defined growing points.

- The response to external stimuli is slow.

Features of Kingdom Animalia

The significant features of the kingdom Animalia are listed here:

- The cell wall is absent.

- There are no inorganic crystals present in their cells.

- Central vacuole is absent.

- Growth is limited and well-defined growing points are not present.

- Heterotrophic mode of nutrition is used.

- Show quick response to external stimuli.

- The muscular system is present.

- Locomotion is present.

- Excretory organs, nervous system and sense organs are present.

- Reserve food as glycogen.

B.   Six Kingdom Classification System

Carl Woese a Professor in the Department of Microbiology, University of Illinois, came up with the Six Kingdom Classification System in the year 1990. It was also known as the three-domain system as in it organism classification was done in three domains, i.e., Archaea, Bacteria and Eukarya.

It majorly used the basic principles of the five kingdom system but divides the Monera into two domains Archaebacteria, Eubacteria and other eukaryotes in the third kingdom.

1. Archaea

Archaea domain includes prokaryotic organisms. These have a monolayer core of lipids in the cell membrane and distinct nucleotides in their RNA. It contains a single kingdom called Archaebacteria. This kingdom includes early prokaryotes. These are methanogens, halophiles and thermoacidophiles.

2. Bacteria

The bacteria domain consists of typical prokaryotes that lack membrane covered cell organelles. These do not have micro chambers for separating various metabolic activities. It also has a single kingdom-Eubacteria.

Kingdom-Eubacteria

The members of this kingdom have peptidoglycan cell wall, naked DNA in coiled form, glycogen food reserves. There is no sap vacuole and ribosomes are present. The members of this kingdom are bacteria, mycoplasma, actinomycetes, rickettsiae, spirochaetes, cyanobacteria, Firmicutes.

3. Eukarya

The domain eukarya contain all the eukaryotes. The four kingdoms of this domain are:

- Protista
- Animalia
- Plantae
- Fungi

Parts of a cell and its corresponding functions

Life takes many forms, from the simplicity of bacteria to the complexity of primates. According to cell theory, all living things are comprised of cells. Complex life forms have more cells and more complexity to their cell structure.

Cell theory goes on to state that cells are the unit of function for organisms. They are responsible for life functions like digestion, circulation, reproduction, and immunity.

The life cycle depends on two different types of organisms, autotrophs and heterotrophs.

Autotroph comes from the Greek language and means self-feeder. Autotrophs produce glucose through photosynthesis and feed themselves and other living beings. They are mainly plants.

Heterotrophs get their nutrition from outside sources. The prefix hetero - means different. Animals eat plants and other animals to survive.

The cell structures of autotrophs and heterotrophs differ.

Prokaryote and Eukaryote cells

There are two basic types of cells that form the building blocks of all organisms, prokaryote and eukaryote cells.

Prokaryote cells are simpler, having no nucleus and lacking some of the complex organelles of eukaryotes. Their DNA is not tightly contained as in a eukaryote nucleus. Prokaryote cells are represented in two types of organisms, bacteria and archaea. Most organisms in these two groups are just a single cell with a flagellum for movement. They replicate themselves through a process called binary fission in which they split apart, creating two exact copies of the same cell.

Eukaryote cells are present in almost all of the abundance of life visible to the eye, from plants and animals to fungi and even some bacteria. They have membrane covered organelles, including a nucleus that holds the cell's DNA. They reproduce through either mitosis or meiosis.

Animal cells

A typical animal cell is filled with cytoplasm within a cell membrane. The cell membrane allows select substances (proteins, enzymes, and chemicals) to pass through while keeping others out. Resting in the cytoplasm are various organelles. Organelles serve to regulate the metabolic functions of the cell.

- The nucleus is the control center of the cell and contains the nucleolus. The cell's DNA is contained in the nucleus, and it delivers information to control the metabolic functions of the cell. The nucleolus produces ribosomes. Ribosomes are found throughout the cell and synthesize proteins.

- The mitochondrion is the energy center of the cell where glucose and oxygen are broken down into water and carbon dioxide. As a result of breaking these chemical bonds, energy in the form of adenosine triphosphate (ATP) is produced.

- The endoplasmic reticulum of a cell is a membrane where proteins, the building blocks of cellular life, are built and stored. Rough endoplasmic reticulum has ribosomes attached, whereas smooth endoplasmic reticulum has none. Working with the Golgi complex, or Golgi apparatus, the endoplasmic reticulum assembles proteins and makes structures with those proteins.

- Centrioles are organelles that assist in cell reproduction, either mitosis or meiosis.

- Lysosomes capture the products of cellular function that the cell cannot use. They break down this cellular waste.

Plant Cells

Plant cells are similar to animal cells in most respects. They have all the same organelles, but they also have a cell wall and contain chloroplasts. Chloroplasts are organelles that aid in photosynthesis, through which plants use water, carbon dioxide, and the sun's energy to create glucose and oxygen.

Cell Reproduction

Cells proliferate in two ways, through mitosis or meiosis. Mitosis is the way that cells proliferate through a sexual reproduction. In mitosis, cells reproduce an exact copy of themselves.

Meiosis is how cells reproduce through sexual reproduction. In this case, each daughter cell has half of the DNA of the original cell. In sexual reproduction, the daughter cells combine with such cells from another individual to form offspring, leading to genetic variation. Cells that are thriving and conducting metabolic functions are considered to be in interphase. During interphase, cells' energy expenditure goes to the function of the organisms.

A. Understanding Mitosis

Mitosis occurs when a cell duplicates itself. This can happen in single-cell organisms, like protozoa or bacteria, and is how they reproduce. It also happens in other living organisms when they grow or heal. New cells are created with the same DNA as the original cells.

When more cells are needed or a sexual stimulus is introduced, chromosomes and centrioles are replicated.

1. Prophase is the first phase of mitosis. In this phase, the nuclear membrane dissolves, allowing the doubled chromosomes to float freely. Spindle fibers congregate around structures known as centrosomes to produce a spindle apparatus, which separates the floating DNA into separate poles.

2. Metaphase sees an orientation of the spindle apparatus, drawn by the centrosomes, to push the DNA to opposite ends of the cell.

3. During anaphase, spindle fibers retract , again influenced by the centrosomes, pulling apart chromosomes into their v-shaped halves.

4. Telophase ushers in a reversal of previous processes, with spindle fibers dissolving and nuclear membranes forming around the new chromosome pairings. At this point mitotic division is all but complete.

5. After telophase, the two daughter cells undergo cytokinesis. This is a simple process in which the two nuclei are divided by cell membranes. There are now identical twin cells with the same DNA ready for interphase.

B. Understanding Meosis

Meiosis is a more complex process than mitosis. Cells in meiosis go through two rounds of prophase, metaphase, anaphase, and telophase. These two stages are called meiosis I and meiosis II.

Prophase I is similar to mitotic prophase in that the nuclear membrane disappears, allowing chromosomes from each parent to mingle. In this case, chromosomes perform a crossing-over in which similar chromosomes from each parent bundle together. An allele from one parent may replace an allele from another, causing genetic variation.

Metaphase I, anaphase I, and telophase I mimic their mitotic counterparts. The new chromosomal pairings, called tetrads, migrate, and cytokinesis begins creating two diploid cells containing a full, but unique, complement of mixed DNA (46 chromosomes in human). These two daughter cells then begin the process of meiosis II.

Prophase II, metaphase II, anaphase II, and telophase II mirror the previous process. Centrosomes and spindle fibers push apart chromosomes. When the spindle fibers retract, chromosomes are pulled apart. When telophase II begins, each daughter nucleus has only one of each pair of chromosomes (23 chromosomes rather 46 in humans). The result is four haploid cells, or gametes.

DNA and RNA

Deoxyribonucleic acid (DNA) and Ribonucleic acid (RNA) are perhaps the most important molecules in cell biology, responsible for the storage and reading of genetic information that underpins all life.

They are both linear polymers, consisting of sugars, phosphates and bases, but there are some key differences which separate the two.

These distinctions enable the two molecules to work together and fulfil their essential roles. Here, we look at 5 key differences between DNA and RNA. Before we delve into the differences, we take a look at these two nucleic acids side-by-side.

Table 3 – Differences between DNA and RNA

	DNA	RNA
Full Name	Deoxyribonucleic Acid	Ribonucleic Acid
Function	DNA replicates and stores genetic information. It is a blueprint for all genetic information contained within an organism	RNA converts the genetic information contained within DNA to a format used to build proteins, and then moves it to ribosomal protein factories.

Structure	DNA consists of two strands, arranged in a double helix. These strands are made up of subunits called nucleotides. Each nucleotide contains a phosphate, a 5-carbon sugar molecule and a nitrogenous base.	RNA only has one strand, but like DNA, is made up of nucleotides. RNA strands are shorter than DNA strands. RNA sometimes forms a secondary double helix structure, but only intermittently.
Length	DNA is a much longer polymer than RNA. A chromosome, for example, is a single, long DNA molecule, which would be several centimeters in length when unraveled.	RNA molecules are variable in length, but much shorter than long DNA polymers. A large RNA molecule might only be a few thousand base pairs long.
Sugar	The sugar in DNA is deoxyribose, which contains one less hydroxyl group than RNA's ribose.	RNA contains ribose sugar molecules, without the hydroxyl modifications of deoxyribose.
Bases	The bases in DNA are Adenine ('A'), Thymine ('T'), Guanine ('G') and Cytosine ('C').	RNA shares Adenine ('A'), Guanine ('G') and Cytosine ('C') with DNA, but contains Uracil ('U') rather than Thymine.
Base Pairs	Adenine and Thymine pair (A-T) Cytosine and Guanine pair (C-G)	Adenine and Uracil pair (A-U) Cytosine and Guanine pair (C-G)

Location	DNA is found in the nucleus, with a small amount of DNA also present in mitochondria.	RNA forms in the nucleolus, and then moves to specialized regions of the cytoplasm depending on the type of RNA formed.
Reactivity	Due to its deoxyribose sugar, which contains one less oxygen-containing hydroxyl group, DNA is a more stable molecule than RNA, which is useful for a molecule which has the task of keeping genetic information safe.	RNA, containing a ribose sugar, is more reactive than DNA and is not stable in alkaline conditions. RNA's larger helical grooves mean it is more easily subject to attack by enzymes.
(UV) Sensitivity	DNA is vulnerable to damage by ultraviolet light.	RNA is more resistant to damage from UV light than DNA.

The key difference are that DNA encodes all genetic information, and is the blueprint from which all biological life is created. And that's only in the short-term. In the long-term, DNA is a storage device, a biological flash drive that allows the blueprint of life to be passed between generations.

RNA functions as the reader that decodes this flash drive. This reading process is multi-step and there are specialized RNAs for each of these steps. Below, we look in more detail at the three most important types of RNA.

There are three types of RNA:

- Messenger RNA (mRNA) copies portions of genetic code, a process called transcription, and transports these copies to ribosomes, which are the cellular factories that facilitate the production of proteins from this code.

- Transfer RNA (tRNA) is responsible for bringing amino acids, basic protein building blocks, to these protein factories, in response to the coded instructions introduced by the mRNA. This protein-building process is called translation.

- Finally, Ribosomal RNA (rRNA) is a component of the ribosome factory itself without which protein production would not occur.

A. Sugar

Both DNA and RNA are built with a sugar backbone, but whereas the sugar in DNA is called deoxyribose the sugar in RNA is called simply ribose. The 'deoxy' prefix denotes that, whilst RNA has two hydroxyl (-OH) groups attached to its carbon backbone, DNA has only one, and has a lone hydrogen atom attached instead. RNA's extra hydroxyl group proves useful in the process of converting genetic code into mRNAs that can be made into proteins, whilst the deoxyribose sugar gives DNA more stability.

B. Bases

The nitrogen bases in DNA are the basic units of genetic code, and their correct ordering and pairing is essential to biological function. The four bases that make up this code are adenine (A), thymine (T), guanine (G) and cytosine (C). Bases pair off together in a double helix structure, these pairs being A and T, and C and G. RNA doesn't contain thymine bases, replacing them with uracil bases (U), which pair to adenine.

C. Structure

Whilst the ubiquity of Francis Crick and James Watson's DNA double helix means that the two-stranded structure of DNA structure is common knowledge, RNA's single stranded format is not as well known. RNA can form into double-stranded structures, such as during translation, when mRNA and tRNA molecules pair. DNA polymers are also much longer than RNA polymers; the 2.3m long human genome consists of 46 chromosomes, each of which is a single, long DNA molecule. RNA molecules, by comparison, are much shorter.

D. Location

Eukaryotic cells, including all animal and plant cells, house the great majority of their DNA in the nucleus, where it exists in a tightly compressed form, called a chromosome. This squeezed format means the DNA can be easily stored and transferred. In addition to nuclear DNA, some DNA is present in energy-producing mitochondria, small organelles found free-floating in the cytoplasm, the area of the cell outside the nucleus.

The three types of RNA are found in different locations. mRNA is made in the nucleus, with each mRNA fragment copied from its relative piece of DNA, before leaving the nucleus and entering the cytoplasm. The fragments are then shuttled around the cell as needed, moved along by the cell's internal transport system, the cytoskeleton. tRNA, like mRNA, is a free-roaming molecule that moves around the cytoplasm. If it receives the correct signal from the ribosome, it will then hunt down amino acid subunits in the cytoplasm and bring them to the ribosome to be built into proteins. rRNA, as previously mentioned, is found as part of ribosomes. Ribosomes are formed in an area of the nucleus called the nucleolus, before being exported to the cytoplasm, where some ribosomes float freely. Other cytoplasmic ribosomes are bound to the endoplasmic reticulum, a membranous structure that helps process proteins and export them from the cell.

Photosynthesis and Cellular respiration

Photosynthesis and cellular respiration are complementary processes by which living things obtain needed substances. They both consume and create the same substances (water, glucose, oxygen, and carbon dioxide) but in different ways. Through these processes, plants obtain the carbon dioxide they need and living organisms obtain the oxygen they need. They are also necessary to the energy exchange that living things need to survive.

Photosynthesis is the process by which green plants create their own food by turning light energy into chemical energy. Chlorophyll in the leaves transform carbon dioxide, water, and minerals into oxygen and glucose. Photosynthesis takes place in the chloroplasts of cells. This process is what gives energy to all living organisms either directly or indirectly. Without it, life on Earth would cease to exist.

Cellular respiration, on the other hand, is the process by which living things convert oxygen and glucose to carbon dioxide and water, thereby yielding energy. It does not require the presence of sunlight and is always occurring in living organisms. Cellular respiration takes place in the mitochondria of cells.

While photosynthesis requires energy and produces food, cellular respiration breaks down food and releases energy. Plants perform both photosynthesis and respiration, while animals can only perform respiration.

Utilize taxonomy

Taxonomic categories

There are eight distinct taxonomic categories. These are: Domain, Kingdom, Phylum, Class, Order, Family, Genus, and Species.

With each step down in classification, organisms are split into more and more specific groups.

For example, all of the animals in the Kingdom Animalia are split into multiple phyla (plural of phylum). All of the animals in the phylum Chordata are split into multiple classes such as mammals, reptiles, and amphibians.

The broadest category splits all organisms into three groups called 'Domains'. The three Domains of life are Bacteria, Archaea and Eukaryota.

Kingdom

For a long time, all life was separated into five or six kingdoms. These included kingdoms such as animals, plants, fungi, protists, archaea, and bacteria.

With new genetic data, we now know that some protists are more closely related to animals, plants, and fungi than they are to other protists. This suggests that the protist kingdom could be separated into multiple kingdoms. Thoughts are similar for the bacteria and archaea kingdoms.

Phylum

A phylum (plural phyla) is still a very broad classification but it splits kingdoms into multiple groups. An example of phyla from the animal kingdom is Arthropoda which includes all insects, spiders, crustaceans, and more. All vertebrate animals belong to one phylum called 'Chordata'. Invertebrates are separated into many different phyla.

Class

A class is the next level down. As mentioned earlier some classes from the phylum Chordata include mammals, reptiles, and amphibians. Arthropod classes include the likes of insects and arachnids (spiders, mites, and scorpions).

Order and Family

From class, organisms are placed into an Order and then a Family. Using grasses as an example from the plant kingdom, they belong to the order Poales and the family Poaceae.

Genus and Species

The final two categories are genus and species. The genus and species that an organism belongs to are how an organism receives its scientific name. This naming system is called 'binomial nomenclature' and was invented by a brilliant biologist named Carl Linnaeus.

An identified species is placed into a specific group in each of these categories. For example, the taxonomic classification of humans is:

- Domain: Eukaryota

- Kingdom: Animalia

- Phylum: Chordata

- Class: Mammalia

- Order: Primates

- Family: Hominidae

- Genus: Homo

- Species: Homo sapiens

To remember the order of the taxonomic hierarchy from domain to species, people often use mnemonics to make it easier. The phrase that I was taught and still use to help me remember is 'King Phillip Came Over From Germany Swimming'. There are many different phrases people have come up with. If you're not keen on the sentence I use and want another one, take a look at these taxonomy mnemonics.

Taxonomy is the practice of identifying different organisms, classifying them into categories, and naming them. All organisms, both living and extinct, are classified into distinct groups with other similar organisms and given a scientific name.

The classification of organisms has various hierarchical categories. Categories gradually shift from being very broad and including many different organisms to very specific and identifying single species.

Carl Linnaeus

Carl Linnaeus was a Swedish naturalist from the 18th century and is considered the father of taxonomy. It was Linnaeus who first began to separate organisms into hierarchical categories. He also developed the system that we use to name new species called 'binomial nomenclature'. Linnaeus is credited with identifying over 10,000 different plant and animal species in his lifetime, more than any other biologist.

Systema Naturae

When Linnaeus developed his system of hierarchical categories, he called it 'Systema Naturae'. It contained three kingdoms, classes, orders, genera, and species. We have since added two more categories – domains and phyla.

Linnaeus's original classification had three kingdoms – animals, plants, and minerals (natural, non-living elements). We now only use this system for classifying organisms and we have since separated all of life into more than two kingdoms.

Binomial Nomenclature

Binomial nomenclature is the method that we use to uniquely name every different organism on Earth, living or extinct. All organisms have a scientific name that includes two Latin words.

The two words are made from the names of the genus the species belongs to and a second word to separate each of the species within the same genus. The second word is known as the 'specific epithet'. Hence, the scientific names of all organisms are made from the name of their genus and a specific epithet.

For example, the scientific name given to humans includes their genus Homo and the specific epithet sapiens. The overall name is Homo sapiens. Scientific names are also written in either italics or underlined.

Taxonomy is not a perfect science and, as you will find out, there is a lot of disagreement and uncertainty about the structure of taxonomic classifications. In general, however, taxonomy is a great way to quickly learn about how an organism slots into the tree of life.

Tree of Life

The tree of life is used to explain the relationships between the different species on Earth. From microorganisms to trees to fungi and animals, life has evolved through time down countless pathways to provide us with the marvelous present-day collection of different species. Some species are closely related and, in other cases, we have to travel back billions of years to connect other species.

The common belief in biology is that all living things evolved from a common ancestor more than 4 billion years ago. Now, many millions of different species call Earth home and, over the past 4 billion years, many more have come and gone.

Many scientists have devoted their lives to the giant task of working out the path life has taken to evolve from a single species into millions of different species. From one common ancestor, life has branched out to create a magnificent tree of life.

The branches of the tree of life are formed from different groups of organisms. Two branches that are close to each other contain closely related organisms. The first and largest branches from the tree of life are formed by three domains. The branches of each domain split into many more branches.

Domains

All of life is currently separated into three different domains: Bacteria, Archaea and Eukaryota. The first two domains, Bacteria and Archaea, consist entirely of microscopic single-celled organisms. The third domain, Eukaryota, includes many microscopic organisms but also contains well-known groups such as animals, plants, and fungi.

Bacteria and archaea are called prokaryotes because their cells do not contain a nucleus. A nucleus is a membrane that surrounds the genetic material of a cell. The genetic material in the cells of bacteria and archaea are not enclosed in a membrane but sit tightly coiled in the center of the cell.

The organisms in the domain Eukaryota have cells with a nucleus. The presence of a nucleus is the defining feature that identifies these organisms as eukaryotes.

1. Bacteria

The origins of bacteria can be traced back to more than 3.5 billion years ago. They are an ancient group of organisms and are still found almost everywhere on Earth – throughout oceans, inside humans, and in the atmosphere.

These single-celled microorganisms are incredibly diverse and are important for a wide range of reasons. Bacteria help to decompose dead plants and animals and help animals to digest food. Many species can convert gas in the atmosphere into nutrients through processes such as photosynthesis. Bacteria can also be deadly and are the cause of a number of diseases in humans. Bacteria split into many branches along the tree of life. Different groups are often separated by their different metabolisms or by the habitat they are found in. For example, one group known as cyanobacteria is able to convert nitrogen gas into nitrates. Acidobacteria is another group and they are found in highly acidic soils.

2. Archea

The domain Archaea consists of many microscopic organisms that we know very little about. All archaea are single-celled organisms.

Although their cells lack a nucleus and they are classed as prokaryotes, archaea are believed to be more closely related to eukaryotes than bacteria.

Archaea cells are structurally diverse and these microorganisms share many characteristics with both bacteria and eukaryotes. They also have many unique features.

They are typically a similar size to bacteria cells and lack a nucleus and organelles just as bacteria do. The membrane that surrounds the cells of archaea microorganisms is different from the membrane of any other cell.

Originally, archaea were thought to only exist in extreme environments such as thermal springs and salt lakes. They are now known to exist in many habitats that are far less difficult to live in.

This domain currently splits the tree of life into four main groups: Korarchaeotes, Euryarchaeotes, Crenarchaeotes, and Nanoarchaeotes. The majority of the knowledge that we have on archaea is from euryarchaeotes and the crenarchaeotes.

The euryarchaeotes includes many species of salt-loving archaea and a group known as methanogens. Methanogens are anaerobic archaea that produce methane gas from carbon dioxide and hydrogen gas. They can be found in places such as the guts of cattle and in flooded soils of wetlands.

3. Eukaryota

The domain for all organisms that have a nucleus in their cell or cells. It is an extremely diverse and variable domain. It includes thousands of microscopic organisms plus all the large animal and plant species that are found on land and in water.

Besides having a nucleus, the cells of eukaryotes almost always have small cellular structures called organelles. Organelles are specialized cellular 'factories' that perform certain functions such as photosynthesis or protein production.

Eukaryotes have the greatest variation in size of the three domains but the least amount of variation in other aspects. The smallest eukaryotic organism is less than 1 μm or 0.0001 cm wide. Compare that to a giant sequoia tree by the name of General Sherman which is over 83m tall, 7.7m wide and has a volume of more than 1,400 m^3 (52,000 cu ft).

The domain Eukaryota is often split into animals, fungi, plants, and protists.

A. Protists

Protists are a broad group of eukaryotes that includes all eukaryotic organisms that are not plants, animals or fungi. They are not necessarily closely related. Protists were once considered to be a distinct kingdom just as plants, animals, and fungi are. It is now well-known that many protists are more closely related to plants, animals or fungi than they are to other protists. The term is still used for convenience to refer to any eukaryote that isn't a plant, animal or fungi.The vast majority of protists are microscopic single-celled organisms. They are a hugely diverse group and many new species have only been identified in the past decade.

Some branches of protists on the tree of life include organisms such as algae (red, green, brown and golden), ameba, slime molds, diatoms, and dinoflagellates.A large number of protists live as parasites of animals and plants. Other species are important photosynthesizers and predators of bacteria.

B. Plants

Plants make up a kingdom of photosynthetic organisms. They are a group of multicellular organisms that dominate the majority of natural landscapes.

Plants make up a branch in the tree of life plants have the ability to make their own food using light energy from the sun. Through the process of photosynthesis, plants convert carbon dioxide and water into sugars and oxygen. The production of sugars by plants provides the foundation of land-based ecosystems such as forests, wetlands, and grasslands. The kingdom Plantae contains around 400,000 species of plants that we currently know exist on Earth. The vast majority are flowering plants known as angiosperms. Other groups of plants include gymnosperms, ferns, lycophytes and non-vascular plants such as mosses.

C. Fungi

Fungi make up another kingdom within the domain Eukaryota. Approximately 100,000 species have been identified by biologists but it is estimated that around 1.5 million species currently exist on Earth.

Fungi were once placed in the plant kingdom but we now know that they are actually more closely related to animals. Unlike plants, fungi are unable to make their own food and instead get nutrients by decomposing organic material such as dead plants and animals.

Fungi come as both single-celled organisms and multicellular organisms. Single-celled fungi have been referred to as yeasts. Some yeasts are used in food industries to make products such as bread, wine, and beer.

The majority of fungi are multicellular. These include fungi that produce mushrooms, molds, and truffles. Around 35,000 of the already identified fungal species produce mushrooms that assist with reproduction.

D. Animals

The kingdom Animalia is the final eukaryotic kingdom. This is the most diverse of all kingdoms, largely due to the huge diversity of insects that have evolved over the last 400 million years.

Animals are multicellular organisms that are unable to make their own food. They rely on eating other organisms, such as plants and fungi, to secure the energy required to survive.

The animal kingdom is often separated into vertebrates and invertebrates. A vertebrate animal is any animal with an internal backbone. Examples include humans, birds, reptiles, and fish. An invertebrate is any animal that lacks an internal backbone. Insects, jellyfish, sponges, and worms are all examples of invertebrate animals.

The animal kingdom contains the most advanced organisms on Earth. Many animals have the ability to think intelligently and solve problems. The heightened intelligence of animals allows them to perform many complex behaviors that are uncommon in other organisms.

Mendel's laws of genetics and the Punnett square

Mendel spent time crossing pea plants. he noticed some patterns to the inheritance of traits from one set of pea plants to the next. By carefully analyzing his pea plant numbers he discovered three laws of inheritance.

Mendel's Laws are:

1. The Law of Dominance

2. The Law of Segregation

3. The Law of Independent Assortment

Chromosomes or genes do not appear in Mendel's work. That is because the role of these things in relation to inheritance & heredity had not been discovered yet. What makes Mendel's contributions so impressive is that he described the basic patterns of inheritance before the mechanism for inheritance (namely genes) was even discovered.

Genotype describes the genes present in the DNA of an organism. I will use a pair of letters (ex: Tt or YY or ss, etc.) to represent genotypes for one particular trait. There are always two letters in the genotype because (as a result of sexual reproduction) one code for the trait comes from mama organism & the other comes from papa organism, so every offspring gets two codes (two letters).

There are three possible genotypes - two big letters (like "TT"), one of each ("Tt"), or two lowercase letters ("tt"). Each combination of these letters has a name for it that I will use from now on.

When we have two capital or two lowercase letters in the genotype (ex: TT or tt) it's called homozygous. When the genotype is made up of one capital letter & one lowercase letter (ex: Tt) it's called heterozygous.

For *Example*:

Table 4 – Possible Genotypes

Genotype = genes present in an organism (usually abbreviated as two letters)		
TT = homozygous	**Tt** = heterozygous	**tt** = homozygous

A phenotype is how the trait physically shows-up in the organism. Examples of phenotypes: blue eyes, brown fur, striped fruit, yellow flowers.

Alleles are alternative forms of the same gene. Alleles for a trait are located at corresponding positions on homologous chromosomes.

For example, there is a gene for hair texture (whether hair is curly or straight). One form of the hair texture gene codes for curly hair. A different code for of *the same gene* makes hair straight. So the gene for hair texture exists as two alleles - one curly code, and one straight code.

For example, if the codes look like the two below:

aBcdeF

ABcDef

In this the two strings of letters represent a pair of homologous chromosomes. Homologous chromosomes are the same size & have the same genetic info (genes). Each letter in the diagram stands for an allele (form of a gene). What's important to notice is that the letters can be in different forms (capital or lowercase) (that is what is meant by allele) and that the letters are lined-up in the same order along each mean homologous chromosome. The "a-forms" are in corresponding positions, so are the "B-forms", the "c" alleles, the "d" alleles. We will use "C" for the curly allele, and a "c" for the straight allele. A person's genotype with respect to hair texture has three possibilities: CC, Cc, or cc. Homozygous means having two of the same allele in the genotype (2 big or 2 little letters --- CC or cc). Heterozygous means one of each allele in the genotype (ex: Cc). This is Mendel's First Law

The Law of Dominance

In a cross of parents that are pure for contrasting traits, only one form of the trait will appear in the next generation. Offspring that are hybrid for a trait will have only the dominant trait in the phenotype. While Mendel was crossing (reproducing) his pea he noticed something interesting. When he crossed pure tall plants with pure short plants, all the new pea plants (referred to as the F1 generation) were tall. Similarly, crossing pure yellow seeded pea plants and pure green seeded pea plants produced an F1 generation of all yellow seeded pea plants. The same was true for other pea traits:

Table 5 –

Parent Pea Plants	F1 Pea Plants
tall stem x short stem	all tall stems
yellow seeds x green seeds	all yellow seeds
green pea pods x yellow pea pods	all green pea pods
round seeds x wrinkled seeds	all round seeds
axial flowers x terminal flowers	all axial flowers

So, what he noticed was that when the parent plants had contrasting forms of a trait (tall vs short, green vs yellow, etc.) the phenotypes of the offspring resembled only one of the parent plants with respect to that trait. He noticed that the tall factor seems to dominate the short factor. For abbreviations, we use the capital "T" for the dominant tall allele, and the lowercase "t" for the recessive short allele.

Table 6- Genotype x Phenotype

Genotype Symbol	Genotype Vocab	Phenotype
TT	homozygous dominant	tall
Tt	heterozygous	tall
tt	homozygous recessive	short

Note: the only way the recessive trait shows-up in the phenotype is if the genotype has 2 lowercase letters (i.e. is homozygous recessive).

Also note: hybrids always show the dominant trait in their phenotype (that, by the way, is Mendel's Law of Dominance in a nutshell).

The Punnet Square

OK, now is as good of time as any to introduce you to a new friend, the Punnett Square. This will assist you in figuring out a multitude of genetics problems.

We will start by using a Punnet Square to illustrate Mendel's Law of Dominance. Recall that he "discovered" this law by crossing a pure tall pea plant & a pure short pea plant. In symbols, that cross looks like this:

Parents (P): TT x tt

where T = the dominant allele for tall stems & t = recessive allele for short stems.

The P-Square for such a cross looks like this:

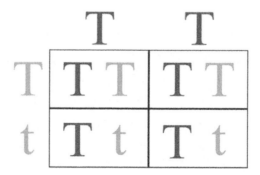

Figure 3 – Putnet Square

Inside the 4 boxes are the possible genotypes (with respect to plant height) of the offspring from these parent pea plants. In this case, the only possible genotype is Tt (heterozygous).

In hybrids, the dominant trait (whatever the capital letter stands for) is the one that appears in the phenotype, so all the offspring from this cross will have tall stems.

To "fill in the boxes" of the Punnett Square, say to yourself "letter from the left & letter from the top". The "t" from the left is partnered with the "T" from the top to complete each of the four squares.

A summary of this cross would be:

Table 7 –

Parent Pea Plants (P Generation)		Offspring (F1 Generation)	
Genotypes:	Phenotypes:	Genotypes:	Phenotypes:
TT x tt	tall x short	100% Tt	100% tall

Apply the periodic table of elements

The periodic table (also known as the periodic table of elements) is organized so scientists can quickly discern the properties of individual elements such as their mass, electron number, electron configuration and their unique chemical properties.

Metals reside on the left side of the table, while non-metals reside on the right.

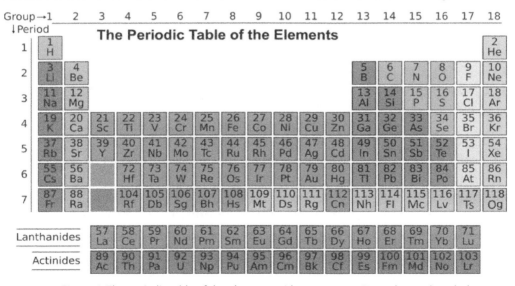

Figure 4: The periodic table of the elements with names, atomic number and symbol

The primary building blocks of atoms are protons, neutrons, and electrons. It is convenient to describe the composition of an atom in terms of the number of protons and neutrons in its nucleus. The term atomic number, conventionally denoted by the symbol Z, indicates number of protons present in the nucleus of an atom, which is also equal to the number of electrons in an uncharged atom. The number of neutrons is represented by the neutron number (N). Because the mass of these nuclear particles is each approximately equal to one unified atomic mass unit (u), the sum of the protons plus neutrons is designated as the mass number (A). The mass of the electron is more than 1800 times smaller than the proton mass and, therefore, can be neglected in calculating the mass number. For any element, the mass number is equal to the atomic weight rounded off to the nearest integer value.

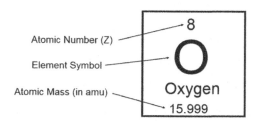

Figure 5 – Properties of the elements shown in the periodic table

Describe the properties of atoms

Atoms and molecules follow the rules of chemistry and physics, even when they're part of a complex, living, breathing being.

If you learned in chemistry that some atoms tend to gain or lose electrons or form bonds with each other, those facts remain true even when the atoms or molecules are part of a living thing.

In fact, simple interactions between atoms played out many times and in many different combinations, in a single cell or a larger organism are what make life possible. One could argue that everything you are, including your consciousness, is the byproduct of chemical and electrical interactions between a very, very large number of nonliving atoms!

So as an incredibly complex being made up of roughly 7,000,000,000,000,000,000,000,000,000 atoms, you'll probably want to know some basic chemistry as you begin to explore the world of biology, and the world in general.

Matter and elements

Matter refers to anything that occupies space and has mass—in other words, the "stuff" that the universe is made of. All matter is made up of substances called elements, which have specific chemical and physical properties and cannot be broken down into other substances through ordinary chemical reactions. Gold, for instance, is an element, and so is carbon. There are 118 elements, but only 92 occur naturally. The remaining elements have only been made in laboratories and are unstable.

Each element is designated by its chemical symbol, which is a single capital letter or, when the first letter is already "taken" by another element, a combination of two letters. Some elements follow the English term for the element, such as C for carbon and Ca for calcium. Other elements' chemical symbols come from their Latin names; for example, the symbol for sodium is Na, which is a short form of natrium, the Latin word for sodium.

The four elements common to all living organisms are oxygen (O), carbon (C), hydrogen (H), and nitrogen (N), which together make up about 96% of the human body. In the nonliving world, elements are found in different proportions, and some elements common to living organisms are relatively rare on the earth as a whole. All elements and the chemical reactions between them obey the same chemical and physical laws, regardless of whether they are a part of the living or nonliving world.

The structure of the atom

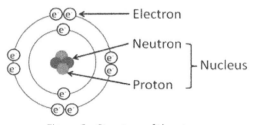

Figure 6 – Structure of the atom

An atom is the smallest unit of matter that retains all of the chemical properties of an element. For example, a gold coin is simply a very large number of gold atoms molded into the shape of a coin, with small amounts of other, contaminating elements. Gold atoms cannot be broken down into anything smaller while still retaining the properties of gold. A gold atom gets its properties from the tiny subatomic particles it's made up of.

An atom consists of two regions. The first is the tiny atomic nucleus, which is in the center of the atom and contains positively charged particles called protons and neutral, uncharged, particles called neutrons. The second, much larger, region of the atom is a "cloud" of electrons, negatively charged particles that orbit around the nucleus.

The attraction between the positively charged protons and negatively charged electrons holds the atom together. Most atoms contain all three of these types of subatomic particles—protons, electrons, and neutrons. Hydrogen (H) is an exception because it typically has one proton and one electron, but no neutrons. The number of protons in the nucleus determines which element an atom is, while the number of electrons surrounding the nucleus determines which kind of reactions the atom will undergo.

Protons and neutrons do not have the same charge, but they do have approximately the same mass, about 1.67×10^{-24}.

Since grams are not a very convenient unit for measuring masses that tiny, scientists chose to define an alternative measure, the Dalton or atomic mass unit (amu). A single neutron or proton has a weight very close to 1 amu. Electrons are much smaller in mass than protons, only about 1/1800 of an atomic mass unit, so they do not contribute much to an element's overall atomic mass. On the other hand, electrons do greatly affect an atom's charge, as each electron has a negative charge equal to the positive charge of a proton. In uncharged, neutral atoms, the number of electrons orbiting the nucleus is equal to the number of protons inside the nucleus. The positive and negative charges cancel out, leading to an atom with no net charge.

Protons, neutrons, and electrons are very small, and most of the volume of an atom—greater than 99 percent—is actually empty space. With all this empty space, you might ask why so-called solid objects don't just pass through one another. The answer is that the negatively charged electron clouds of the atoms will repel each other if they get too close together, resulting in our perception of solidity.

Properties of matter

All matter has physical and chemical properties. Physical properties are characteristics that scientists can measure without changing the composition of the sample under study, such as mass, color, and volume (the amount of space occupied by a sample). Chemical properties describe the characteristic ability of a substance to react to form new substances; they include its flammability and susceptibility to corrosion.

All samples of a pure substance have the same chemical and physical properties. For example, pure copper is always a reddish-brown solid (a physical property) and always dissolves in dilute nitric acid to produce a blue solution and a brown gas (a chemical property).

Physical properties can be extensive or intensive. Extensive properties vary with the amount of the substance and include mass, weight, and volume. Intensive properties, in contrast, do not depend on the amount of the substance; they include color, melting point, boiling point, electrical conductivity, and physical state at a given temperature.

For example, elemental sulfur is a yellow crystalline solid that does not conduct electricity and has a melting point of 115.2 °C, no matter what amount is examined. Scientists commonly measure intensive properties to determine a substance's identity, whereas extensive properties convey information about the amount of the substance in a sample.

Because they differ in size, the two samples of sulfur have different extensive properties, such as mass and volume. In contrast, their intensive properties, including color, melting point, and electrical conductivity, are identical.

Although mass and volume are both extensive properties, their ratio is an important intensive property called density (ρ). Density is defined as mass per unit volume and is usually expressed in grams per cubic centimeter (g/cm^3). As mass increases in a given volume, density also increases.

For example, lead, with its greater mass, has a far greater density than the same volume of air, just as a brick has a greater density than the same volume of Styrofoam. At a given temperature and pressure, the density of a pure substance is a constant:

Density ρ = mass x volume = mV

Pure water, for example, has a density of 0.998 g/cm^3 at 25 °C. The average densities of some common substances are listed below.

Substance	Density at 25 °C (g/cm^3)
honey	1.420
blood	1.035
whole milk	1.030
corn oil	0.922
body fat	0.918
mayonnaise	0.910

Physical Property and Change

Physical changes are changes in which no chemical bonds are broken or formed. This means that the same types of compounds or elements that were there at the beginning of the change are there at the end of the change. Because the ending materials are the same as the beginning materials, the properties (such as color, boiling point, etc.) will also be the same. Physical changes involve moving molecules around, but not changing them. Some types of physical changes include:

- Changes of state (changes from a solid to a liquid or a gas and vice versa)
- Separation of a mixture
- Physical deformation (cutting, denting, stretching)
- Making solutions (special kinds of mixtures).

As an ice cube melts, its shape changes as it acquires the ability to flow. However, its composition does not change. Melting is an example of a physical change since some properties of the material change, but the identity of the matter does not. Physical changes can further be classified as reversible or irreversible. The melted ice cube may be refrozen, so melting is a reversible physical change.

Physical changes that involve a change of state are all reversible. Other changes of state include vaporization (liquid to gas), freezing (liquid to solid), and condensation (gas to liquid). Dissolving is also a reversible physical change. When salt is dissolved into water, the salt is said to have entered the aqueous state. The salt may be regained by boiling off the water, leaving the salt behind.

Ice Melting is a physical change. When solid water (H_2O) as ice melts into a liquid (water), it appears changed. However, this change is only physical as the composition of the constituent molecules is the same: 11.19% hydrogen and 88.81% oxygen by mass.

Chemical Properties and Change

Chemical changes occur when bonds are broken and/or formed between molecules or atoms. This means that one substance with a certain set of properties (such as melting point, color, taste, etc.) is turned into a different substance with different properties. Chemical changes are frequently harder to reverse than physical changes.

One good example of a chemical change is burning paper. In contrast to ripping paper, burning paper actually results in the formation of new chemicals (carbon dioxide and water). Another example of chemical change occurs when water is formed. Each molecule contains two atoms of hydrogen and one atom of oxygen chemically bonded.

Another example of a chemical change is what occurs when natural gas is burned in your furnace. This time, before the reaction we have a molecule of methane, CH_4, and two molecules of oxygen, O_2, while after the reaction we have two molecules of water, H_2O, and one molecule of carbon dioxide, CO_2. In this case, not only has the appearance changed, but the structure of the molecules has also changed. The new substances do not have the same chemical properties as the original ones. Therefore, this is a chemical change.

The combustion of magnesium metal is also chemical change (Magnesium + Oxygen → Magnesium Oxide):

$2\ Mg + O_2 \rightarrow 2\ MgO$

as is the rusting of iron (Iron + Oxygen → Iron Oxide/ Rust):

$4\ Fe + 3\ O_2 \rightarrow 2\ Fe_2 2O_3$

Using the components of composition and properties, we have the ability to distinguish one sample of matter from the others.

Calculate diffusion rates and molarity

Diffusion takes place because of particle motion. Particles in random motion, like gas molecules, bump into one another, following Brownian motion, until they disperse evenly in a given area. Diffusion then is the flow of molecules from an area of high concentration to that of low concentration, until equilibrium is reached. In short, diffusion describes a gas, liquid or solid dispersing throughout a particular space or throughout a second substance. Diffusion examples include a perfume aroma spreading throughout a room, or a drop of green food coloring dispersing throughout a cup of water. There a number of ways to calculate diffusion rates.

Remember that the term "rate" refers to the change in a quantity over time.

As diffusion takes place against a concentration gradient, there must be some form of energy that facilitates the diffusion. Consider how water, carbon dioxide and oxygen can easily cross cell membranes by passive diffusion (or osmosis, in the case of water). But if a large, non-lipid soluble molecule has to pass through the cell membrane, then active transport is required, which is where the high-energy molecule of adenosine triphosphate (ATP) steps in to facilitate the diffusion across cellular membranes.

Interpret pH scale values

Whether a solution is acidic or alkali is all to do with hydrogen ions (abbreviated with the chemical symbol H^+). In water (H_2O), a small number of the molecules dissociate (split up).

Some of the water molecules lose a hydrogen and become hydroxide ions (OH^-). The "lost" hydrogen ions join up with water molecules to form hydronium ions (H_3O^+). For simplicity, hydronium ions are referred to as hydrogen ions H^+. In pure water, there are an equal number of hydrogen ions and hydroxide ions. The solution is neither acidic or basic.

An acid is a substance that donates hydrogen ions. Because of this, when an acid is dissolved in water, the balance between hydrogen ions and hydroxide ions is shifted. Now there are more hydrogen ions than hydroxide ions in the solution. This kind of solution is acidic.

A base is a substance that accepts hydrogen ions. When a base is dissolved in water, the balance between hydrogen ions and hydroxide ions shifts the opposite way. Because the base "soaks up" hydrogen ions, the result is a solution with more hydroxide ions than hydrogen ions. This kind of solution is alkaline.

Acidity and alkalinity are measured with a logarithmic scale called pH. a strongly acidic solution can have one hundred million million, or one hundred trillion (100,000,000,000,000) times more hydrogen ions than a strongly basic solution! The flip side, of course, is that a strongly basic solution can have 100,000,000,000,000 times more hydroxide ions than a strongly acidic solution. Moreover, the hydrogen ion and hydroxide ion concentrations in everyday solutions can vary over that entire range.

In order to deal with these large numbers more easily, scientists use a logarithmic scale, the pH scale. Each one-unit change in the pH scale corresponds to a ten-fold change in hydrogen ion concentration.

The pH scale is theoretically open-ended but most pH values are in the range from 0 to 14. It's a lot easier to use a logarithmic scale instead of always having to write down all those zeros! By the way, notice how one hundred million million is a one with fourteen zeros after it? It is not coincidence, it is logarithms!

To be more precise, pH is the negative logarithm of the hydrogen ion concentration:

$$pH = -\log [H^+]$$

The square brackets around the H^+ automatically mean "concentration" to a chemist. What the equation means is just what we said before: for each 1-unit change in pH, the hydrogen ion concentration changes ten-fold. Pure water has a neutral pH of 7. pH values lower than 7 are acidic, and pH values higher than 7 are alkaline (basic).

Table 8 - Examples of substances with different pH values

pH Value	H⁺ Concentration Relative to Pure Water	Example
0	10 000 000	battery acid
1	1 000 000	gastric acid
2	100 000	lemon juice, vinegar
3	10 000	orange juice, soda
4	1 000	tomato juice, acid rain
5	100	black coffee, bananas
6	10	urine, milk
7	1	pure water
8	0.1	sea water, eggs
9	0.01	baking soda
10	0.001	Great Salt Lake, milk of magnesia
11	0.000 1	ammonia solution
12	0.000 01	soapy water
13	0.000 001	bleach, oven cleaner
14	0.000 000 1	liquid drain cleaner

Determine force and motion

Forces and their effects are all around us. They keep us firmly rooted to the ground, they make us move and they stop us slipping and sliding. Forces are vital to life and the universe.

However, forces only do three very simple things. They change:

- The shape of an object

- The direction of an object

- The speed of an object

Force is measured in the unit called Newton's (N) – named after the first scientist to quantify forces, Sir Isaac Newton.

We can measure force using a special piece of equipment called the Newton Balance.

Friction

Friction is a force that opposes motion. It is present whenever two surfaces rub over each other, such as when you rub your hands together, or when you apply the brakes on a bike or in a car. Friction also prevents an object from starting to move, such as a shoe placed on a ramp. When friction acts between two surfaces that are moving over each other, some kinetic energy is transformed into heat energy.

Friction can sometimes be useful. For example, we rely on the soles of our shoes to not slip over the ground that we are walking on, and the friction between a car tire and the road surface helps cars to speed up, slow down and turn corners. Sometimes though, friction can be a nuisance. For example, the friction between a wheel and the axle that it rotates on wastes energy, so we try to minimize the friction using bearings and lubricants.

Balanced and unbalanced forces

'Unchanging motion' is when the body is at rest or is moving with a steady speed in a straight line. Balanced forces are responsible for unchanging motion. Balanced forces are forces where the effect of one force is cancelled out by another. A tug of war, where each team is pulling equally on the rope, is an example of balanced forces. The forces exerted on the rope are equal in size and opposite in direction. The rope will have an acceleration of zero under the action of these balanced forces. It will therefore remain stationary (or moving at a constant velocity – if it was to be moving before the teams started pulling).

Sir Isaac Newton, in his laws of motion, made statements about the effect of balanced and unbalanced forces.

Newton's first law is concerned with balanced forces. The first law states that if a body is at rest and the forces acting on it are balanced then the body will remain at rest. However if the body is moving and the forces acting are balanced then the body will keep moving at constant speed in a straight line.

Newton's First Law

Newton's second law is concerned with unbalanced forces. Unbalanced forces produce acceleration. The bigger the unbalanced force the bigger the acceleration. This law is usually written as an equation F = ma.

Weight, mass and gravity

The weight of an object is the force on it due to the gravitational pull of gravity at that point. Since it is a force, weight is measured in Newton's (not kilograms).

Gravity is different on different planets, so the weight of an object on different planets (or moons) is different from its weight on Earth.

The mass of an object is the amount of matter that makes up the object and is measured in kilograms. The mass of an object remains the same no matter where the object is in the universe.

Gravitational field strength

The gravitational field strength (g) of a planet is the weight per unit mass of an object on that planet. It has the units, Newton's per kilogram, Nkg^{-1}

Examples:

- Earth g = 9.8 Nkg^{-1}

- Mars g = 3.7 Nkg^{-1}

- Moon g = 1.6 Nkg^{-1}

Calculating weight

The weight of an object can be calculated on different planets so long as we know that object's mass and the gravitational field strength of the planet.

We can calculate weight using the following formula.

W = mg

Where W = weight and is measured in Newtons (N)

m = mass and is measured in kilograms (kg)

g = gravitational field strength and is measured in Newtons per kilogram (N kg^{-1})

Newton's Second Law of motion

Newton's Second Law of Motion is concerned with the effect that unbalanced forces have on motion. An unbalanced force acting on an object causes it to accelerate. There are two points to note about the acceleration of an object when an unbalanced force acts on it.

The bigger the unbalanced force acting on the object the bigger the acceleration of the object.

The more mass the object has, the more inclined it is to resist any change to its motion. For example, if you apply the same unbalanced force to a mass of 1000 kg and a mass of 1 kg, the acceleration (change in motion) of the 1000 kg mass will be much less than that of the 1 kg mass.

Newton's second law provides a relationship between the unbalanced force on the object, the mass of the object and the acceleration that is produced. The amazing thing is that the relationship can be expressed neatly by a straightforward mathematical equation.

unbalanced\,force = mass\times acceleration

F = ma

The unbalanced force F is measured in Newtons (N), the mass m is measured in kilograms (kg) and acceleration a is measured in meters per second per second.

Describe the parts of an experiment

In an experiment, a researcher manipulates one or more variables, while holding all other variables constant. By noting how the manipulated variables affect a response variable, the researcher can test whether a causal relationship exists between the manipulated variables and the response variable.

Parts of an Experiment

All experiments have independent variables, dependent variables, and experimental units.

- ### Independent variable

An independent variable (also called a factor) is an explanatory variable manipulated by the experimenter.

Each factor has two or more levels (i.e., different values of the factor). Combinations of factor levels are called treatments.

In a hypothetical experiment, the researcher is studying the possible effects of Vitamin C and Vitamin E on health. There are two factors - dosage of Vitamin C and dosage of Vitamin E. The Vitamin C factor has three levels - 0 mg per day, 250 mg per day, and 500 mg per day. The Vitamin E factor has 2 levels - 0 mg per day and 400 mg per day. The experiment has six treatments. Treatment 1 is 0 mg of E and 0 mg of C, Treatment 2 is 0 mg of E and 250 mg of C, and so on.

- ### Dependent variable

In the hypothetical experiment, the researcher is looking at the effect of vitamins on health. The dependent variable in this experiment would be some measure of health (annual doctor bills, number of colds caught in a year, number of days hospitalized, etc.).

- ### Experimental units

The recipients of experimental treatments are called experimental units. The experimental units in an experiment could be anything - people, plants, animals, or even inanimate objects.

In the hypothetical experiment above, the experimental units would probably be people (or lab animals). But in an experiment to measure the tensile strength of string, the experimental units might be pieces of string. When the experimental units are people, they are often called participants; when the experimental units are animals, they are often called subjects.

Characteristics of a Well-Designed Experiment

A well-designed experiment includes design features that allow researchers to eliminate extraneous variables as an explanation for the observed relationship between the independent variable(s) and the dependent variable. Some of these features are listed below.

- Control.

Control refers to steps taken to reduce the effects of extraneous variables (i.e., variables other than the independent variable and the dependent variable). These extraneous variables are called lurking variables. Control involves making the experiment as similar as possible for experimental units in each treatment condition. Three control strategies are control groups, placebos, and blinding.

A. Control group.

A control group is a baseline group that receives no treatment or a neutral treatment. To assess treatment effects, the experimenter compares results in the treatment group to results in the control group.

B. Placebo

Often, participants in an experiment respond differently after they receive a treatment, even if the treatment is neutral. A neutral treatment that has no "real" effect on the dependent variable is called a placebo, and a participant's positive response to a placebo is called the placebo effect. To control for the placebo effect, researchers often administer a neutral treatment (i.e., a placebo) to the control group. The classic example is using a sugar pill in drug research. The drug is considered effective only if participants who receive the drug have better outcomes than participants who receive the sugar pill.

C. Blinding.

Of course, if participants in the control group know that they are receiving a placebo, the placebo effect will be reduced or eliminated; and the placebo will not serve its intended control purpose.

Blinding is the practice of not telling participants whether they are receiving a placebo. In this way, participants in the control and treatment groups experience the placebo effect equally. Often, knowledge of which groups receive placebos is also kept from people who administer or evaluate the experiment.

This practice is called double blinding. It prevents the experimenter from "spilling the beans" to participants through subtle cues; and it assures that the analyst's evaluation is not tainted by awareness of actual treatment conditions.

- **Randomization.**

Randomization refers to the practice of using chance methods (random number tables, flipping a coin, etc.) to assign experimental units to treatments. In this way, the potential effects of lurking variables are distributed at chance levels (hopefully roughly evenly) across treatment conditions.

- **Replication.**

Replication refers to the practice of assigning each treatment to many experimental units. In general, the more experimental units in each treatment condition, the lower the variability of the dependent measures.

- **Confounding**

Confounding occurs when the experimental controls do not allow the experimenter to reasonably eliminate plausible alternative explanations for an observed relationship between independent and dependent variables.

Consider this example: A drug manufacturer tests a new cold medicine with 200 participants - 100 men and 100 women. The men receive the drug, and the women do not. At the end of the test period, the men report fewer colds.

This experiment implements no controls! As a result, many variables are confounded, and it is impossible to say whether the drug was effective. For example, gender is confounded with drug use. Perhaps, men are less vulnerable to the particular cold virus circulating during the experiment, and the new medicine had no effect at all. Or perhaps the men experienced a placebo effect.

This experiment could be strengthened with a few controls. Women and men could be randomly assigned to treatments. One treatment group could receive a placebo, with blinding. Then, if the treatment group (i.e., the group getting the medicine) had sufficiently fewer colds than the control group, it would be reasonable to conclude that the medicine was effective in preventing colds.

Interpret scientific arguments

You already know what an argument is: a disagreement between people about some issue they feel is important. A scientific argument is defined as people disagreeing about scientific explanations (claims) using empirical data (evidence) to justify their side of the argument. A scientific argument is a process that scientists follow to guide their research activities.

Scientists identify weaknesses and limitations in others arguments, with the ultimate goal of refining and improving scientific explanations and experimental designs. This process is known as evidence-based argumentation.

Below explains the three components of a scientific argument - the claim, the evidence, and the rationale.

Hence, scientific argumentation requires scientists to support their claims (either for or against a particular idea or explanation) with evidence that has been gathered through observation or experimentation and then to use logic and reason to justify why that evidence supports their claims.

Scientific arguments use evidence and data rather than belief or opinion to support a claim because evidence and data can be empirically reexamined and retested, whereas beliefs and opinions (no matter how strongly held) cannot be empirically verified.

Learning how to construct a valid scientific argument will help you recognize arguments that are unscientific — those based wholly or in part on emotion, ignorance, misinterpretation of scientific evidence, or denial.

But the truth is, you can think of it as more of a nonfiction, critical reading, and thinking section. In actuality, the Science section does not test your knowledge of advanced scientific concepts. Instead, it is intended to test your ability to solve problems using scientific analysis and reasoning with the information you're given. Although it does require a base level of knowledge and grasp of science terms, most of the information that you need to apply your scientific thinking and analysis will be provided in the passages.

The Scientific Method is a rigorous step-by-step process used to test hypotheses and establish facts. First you need to ask a question, often referred to as making a hypothesis, this question is in the nature of an "educated guess:" something the questioner suspects is true but has not been tested.

For example, Jade's two cats have become overweight eating SuperHungry Cat Food. She wonders if they might lose some of that weight if she switches them to Vegan Kitty Chow.

Set Up and Conduct an Experiment.

An experiment sets up a situation to test the questioner's initial guess. It often involves using a "control," or unchanged situation, to measure the success or failure of the experiment. In Jade's case, she gives one cat, Hyde, one cup of Vegan Kitty Chow per day instead of one cup of SuperHungry Cat Food. Jade's other cat, Jeckle, is the control; he gets one cup of SuperHungry Cat Food every day. In order for her results to be valid, Jade will need to make sure neither cat eats out of the other's bowl and that she doesn't give them other snacks on top.

Collect and Interpret Data.

Jade should be very careful with Hyde and Jeckle's food. She needs to carefully monitor each cat's intake. It would also be a good idea for her to record her findings on a regular basis.

Draw Conclusions.

When the experiment is over, Jade should have enough data to answer the question "Did switching to Vegan Kitty Chow cause my cat to lose weight?" She can then decide if she wants to use that information.

That's a very simple overview of the scientific method, but as you can see, it's not really anything to be scared of, it's just following a logical route, there's not an extreme amount of required scientific knowledge of biology, chemistry, and physics. It's basically a test that measures how well you can interpret charts, tables, and graphs. The sort of questions you may get are below:

1. **Specific Detail Questions**

These questions ask you to locate and consider the significance of a specific detail contained within a graph, chart, table, or passage. They're incredibly easy and very straightforward, and they're designed to test your ability to quickly locate information. Be certain that you're searching in the correct location. If the question directs you to "Table 2," make sure that's where you're looking. Pay attention to whether the table name is displayed above or below the table itself.

2. **Pattern Recognition Questions**

These questions are designed to test your ability to identify and interpret the significance of patterns. You'll be asked to observe a trend or relationship among data. Are temperatures going up as you approach the equator? Are elk leaving the east coast at a constant rate? You might be asked to predict what will happen beyond the parameters of the given data. That's no problem, if you're able to spot the trend. To solve these questions, look at what's being measured and ask yourself how those factors correlate.

3. **Drawing Inferences Questions**

These questions require that you draw inferences based on the data presented. You may need to consider the experiment or study as a whole, and consult multiple charts and graphs. You might also be asked how the results of the experiment or study might change if a new factor were introduced. To solve these questions, make sure you understand the conditions of the experiment and the relationship between data.

4. **Assessing the Scientific Method Questions**

These questions test your understanding of the scientific method as it applies to specific experiments. They ask you to consider how the experiment is designed or conducted, what the implications of the hypothesis are, how data is measured and interpreted, what conclusions the scientists draw, and so on. They might, for example, ask you to identify the independent and dependent variables in an experiment.To solve scientific method questions, read the introductory paragraph before each experiment. Consider the data presented and form an impression of how the hypothesis and testing procedure relate to the outcome.

5. Compare and Contrast Questions

On the Conflicting Viewpoints passages, you will analyze and compare incompatible analyses based on different or incomplete data. Questions will assess whether you understand each viewpoint, and ask you to compare them.

A Guide to the Science Section of the ATI TEAS

The Science section of the ATI TEAS consists of 40 multiple-choice questions that you'll answer over the course of 35 minutes. This section is the final required part of the ATI TEAS You may find that when they arrive at this part of the test, they are beginning to feel tired, bored and lacking in concentration. If you find that during practice tests, this happens to you, it may be worth finding time in the break beforehand to reset. Drink some water etc., find what works for you as a break.

Many of the passages will also include charts, tables, graphs, or figures, and you will often be asked to interpret these. Although some basic computational skills may be required, they are not directly assessed and the use of a calculator is not allowed on the Science section of the ATI TEAS.

Just like the other sections of the ATI TEAS, the score that you receive on the Science section of the ATI TEAS will be a scaled score ranging from 1-36. This number is scaled from your raw score, which is the number of questions that you got correct on the Science section. Your scaled score ranging from 1-36 on the Science section is the number that will be used to average into your overall composite ATI TEAS score. Each section of the test is weighed equally and averaged to calculate your composite score.

In the Detailed Results portion of your score report, you will see a series of sub scores underneath your Science score. These include Interpretation of Data, Scientific Investigation, and Evaluation of Models, Inferences & Experimental Results.

Strategies for ATI TEAS Science

Don't try to understand the entire passage your reading comprehension skills on the Science section of the ATI TEAS are assessed more sporadically and through more specific questions.

Remember, the test assesses your ability to apply your knowledge about what's presented, not summarize complete passages. Don't spend too much time or energy trying to wrap your head around every detail of the text. Instead, wait until you know what details are important for answering the questions.

Your time is best spent skimming the passages to get the general idea of their content, and then reading the questions and selectively reviewing the passage in more detail as necessary. In fact, sometimes, especially on Data Representation portions, the questions will apply solely to informational graphics without any mention of the passage at all.

With that in mind you need to master the art of reading graphs, charts, and figures this is one of the two skills most explicitly tested on the Science section of the ATI TEAS. There will definitely be several questions, if not more, that ask you to read and interpret information that is presented graphically. And some of the graphs can be fairly complex.

Make sure that you are familiar with various graphs, charts, maps, and figures. Each time you evaluate one, be sure to read the title and labels carefully. Know what each axis represents and understand the relationship between them. Look for trends or anomalies. The informational graphics on the Science section of the ATI TEAS are often selected for their complexity, so make sure to take lots of practice tests to familiarize yourself with them.

Remember that any question about a value relating to a graph or chart will have that value represented on the graphic somewhere. If you can locate it, you'll get the answer correct. If the value of an answer option is not represented anywhere on the graph, you should cross it off immediately. It is not a feasible answer.

Get to know, and really understand, the scientific method; a key skill that is tested on the Science section of the ATI TEAS. Much of the Research Summary portion will directly or indirectly relate to the scientific method. You should know each step of it in detail and be able to offer critiques of its effectiveness as applied to sample research.

Common questions related to the scientific method will include identifying independent and dependent variables, why the scientists made certain choices during their experiment, and how hypothetical changes to the experiment might affect the results. You will need to be comfortable differentiating between experimental and observational studies, recognizing how variables are isolated, and interpreting how experimental design affects results

It is still worth the time to brush up on your content knowledge. Although not much of the Science section of the ATI TEAS relies on pre-existing knowledge, there will be some questions on each test that do. In order to really maximize your chances of achieving the highest score possible, you should spend some time reviewing key concepts such as basic atomic structure, fundamentals of cell biology including photosynthesis, basic genetics with an understanding of alleles, traits, and inheritance, and basic physics concepts regarding kinetic and potential energy and mass versus weight.

Science Exercises

Passage I

The ninth planet of our solar system, Pluto, was discovered in 1930. It is the smallest planet in the solar system, with a surface area more than 300 times smaller than Earth's. Recently, Pluto's categorization as a planet has been debated. Two scientists discuss whether Pluto is a planet or another celestial object.

Scientist 1

Pluto is most certainly a planet. Some astronomers have suggested that Pluto be stripped of its planetary status, arguing that it is more accurately categorized as an asteroid or comet. However, with a 1,413-mile diameter, Pluto is almost 1,000 times bigger than an average comet, and it does not have a tail of dust and gas as comets do. A planet can be described as a non-moon, sun-orbiting object that does not generate nuclear fusion and is large enough to be pulled into a spherical shape by its own gravity. Strictly by definition alone, Pluto is a planet. Pluto is clearly not a moon, as it does not orbit another planet. Although Pluto's orbital path is irregular as compared with the other planets of the solar system, it undisputedly orbits the sun. Pluto does not generate heat by nuclear fission, distinguishing it from a star. It is large enough to be pulled into a spherical shape by its own gravitational force, distinguishing it from either a comet or an asteroid.

Scientist 2

There are many facts about Pluto suggesting that it is actually not a planet but a member of the Kuiper Belt, a group of sizable comets that orbit the sun beyond Neptune. First, Pluto is composed of icy material, as are the comets in the Kuiper Belt, while the other planets of the solar system fall into one of two categories: rocky or gaseous. The four inner planets, Mercury, Venus, Earth, and Mars are rocky planets; Jupiter, Saturn, Uranus, and Neptune are gaseous. Pluto is neither rocky nor gaseous but has an icy composition. In addition, Pluto is much too small to be a planet. It is less than half the diameter of the next smallest planet, Mercury. The Earth's moon is even larger than Pluto. Finally, the eccentricity of Pluto's orbit indicates that it is not a planet. Pluto is generally considered the ninth planet, but for twenty years of its 249-year orbit, it is actually closer to the sun than is Neptune, making it the eighth planet during that period of time. This irregular orbit is shared by over seventy Kuiper Belt comets.

1. Which of the following phrases best describes the major point of difference between the two scientist's viewpoints?

    A. The actual location of Pluto in the solar system.

    B. The length of Pluto's orbit.

    C. The shape of Pluto's orbit.

    D. The classification of Pluto as a planet.

2. According to Scientist 2's viewpoint, compared to other planets of the solar system, Pluto's surface is:

A. less icy.

B. more icy.

C. more gaseous.

D. more rocky.

3. Scientist 1's viewpoint indicates that Pluto differs from asteroids and comets in all of the following ways EXCEPT:

A. Pluto can generate heat through nuclear fission.

B. Pluto is pulled into a spherical shape by its own gravitational force.

C. asteroids and comets have a tail of gas and dust particles.

D. asteroids and comets are much smaller than Pluto.

4. The polar ice caps on Pluto's surface melt one time during every 249-year orbit, exposing Pluto's truly rocky surface, which is similar to that of Mars. Based on the information provided, this finding, if true, would most likely weaken the position(s) of:

A. Scientist 1 only.

B. Scientist 2 only.

C. both Scientist 1 and Scientist 2.

D. neither Scientist 1 nor Scientist 2.

5. With which of the following statements would both scientists most likely agree?

A. The size of Pluto indicates that it could actually be a satellite of another planet.

B. Pluto should be classified as neither a planet nor a comet; a new category is indicated.

C. The surface composition of Pluto is irrelevant and should not be considered in its classification.

D. Pluto's erratic orbit differentiates it from all other planets in the solar system.

6. Scientist 1's viewpoint would be weakened by which of the following observations, if true?

A. Scientists have recently discovered a Kuiper Belt comet with a radius of almost 1,500 miles.

B. Pluto only has one moon, Charon, which is half the size of Pluto.

C. Planets can be distinguished from comets by the lack of gas and dust particles in the wake of their orbits.

D. Comets and asteroids are capable of generating nuclear fission.

7. Which of the following statements best describes how Scientist 2 likens Pluto to a Kuiper Belt comet?

A. Neither Pluto nor Kuiper Belt comets have identifiable atmospheres.

B. Neither Pluto nor Kuiper Belt comets are trailed by a cloud of gases and

C. Both Pluto and Kuiper Belt comets have similar eccentric orbital patterns.

D. Both Pluto and Kuiper Belt comets are roughly half the size of the next smallest planet, Mercury.

PASSAGE II

A solute is any substance that is dissolved in another substance, which is called the solvent. A student tested the solubility (a measure of how much solute will dissolve into the solvent) of six different substances. The solubility of a substance at a given temperature is defined as the concentration of the dissolved solute that is in equilibrium with the solvent.

Table 1 represents the concentration of dissolved substances in 100 grams of water at various temperatures. The concentrations are expressed in grams of solute per 100 grams of water.

Table 1						
Temp ($^\circ$C)	\multicolumn{6}{c}{Concentration of solute (g/100 g H_2O)}
	KCl	$NaNO_3$	HCl	NH_4Cl	NaCl	NH_3
0	28	72	83	29	37	90
20	33	86	72	37	37	55
40	39	105	63	46	38	36
60	45	125	55	55	38	23
80	51	145	48	66	39	14
100	57	165	43	77	40	8

1. According to Table 1, the concentrations of which of the following substances varies the least with temperature?

    A. HCl

    B. NH$_3$

    C. NaCl

    D. KCl

2. The graph below best represents the relationship between concentration and temperature for which of the following substances?

    A. HCl

    B. NaNO$_3$

    C. NaCl

    D. KCl

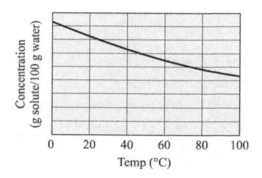

3. The data shown in Table 1 support the conclusion that, for a given substance, as the temperature of the water increases, the amount of solute that can be dissolved:

    A. increases only.

    B. decreases only.

    C. varies, but there is a trend depending on the substance.

    D. varies, but with no particular trend.

4. According to Table 1, HCl would most likely have which of the following concentrations at 70°C?

    A. 25.5 g/100g H_2O

    B. 37.0 g/100g H_2O

    C. 45.5 g/100g H_2O

    D. 51.5 g/100g H_2O

5. A scientist wants to dissolve at least 50 grams of NH_4Cl in 100 g of water in order for the solution to be the   proper concentration for use in an experiment. A reasonable minimum temperature for the solution would be:

    A. 25°C

    B. 30°C

    C. 35°C

    D. 50°C

Answers

Passage I

1. Correct Answer: D

The two scientists are discussing how the planet Pluto should be classified: as a planet, or as some other celestial object. Scientist 1 believes Pluto should retain its status as a planet, while Scientist 2 believes Pluto would be more accurately categorized as a Kuiper Belt comet. This best supports answer choice D.

2. Correct Answer: B

Scientist 2 explains that currently two categorizations of planets exist: rocky and gaseous. The scientist then goes on to say that Pluto does not fit into either of these categories because it is composed of an icy material. This best supports answer choice B.

3. Correct Answer: A

The question asks for the identification of the characteristic that does not differentiate Pluto from asteroids and comets. Neither Pluto nor asteroids and comets can generate heat through nuclear fission, so this is not a differentiating characteristic, making this answer choice the best.

4. **Correct Answer: B**

The best answer is B. Scientist 2 maintains that Pluto is not like the other planets due to its icy surface. If the ice melted and revealed that Pluto's surface was similar to Mars, Scientist 2's argument would be significantly weakened.

5. **Correct Answer: D**

Both scientists mention the irregularity of Pluto's orbit in their respective arguments. Scientist 1 states, "Pluto's orbital path is irregular as compared with the other planets of the solar system, and Scientist 2 also makes note of the "eccentricity of Pluto's orbit."

6. **Correct Answer: A**

One of the arguments that Scientist 1 makes for Pluto not being a comet is that Pluto is far too massive. If a comet were discovered with a diameter of 1,500 miles, it would be even larger than Pluto, which has a diameter of 1,413 miles. This would nullify the scientist's argument that Pluto cannot be a comet because comets are much smaller than Pluto.

7. **Correct Answer: C**

The best answer is C. One reason that Scientist 2 offers to support the argument for Pluto to be a Kuiper Belt object is that both have strange, atypical orbital patterns.

Passage II

1. **Correct Answer: C**

The question asks you to look at the overall trends of the data sets for each substance. A good way to measure the degree to which data varies would be to find the range, meaning subtract the lowest value from the highest value for each individual substance. In this problem it is clear that NaCl varies the least with temperature.

2. Correct Answer: A

In this question you are asked to look at the trends of the substances, especially at how their concentrations change with increasing temperature. In the data set, some substances become more soluble with increasing temperature, while some become less soluble. The graph represents the solubility curve for a substance that gets less soluble with increasing temperature. Looking at the possible answer choices, HCl is the only logical choice.

3. Correct Answer: C

It is clear from the table that each substance reacts differently in its solubility depending on the temperature. However, each substance does show a clear trend in whether it gets more or less soluble with increasing temperature.

4. Correct Answer: D

According to Table 1, HCl has a concentration of 55 g/100 g H_2O at 60°C, and a concentration of 48 g/100 g H_2O at 80°C.

Therefore, at 70°C it would likely have a concentration of $55 + 48 \div 2 = 51.5$ g/100 g H_2O.

5. Correct Answer: D

By looking at the trend in concentration for NH_4Cl, 50g are dissolved between the 40° and 60°C measurements. The logical answer choice would then be 50°C.

Practice test

Sit this test like the real thing, as much as possible. Do it in a quiet space without distractions. Do not look up answers. Answer within the timeframes given.

ATI TEAS English Language and Usage

General Informations: 28 questions (24 Scored)

Timing: 28 minutes

Directions: In the passages that follow, certain words and phrases are underlined and numbered. In the right-hand column, you will find alternatives for the underlined part. In most cases, you are to choose the one that best expresses the idea, makes the statement appropriate for standard written English, or is worded most consistently with the style and tone of the passage as a whole. If you think the original version is best, choose "NO CHANGE." In some cases, you will find in the right-hand column a question about the underlined part. You are to choose the best answer to the question.

You will also find questions about a section of the passage, or about the passage as a whole. These questions do not refer to an underlined portion of the passage, but rather are identified by a number or numbers in a box.

Passage

Building the Plaza de Toros

Thousands of tourists from all over the world gather in Seville, Spain each year, two weeks after Easter Holy Week, to witness the La Real Maestranza. La Real Maestranza is part of the Seville Fair, **and the Fair** (1) originated back in 1847 **when** (2) it was originally organized as a livestock fair. Of central importance to the festival are the bullfights that **took place** (3) in the Plaza de Toros, a circular ring on Baratillo Hill.

Construction on the **stunning and beautiful** (4) Plaza de Toros first **begun in 1749 but had not completed** (5) for many years after. The inner facade of the plaza (called the Palco del Príncipe or Prince's Box) was completed in 1765, and this box consists of two **parts; the (6)** access gate through which the successful bullfighters **exited (7),** and the theater box itself, which was reserved for the exclusive use of **not only the Spanish King and Queen, but for (8)** other members of the Royal Family. **(9)**

When monarch Carlos III prohibited bullfighting celebrations in 1786, work halted, **and (10)** only one-third of the plaza **had been completed (11)** at the time. The construction of the ring was finally completed in **1881, two thirds (12)** were constructed in stone, the rest in wood.

Choosing to redo them in brick, the stone grandstands were replaced between 1914 and 1915 by architect Anival Gonzalez. (13) All the rows were reconstructed with a smoother slope. Ten to twelve rows of shaded seating were constructed as well as fourteen rows in the sun and three rows of barrier. A row of armchairs was built in the superior part of the shaded area, and **they (14)** were placed in front of the theater boxes. **(15)**

1.

    A. NO CHANGE

    B. which originated

    C. which did originate

    D. and the Fair originated

2.

    A. NO CHANGE

    B. in which

    C. after which

    D. As

3.

    A. NO CHANGE

    B. had taken place

C. did take place

D. take place

4.

A. NO CHANGE

B. stunning yet beautiful

C. Beautiful

D. stunning, however beautiful,

5.

A. NO CHANGE

B. was begun in 1749 and was not completed

C. had begun in 1749 and had completed

D. began in 1749 but was not completed

6.

A. NO CHANGE

B. parts: the

C. parts, the

D. parts the

7.

A. NO CHANGE

B. did exit

C. are exiting

D. will exit

8.

A. NO CHANGE

B. not only the Spanish King and Queen, yet for

C. not only the Spanish King and Queen, but also for

D. not the Spanish King and Queen, but also for

9. Which of the sentences below does not belong anywhere in the second paragraph?

A. The bullring is the oldest bullring constructed entirely of stone, because most others were constructed with a combination of stone and brick.

B. The stands were constructed in two levels of seating of 5 raised rows per level and 136 Tuscan sandstone columns.

C. Seville's fair is officially known as the April Fair, but in fact, it hasn't always been celebrated entirely in April and once, it even had to be celebrated in May.

D. The Royal Box has a sloping roof covered in Arabic tiles.

10.

A. NO CHANGE

B. Nevertheless

C. Because

D. even though

11.

A. NO CHANGE

B. were completed

C. will complete

D. are completed

12.

    A. NO CHANGE

    B. 1881; two thirds

    C. 1881, two thirds,

    D. 1881—two thirds

13.

    A. NO CHANGE

    B. Choosing to redo them in brick, between 1914 and 1915 architect Anival Gonzalez replaced the stone grandstands.

    C. Choosing to redo them in brick, architect Anival Gonzalez replaced the stone grandstands between 1914 and 1915.

    D. Choosing, between 1914 and 1915, to redo them in brick, architect Anival Gonzalez replaced the stone grandstands.

14.

    A. NO CHANGE

    B. Those

    C. these chairs

    D. It

15. Which of the following sentences best completes the passage?

    A. Today spectators from around the world enjoy watching this traditional Spanish sport in this world-class ring.

    B. Between 1729 and 1733 Felipe V stayed in Seville and received support from the Corporation in spite of being French and the first Bourbon king of Spain.

C. More than 12,500 spectators can watch the fight between the torero and the bull in this ring.

D. During the Seville Festival, men and women dress up in their finery, ideally the traditional "traje corto" (short jacket, tight trousers and boots) for men and the "faralaes" or "trajes de flamenca" (flamenco style dress) for women.

Illinois Prairies

There are different kinds of prairies in Illinois depending on the moisture gradient and soil type. The different kinds of prairie **wildflowers, are often** (16) associated with these different moisture gradients and soil types. As an ecological habitat, grasses and herbaceous wildflowers, rather than trees and shrubs, or areas with more or less permanent water, **dominated** (17) prairies.

(18) High quality prairies are interesting and colorful places to visit during the growing season **because they demonstrate high biodiversity** (19). Black soil prairie was the dominant type of prairie in central and northern **Illinois, until** (20) it was almost totally destroyed by agricultural development during the 19th century. The landscape of such prairies is rather flat. A high-quality black soil prairie has lots of wildflowers in bloom from late spring until the middle of fall. Today, small remnants of original black soil prairie can be found in pioneer **cemeteries, or at construction sites** (21)

Gravel and dolomite prairies were never very common in Illinois, and can be found primarily in northern Illinois. Gravel and dolomite prairies can be rather flat, or slightly hilly. **Yet** (22) the original gravel and dolomite prairies have been largely destroyed by modern development. They tend to be rather dry and well drained. More recently, such prairies have been found along the gravelly ballast of railroads, where they probably did not formerly exist. **(23)** In this case, they are degraded and **often contain flora** (24) from Western states **(25)**

Hill prairies occur primarily along the Illinois and Mississippi **rivers, hills (26)** prairies are very dry and exposed to prevailing winds from the south or west. The wild-flowers of hill prairies are similar to those **who are found (27)** found in the drier areas of gravel and dolomite prairies.

Some species that are found in hill prairies is typical **(28)** of western areas.

Sand prairies can be moist mesic or dry and their landscape is either flat or slightly hilly. They usually occur near current or former bodies of water. Their vegetation is sparser that that of black soil prairies.

16.

    A. NO CHANGE

    B. wildflowers are often

    C. wildflowers often

    D. wildflowers: often

17.

    A. NO CHANGE

    B. Dominates

    C. Dominating

    D. Dominate

18. At this point in the opening paragraph, the writer is considering adding the following true statement: In Iowa, six different types of coneflowers sway in summer breezes. Should the writer make this addition here?

    A. Yes, because it helps establish that the essay is set in the Midwest.

    B. Yes, because it helps reinforce the main idea of the paragraph.

    C. No, because it does not make clear whether coneflowers grow in every state.

    D. No, because it distracts from the main focus of the paragraph.

19. The writer is considering deleting the underlined portion from the sentence. Should the phrase be kept or deleted?

    A. Kept, because it provides supporting details that reinforce the main idea of the sentence.

B. Kept, because it establishes that prairies contain more biodiversity than any other habitat.

C. Deleted, because it has already been established earlier in the paragraph that prairies have low biodiversity.

D. Deleted, because it draws attention away from the different types of prairies.

20.

A. NO CHANGE

B. Illinois,

C. Illinois: until

D. Illinois. Until

21. Given that all choices are grammatically correct, which one best establishes that black soil prairies are difficult to find today?

A. NO CHANGE

B. cemeteries or along old railroads.

C. cemeteries, state parks, and surrounding farmland.

D. cemeteries and in many neighborhoods.

22.

A. NO CHANGE

B. However,

C. Unfortunately,

D. Accordingly,

23. The writer is considering deleting the phrase "where they probably did not formerly exist" from the preceding sentence (and placing a period after the word *railroads*). Should the phrase be kept or deleted?

A. Kept, because the information helps to establish the rampant proliferation of gravel and dolomite prairies in Illinois.

B. Kept, because it strengthens the paragraph's focus on the unchanging landscape of prairies.

C. Deleted, because it is not relevant to the description of gravel and dolomite prairies found in Illinois.

D. Deleted, because the speculation is inconsistent with the claim made earlier in the paragraph that the prairies have been largely destroyed.

24.

A. NO CHANGE

B. and many bird species migrate to them

C. consisting of a mix of native grasses and flowers and flora

D. and are of particular interest to tourists

25. For the sake of the logic and coherence of this paragraph, Sentence 4 should be placed:

A. where it is now.

B. before Sentence 1.

C. before Sentence 3.

D. before Sentence 6.

26.

A. NO CHANGE

B. rivers. hill

C. rivers hill

D. rivers; hill

27.

    A. NO CHANGE

    B. which are finding

    C. if found

    D. that can be found

28.

    A. NO CHANGE

    B. are more typical

    C. typify

    D. are more usual

ATI TEAS Math

General Informations: 36 Questions (32 scored)

Timing: 54 minutes

1. Assume l and m are parallel horizontal lines where l is above m. A third straight line k intersects both lines l and m, creating a total of 4 different angles on each of the two intersections. The intersections of lines l and m contain angles a, b, c, d and w, x, y, z, respectively. The angle layouts start with a and w in the top left position with the other angles following in alphabetical order in the clockwise direction. What is the degree value of angle z if angle c has a value of 67 degrees?

   A. 90 degrees

   B. 180 degrees

   C. 67 degrees

   D. 113 degrees

2. How to Find the Angle of Two Lines

   Angle $\angle ABC$ measures 20°

   BD$-\rightarrow-$ is the bisector of $\angle ABC$

   BE$-\rightarrow$ is the bisector of $\angle CBD$

   What is the measure of $\angle ABE$?

Possible Answers:

   A. 5°

   B. 15°

   C. 40°

   D. 30°

3. Aristotle High School has an unusual track in that it is shaped like a regular pentagon with a perimeter one third of a mile. Jessica starts at Point A and runs clockwise until she gets halfway between Points D and E. Which of the following choices is closest to the number of feet she runs?

Possible Answers:

    A. 1,300 feet

    B. 1,200 feet

    C. 1,100 feet

    D. 1,000 feet

4. Aristotle High School has an unusual track in that it is shaped like a regular pentagon. Each side of the pentagon measures 264 feet.

Benny runs at a steady speed of eight miles an hour for ten minutes, starting at point A and working his way clockwise. When he is finished, which of the following points is he closest to?

Possible Answers:

    A. Point A

    B. Point E

    C. Point D

    D. Point C

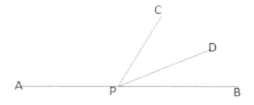

Figure not drawn to scale.

5. In the figure above, APB forms a straight line. If the measure of angle APC is eighty-one degrees larger than the measure of angle DPB, and the measures of angles CPD and DPB are equal, then what is the measure, in degrees, of angle CPB?

Possible Answers:

　A.　66

　B.　114

　C.　50

　D.　40

6. One-half of the measure of the supplement of angle ABC is equal to the twice the measure of angle ABC. What is the measure, in degrees, of the complement of angle ABC?

Possible Answers:

　A.　18

　B.　36

　C.　90

　D.　54

7. In the diagram, AB || CD. What is the value of a+b?

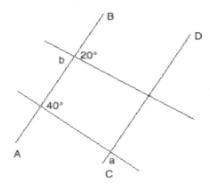

Possible Answers:

    A. 60°

    B. 140°

    C. 80°

    D. 160°

8. In a rectangle ABCD, both diagonals are drawn and intersect at point E.

Let the measure of angle AEB equal x degrees.

Let the measure of angle BEC equal y degrees.

Let the measure of angle CED equal z degrees.

Find the measure of angle AED in terms of x, y, and/or z.

Possible Answers:

    A. $360 - x + y + z$

    B. $180 - 2(x + z)$

    C. $180 - 1/2(x + z)$

    D. $180 - (x + y + z)$

9. A student creates a challenge for his friend. He first draws a square, the adds the line for each of the 2 diagonals. Finally, he asks his friend to draw the circle that has the most intersections possible. How many intersections will this circle have?

Possible Answers:

    A. 4

    B. 6

    C. 8

    D. 12

10. Two pairs of parallel lines intersect:

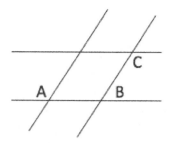

If A = 135°, what is 2 x |B-C| = ?

Possible Answers:

    A. 180°

    B. 140°

    C. 160°

    D. 170°

11. Lines AC and BD are parallel. ∠HFC=10°, ∠DGI=50°, ΔEFG is a right triangle, and EG has a length of 10. What is the length of EF?

Possible Answers:

    A. 15

    B. 12

    C. 5

    D. 20

12. If ∠A measures (40–10x)°, which of the following is equivalent to the measure of the supplement of ∠A ?

Possible Answers:

A. (100x)°

B. (50–10x)°

C. (10x+140)°

D. (10x+50)°

13. In the following diagram, lines b and c are parallel to each other. What is the value for x?

Possible Answers:

A. 60°

B. 30°

C. It cannot be determined

D. 80°

14. The measure of the supplement of angle A is 40 degrees larger than twice the measure of the complement of angle A. What is the sum, in degrees, of the measures of the supplement and complement of angle A?

Possible Answers:

A. 40

B. 90

C. 140

D. 190

15. If $8a - 2 = 22$, then $4a - 1 =$

A. 2

B. 14

C. 11

D. 12

16. Twenty percent of the sweaters in a store are white. Of the remaining sweaters, 40 percent are brown, and the rest are blue. If there are 200 sweaters in the store, then how many more blue sweaters than white sweaters are in the store?

  A. 56

  B. 54

  C. 23

  D. 64

17. Jill has received 8 of her 12 evaluation scores. So far, Jill's average (arithmetic mean) is 3.75 out of a possible 5. If Jill needs an average of 4.0 points to get a promotion, which list of scores will allow Jill to receive her promotion?

Indicate all such sets.

  A. 3.0, 3.5, 4.75, 4.75

  B. 3.5, 4.75, 4.75, 5.0

  C. 3.25, 4.5, 4.75, 5.0

  D. 3.75, 4.5, 4.75, 5.0

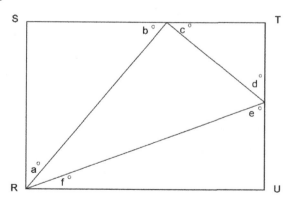

18. In the figure above, if *RSTU* is a rectangle, what is the value of $a + b + c + d + e + f$?

  A. 270

B.   180

C.   90

D.   360

19. All first-year students at Red State University must take calculus, English composition, or both. If half of the 2,400 first-year students at Red State University take calculus and half do not, and one-third of those who take calculus also take English composition, how many students take English composition?

   A.   400

   B.   800

   C.   1,200

   D.   1,600

20. If the probability of choosing 2 red marbles without replacement from a bag of only red and blue marbles is 3/55 and there are 3 red marbles in the bag, what is the total number of marbles in the bag?

   A.   10

   B.   11

   C.   55

   D.   110

21. $5x + 3 = 7x - 1$. Find x

   A.   1/3

   B.   1/2

   C.   1

   D.   2

22. $5x + 2(x + 7) = 14x - 7$. Find x

A. 1

B. 2

C. 3

D. 4

23. 12t − 10 = 14t + 2. Find t

A. -6

B. -4

C. 4

D. 6

24. 5(z + 1) = 3(z + 2) + 11 Solve for z

A. 2

B. 4

C. 6

D. 12

25. The price of a book went up from $20 to $25. By how many percent did the price increase?

A. 5

B. 10

C. 20

D. 25

26. The price of a book decreased from $25 to $20. By how many percent did the price decrease?

A. 5

B. 10

C. 20

D. 25

27. After taking several practice tests, Brian improved the results of his ATI Teas test by 30%. Given that the first time he took the test Brian had answered 150 questions correctly, how many correct answers did he answer in the second test?

    A. 105

    B. 120

    C. 180

    D. 195

28. A number is increased by 2 and then multiplied by 3. The result is 24. What is this number?

    A. 4

    B. 6

    C. 8

    D. 10

29. My father's age divided by 5 is equal to my brother's age divided by 3. My brother is 3 years older than me. My father's age is 3 less than 2 times my age. How old is my father?

    A. 34

    B. 45

    C. 56

    D. 61

30. $(x - 2) / 4 - (3x + 5) / 7 = -3$, x =?

    A. 6

    B. 7

C. 10

D. 13

31. $1 / (1 + 1 / (1 - 1/x)) = 4$, x =?

A. −3/4

B. 3/7

C. 4/7

D. 3/4

32. Angle A and B are complementary. The measure of angle B is three times the measure of angle A. What is the measure of angle A and B in degrees?

A. A=22.5 and B=67.5

B. A=21.5 and B=69

C. A=21 and B=69

D. A=10 and B=80

33. What does 68% equal?

A. 6.8

B . 0068

C. 6800

D. 0.68

34. What is the missing number in the sequence: 4, 6, 10, 18, ____, 66?

A. 54

B. 34

C. 22

D. 45

35. Simplify the expression below. Which of the following is correct?

5,344–57

A. 5,277

B. 5,283

C. 5,287

D. 5,288

36. Solve the equation below. Which of the following is correct?

$3(x-4) = 18$

A. $x = 32$

B. $x = 223$

C. $x = 6$

D. $x = 1$

ATI TEAS Reading

General Informations: 53 Questions(47 scored)

Timing: 64 Minutes

Directions: Read each passage and answer the questions that follow it. Some questions may have more than one answer that looks correct. In that case, pick the one that answers the question most completely and correctly. Don't assume anything that isn't stated in the passage or the questions. All the information you need to answer the questions is contained in the passage, questions, and answer choices.

Questions 1 - 6 refer to the following passage:

Black Apollo, by Kenneth Mannin, describes the life of Ernest Everett Just, one of the first black scientists in America. Manning recounts Just's impoverished origins in South Carolina, his adaptations to a white educational system, and hiss careers as a zoology professor at Howard University and as an embryologist at Marine Biological Laboratory. Despite countless difficulties imposed upon him by a world in which a black person was not supposed to practice science. Just became an internationally esteemed biologist. His story is one of courage determination. And dedication to science but Manning's goals are more far-reaching than to simply tell a story or describe one man's life. Alter all, though just was a brilliant biologist. He was not ultimately pivotal to the development of either science or race relations in the 20th century. The Issues brought out in his story however, are pivotal. A comprehensive appreciation of the conditions that Just faced in his daily work offers a powerful lens through which to examine the development of science and racial boundaries in America.

Manning wrote Just's story as a biography. In some respects, biography does not seem to be a promising medium for great historical work. Biographies simply tell a story. Most students receive their introductions to history in science in the worship full biographies of past scientific giants. Benjamin Franklin and Albert Einstein offer excellent examples to young students of how scientists contribute to society. Biographies are popular for children's reading lists (and bestseller lists) because they have simple subjects, can present clear moral statements and manage to teach a little history at the same time. This simplicity of form, however does not preclude the biography from being a powerful medium of historical work and social commentary.

The biography yields particular rewards for the historian of science, indeed a central reason for the discipline is to show that science is a product of social forces. This principle implies that historians and sociologists have insights on the practice of science that scientists to whom the subject would otherwise fall, are less likely to produce. Moreover, if society does influence science, then it behaves historians to explain how such an important process works. The human orientation of the biography makes it an excellent medium in which historians can do this work. Were a researcher to investigate the development of scientific theory solely by reading the accounts written of a laboratory's experiments, by looking only at the science – the researcher would likely see a science moved by apparently rational forces toward a discernible goal. But this picture is incomplete and artificial. If that researcher examines a science the through people who generated it, a richer mosaic of actors emerges. The science biography has the potential to reveal both the person through the science and the science through the person. From these perspectives, the forces of politics, emotions and economics, each of which can direct science as much as rational thought, are more easily brought to light. Black Apollo is a riveting example of what a historian can accomplish with a skillful and directed use of biography.

1. Which one of the following most accurately states the main point of the passage?

   A. Ernest Everett Just was an extremely important biologist during the 20th century, both because of his contributions to the field of embryology and because of his race.

   B. Scientists tend to ignore the social, historical, and political forces that surround all scientific research and discovery, which makes their interpretations of scientific events incomplete.

   C. Biographies are a popular genre for children's books because they can tell discrete stories in an accessible fashion, incorporating scientific knowledge into a person's life and thereby making it more interesting to readers.

D. Manning's work exemplifies how biography can be a powerful tool for a historian of science, who can use the genre to explore the effects of politics, economics, and emotions on the direction of scientific development.

2. According to the passage, the main goal of the discipline called history of science is to

   A. illuminate the effects of social forces on scientists in a way that scientists themselves are unlikely to do

   B. explain scientific discoveries in a manner that is easily understood by non-scientists

   C. write biographies of important scientific figures that portray their work against a social and political background

   D. influence scientific research by identifying the most important scientific contributions in history

3. What is the primary purpose of the second paragraph?

   A. to describe the many things Ernest Everett Just accomplished despite the racial prejudice he faced

   B. to suggest that biography is really too simple a historical form for the historian of science to use to convey complex ideas

   C. to explain why biography is both a popular historical genre and a powerful medium for explaining the significance of scientific discoveries

   D. to argue against using biographies to teach children about scientific figures from the past

4. The author of the passage would be most likely to agree with which one of the following statements?

   A. One of the best ways to come to an understanding of the realities of race relations and scientific development in the 20th century is to read an in-depth account of the life of one of the people who lived and worked in that world.

B. The goal of a historian of science is to glorify the accomplishments of his historical subjects, embellishing them if need be.

C. A scientific historian should pay close attention to the social and literary aspects of a scientific biography and play down the actual science, because readers can turn to scientific reports to get that information.

D. Ernest Everett Just was likely the most important black biologist, and in fact one of the most important biologists, of the 20th century.

5. According to the passage, why is Ernest Everett Just significant enough to warrant a biography?

A. Just was one of the first professional black scientists in the United States.

B. Just grew up in poverty but overcame this initial adversity to attend Howard University and then become a professional scientist.

C. Just was a biologist whose work was known and respected internationally.

D. Just's daily experiences illuminate the conditions characterized by both scientific research and racial relations during his lifetime.

6. What does the author mean by the phrase "simplicity of form" (Line 38)?

A. the simple language used by many biographical writers

B. the easy-to-read page design used by most publishers of biographies

C. a writing style that is easy for schoolchildren to read and understand

D. the straightforward organization of a biography, which follows the course of the subject's life

Questions 7 - 13 refer to the following passage:

Sodium lauryl sulfate (SLS) is an emulsifier and surfactant that produces lather and foam that can dissolve oil and dirt on skin and hair. SLS and another similar detergent, sodium laureth sulfate (SLES), are commonly used as foaming agents in cleaners, shampoos, and toothpaste.

Both of these substances are derived from coconut oil. They make liquid and paste cleansers more effective at cleansing because they allow the cleanser to disperse more readily over the object being cleaned and make it easier to rinse the cleanser away. SLS and SLES have been used for years in numerous products sold to consumers. Other foaming agents are available, SLS and SLES have remained popular because of their low cost, effectiveness, lack of taste and odor and long history of safe use.

The use of SLS and SLES comes with a few minor risks. The substances burn human eyes, a phenomenon well known to anyone who has ever gotten a drop of shampoo in her eye. A high enough concentration of SLS will burn skin if it remains in contact with the skin for a long time, though normally this is not a problem because the products containing SLES or SLS are diluted with water and quickly washed away. SLS in toothpaste can cause diarrhea in someone who swallows a large quantity of it, but it is not known to be toxic if ingested in small quantities.

Many people have become afraid of SLS and SLES in recent years, largely as a result of widespread rumors circulated on the internet that blame SLS and SLES for causing numerous ailments in humans, including hair loss, dry skin, liver and kidney disease, blindness in children and cancer, SLS has been called one the most dangerous substances used in cosmetic products. Rumors wasn't that SLS and SLES can react with other ingredients in products to form nitrates which are potential carcinogens.

Detractors of SLS and SLES point out that these substances are used in cleansers intended for the floors of garages and bathrooms and in engine degreasers. This is true; it is also true that household and garbage cleaners are not sold for cosmetic use, come with warnings of possible skin and eye irritation and are perfectly safe to use for their intended purposes.

These internet warnings of the dangers of SLS and SLES are absurd and unsubstantiated. The US food and drug administration (FDA) has approved the use of SLS and SLES in a number of personal care products. The Occupational Safety and Health Administration (OSHA), the International Agency for research on cancer, and the American Cancer Society have all done extensive research on SLS and SLES and concluded that they do not cause cancer.

7. Which one of the following best summarizes the main idea of the passage?

A. A few minor risks are associated with the use of SLS and SLES, but consumers should feel safe in using products containing these substances because the FDA has approved them for use in personal care products.

B. Manufacturers of shampoos and toothpastes include the artificial chemicals SLS and SLES in their products because they are cheap and effective surfactants, despite the known dangers associated with them.

C. SLS and SLES are detergents that are commonly used in personal care products because they are effective and safe, despite unsubstantiated rumors to the contrary.

D. Widespread rumors circulated on the Internet blame SLS and SLES for numerous ailments in humans, including hair loss, dry skin, liver and kidney disease, blindness in children, and cancer.

8. According to the passage, what are some of the household products that commonly contain SLS or SLES?

A. shampoo, mouthwash, sunscreen, and hair dye.

B. shampoo, toothpaste, bathroom cleaners, and engine degreasers.

C. toothpaste, engine degreasers, engine lubricants, and garage cleaners.

D. mouthwash, facial moisturizers, and baby wipes.

9. The author mentions the FDA in the last paragraph most likely to:

A. point out that the FDA has approved the use of SLS and SLES in personal care products.

B. suggest that the FDA has the best interests of consumers at heart.

C. imply that the FDA's opinion that SLS and SLES are safe for use in personal care products excuses manufacturers from testing their personal care products for safety

D. refute claims that SLS and SLES are dangerous.

10. According to the passage, what are some of the widely accepted risks of SLS exposure?

A. cancer, blindness, cataracts, dry skin, and diarrhea.

B. burning eyes, burned skin after long exposure, liver disease, and kidney disease.

C. skin irritation, eye irritation, hair loss, and diarrhea if ingested in large quantities.

D. burning eyes, burned skin after long exposure, and diarrhea if ingested in large quantities.

11. Which one of the following best describes the organization of the passage?

A. a list of known risks of exposure to SLS and SLES; a list of unsubstantiated risks of exposure to SLS and SLES; a conclusion stating that SLS and SLES are perfectly safe.

B. a description of several common surfactants and the way in which they work; several anecdotal accounts of injuries and illnesses allegedly caused by SLS and SLES; a call for the government to ban the use of SLS and SLES in consumer care products.

C. a description of the chemical composition of SLS and SLES; a list of evidence against the use of SLS and SLES in personal care products; a proposal to manufacturers suggesting that they use only naturally occurring substances in their products.

D. a description of SLS and SLES and their uses; known risks of SLS and SLES; criticisms aimed at SLS and SLES by detractors on the Internet; evidence that SLS and SLES are safe and the rumors unfounded

12. The primary purpose of the third paragraph is:

A. to criticize makers of personal cleansing products for including harsh chemicals in their shampoos, toothpastes, and other offerings.

B. to describe the way SLS and SLES work and explain why they are commonly used in various foaming products.

C. to warn readers of the dangers associated with exposure to SLS and SLES, which include cancer, skin irritation, blindness, and kidney and liver ailments.

D. to explain why some people fear SLS and SLES and to list the diseases that Internet rumors have linked to the substances.

13. It can be inferred from the passage that the author would be most likely to agree with which one of the following statements?

A. It is unreasonable for people to be afraid of substances that have been deemed safe by the FDA and several other major organizations, and that have a long history of safe use, simply on the basis of unsubstantiated rumors.

B. Consumers can trust the FDA to make sure that all consumer products are safe because the FDA is funded by tax dollars and takes seriously its mission to ensure the health of American citizens.

C. The Internet is not a very reliable source of information on health topics unless that information has been posted by government agencies or major advocacy groups.

D. SLS and SLES are cheap and effective surfactants and emulsifiers, but they aren't especially safe to use in products intended for direct physical contact with human skin.

Questions 14 - 19 refer to the following two passages. The first is adapted from Forensic Psychology and Law, by Ronald Roesch, Patricia A. Zapf, and Stephen D. Hart (Wiley). The second is adapted from Forensic Psychology: Crime, Justice, Law, Interventions, 2nd Edition, edited by Graham Davies and Anthony Beech (Wiley).

Passage A

There are many factors that may account for mistaken eyewitness identification. Wells distinguished between system variables and estimator variables. System variables affect the accuracy of eyewitness testimony that the criminal justice system has some control over. For example, the way a question is worded or the way a lineup is constructed may impact the accuracy of eyewitness identification. In these instances, the justice system has some control over these variables. Estimator variables, on the other hand, are those that may affect the accuracy of eyewitness testimony but that the criminal justice system does not have any control over. These variables have to do with the characteristics of the eyewitness or the circumstances surrounding the event witnessed. For example, the amount of attention that an eyewitness paid to a perpetrator, how long an eyewitness viewed a perpetrator, or the lighting conditions under which a perpetrator was viewed would he examples of estimator variables since they have to do with the eyewitness or the circumstances surrounding the event. The criminal justice system does not have any control over these variables. The vast majority of the research on eyewitness identifications deals with system variables since they are under the control of the justice system and thus can be modified accordingly to improve the accuracy of eyewitness identifications and testimony. Much research has shown that asking an eyewitness misleading questions will influence his or her subsequent reports of a prior observed event. Sonic theorists contend that the misleading questions serve to alter the original memory trace. Thus, a stop sign. for example, is replaced in memory with a yield sign or an empty field is replaced in memory with a field containing a red barn. Race, gender, and age are three characteristics that have been examined to determine the extent to which they impact eyewitness accuracy. Each is an estimator variable and, there-fore, out of the control of the justice system. With respect to age; the majority of the research has examined the differences between adults and children in terms of eyewitness testimony. Research on gender differences in eyewitness identification indicates that there is no evidence that females are any better or worse than males. Similarly, there is no evidence that members of one race arc better or worse at eyewitness identification than members of another race. However, there is evidence to suggest that people are better at recognizing the faces of members of their own race than they are at recognizing the faces of members of other races.

Passage B

Human cognitive abilities are incredible. Consider the task faced by an eyewitness who is present during a street crime. The cognitive system allows the witness to transform characteristics of the light reflected towards her eyes into visual information and characteristics of perturbations in the air made by the culprit's vocal system into auditory information. The person synchronizes these sources of information (and sometimes smells, tastes, and tactile information) with a highly functional knowledge base of past experiences. At later points in time, the witness is able to use this continually adapting knowledge base to bring that distant information into the present. The witness may even be able to travel back to the past mentally to relive the event. What Tulving called episodic memory. As amazing as these cognitive abilities are, they are not perfect. Information is forgotten and distorted, and the past century of memory research has revealed some systematic patterns for these deficits.

To understand how findings from memory research can be applied to a forensic context, it is necessary to understand how memory science works. Within a criminal context, eyewitness memory is a tool that. if reliable, should be diagnostic of guilt or innocence. By this we mean that presenting eyewitness evidence should usually make guilty people seem more likely to be guilty, and innocent people seem more likely to be innocent. To be reliable, evidence does not have to always be correct but it should usually be correct. In the US supreme court's Daubert (1993) ruling, the court argued that, for scientific evidence to be presented, there should be a known error rather, the courts do not state what the maximum error rate (or the minimum reliability) should be to allow evidence to be presented in court because this threshold would likely depend on peculiarities of an individual case.

One of the main goals for eyewitness researchers is to estimate this error rate and show how it varies by different factors. Ultimately, to estimate the reliability of any forensic tool as complex and context dependent as eye witness memory, it is necessary to understand how the system works.

If a science was trying to determine the reliability of a tool to detect, for example the explosive material from a body scan device, the scientist would have the advantage that humans created the device, so the scientist could look at the blue prints. It is more difficult to understand the human cognitive system because it is the ongoing product of ad hoc engineering, a process of trial and error called evolution.

14. The author of Passage A cites research conducted to determine how all the following affect the accuracy of an eyewitness's testimony EXCEPT:

A. the eyewitness's race

B. the eyewitness's gender

C. the types of questions the eyewitness is asked

D. the amount of time that has passed since the eyewitness experienced the event

15. Which one of the following statements is most strongly supported by both passages?

A. Eyewitness testimony is highly accurate considering the complexity of human memory.

B. Eyewitness testimony is often flawed because it is influenced by a variety of factors.

C. The human memory follows an arc pattern over one's lifetime, strengthening through adulthood and then weakening as one enters old age.

D. Little if any evidence supports the fact that males provide more accurate eyewitness testimony than females.

16. Which one of the following claims about eyewitness testimony is NOT suggested by Passage A?

A. How the lighting in a particular event affects the reliability of eyewitness identification is a variable that warrants a good amount of study.

B. The accuracy of eyewitness identification can be negatively affected by the eyewitness's race.

C. The many factors that can lead to mistaken eyewitness identification can be grouped into two main categories.

D. Much research has been done to assess how the order of a lineup may affect eyewitness identification.

17. The passages have which of the following aims in common?

A. to express the need for researchers to come up with a calculable error rate to determine whether eyewitness evidence may be admissible in court.

B. to define episodic memory and explain how it may come into play in judicial proceedings.

C. to identify the differences between system and estimator variables.

D. To understand how memory and human cognitive abilities are affected by a variety of different factors

18. Which of the following statements most accurately characterizes a difference between the two passages?

A. Passage A discusses how misleading questions can affect the accuracy of eyewitness testimony, whereas Passage B dismisses the importance of how a witness is questioned.

B. Passage A emphasizes the importance of forensic research; Passage B is primarily concerned with the way that same research influences how system variables, such as controlling lineups, are manipulated by judicial proceedings.

C. Passage A discusses the role that race plays in greater detail than does Passage B.

D. Both passages concern improving eyewitness accuracy, but Passage A focuses on controlling variables and Passage B concentrates on understanding the science behind human recollection.

19. Each of the following is supported by one or both of the passages EXCEPT:

A. Human memory sometimes fails to recollect events exactly how they happened.

B. The cognitive system is remarkable because it is able to match sensory stimuli with previous experience.

C. Testimony based on a witness's memory ideally should provide confirmation of a culprit's guilt.

D. Lighting issues and the length of time someone witnessed an event are examples of system variables.

Questions 20 - 26 refer to the following passage:

Public education as it is currently known was created by a German government worried about the dangers of work uprisings that were transformed by Enlightenment and Romantic educational theories into an institution genuinely concerned with developing human minds. Before the 1700s, Europe had no public education. Parents who wanted their children to be educated paid for private schools or private tutors. The rest of the children in Europe worked. Many of them worked alongside their parents in spinning factories, producing thread for Germany's burgeoning textile industry. The textile mill owners blatantly exploited their workers, which led to increasing levels of unrest on the part of the peasants. During the 1750s

King Frederick II asked his minister of Silesia, Ernest Wilhelm von Schlabrendorff, to find a way to channel the energy of the restless peasant into something that would be less dangerous to the throne.

Schlabrendorff suggested that the king could mold a compliant citizenry if he created a system of state-run schools. These schools could teach the children of the peasantry that their lot was obtained by God, that they should not try to improve it, that the government was good to them, and that they should not question authority, along with teaching them reading, writing and arithmetic. School would be compulsory, and children who did not attend could be punished by truant officers. This would shift children's primary loyalty from their parents and families to the state. Their parents would be powerless against the truant officers and thus would be forced to send their children to school whether they wanted to or not. Aristocrats liked this idea, they liked the thought of school making peasants more docile and patriotic, and they appreciated the way state-run schools would teach children of lower social classes to accept their position in life. In 1763, Frederick gave Schlabrendorff the go ahead to start opening schools and soon every child in Silesia between the ages of 7 and 15 was attending school. These earliest of school, called Spinnschulen, combined work with education. Children took classes in the mornings and spun thread in the afternoons.

By the 1800s, the Spinnschulen had metamorphosed into full day schools with state certified teachers who taught a state approved curriculum theory, much of it influence by 19th century Romanticism that directly contradicted the principle that had led to the foundation of public schools in the 1700s Johann Bernhard Basedow use the work of Enlightenment scholars to argue that education should be a holistic pursuit, incorporating physical movement, manual training, realistic teaching and the study of nature. Freidrich Froebel invented kindergarten in the mid-1800s, creating a children's garden, based on the belief that children are naturally creative and productive, and he develop special toys designed to teach specific skills and motions. Wilhelm von Humboldt specialized ins secondary and university education theory, insisting that advanced students should pursue independent research and prizing above all three educations principle: self-government by teachers, unity of teaching and academic freedom.

20. The passage is primarily concerned with discussing which one of the following?

    A. the use of public schools to disseminate political messages, as exemplified by German public schools in the 18th and 19th centuries

    B. the exploitation of the working class by German aristocracy in the 18th century and the use of public education to justify this practice

    C. the philosophical origins of public schools in 18th century Germany and the transformation in educational thinking in the 19th century

    D. the thinking of German educational theorists and their influence on modern educational practices

21. The passage suggests which one of the following about the owners of textile mills in the 1700s?

    A. They wanted their child workers to have the benefit of an education, so they opened schools within their factories and required all young workers to attend classes.

    B. Because they could pay children less than adults, they preferred to hire young workers whenever they could.

    C. They were indifferent to the well-being and needs of their workers, caring only to maximize production and profits no matter what it cost their employees.

    D. They were all aristocrats who believed their authority was divinely ordained and that, as a result of this divinely ordained position, they had a duty to care for the less fortunate people in their communities by providing work and education for them.

22. According to the passage, how did 19th-century schools differ from 18th-century schools?

    A. Eighteenth-century schools were intended to make textile mills run more efficiently by making workers become more skilled at their jobs; 19th-century schools were no longer attached to textile factories.

B. Eighteenth-century schools were concerned primarily with teaching working-class children to accept their fate and love their ruler; 19th-century schools began to focus on developing the full human potential of students.

C. Eighteenth-century schools were open only to children of the aristocracy whose parents could pay their tuition. By the 19th century, schools were open to all free of charge, but poorer students had to pay their way by working in spinning factories in the afternoons.

D. Eighteenth-century schools were designed to instill patriotic ideals in the peasantry and make them docile and compliant; 19th-century schools instead tried to develop all children into freethinkers.

23. What does the author mean by the phrase "increasing levels of unrest" in Line 15?

A. riots and other forms of violence against the owners of textile factories by peasants unhappy at their treatment

B. political speeches and demonstrations by politicians trying to earn the working-class vote

C. aggression from neighboring countries looking to invade Germany

D. religious turmoil between Catholics and Protestants

24. According to the passage, what did German aristocrats think about the idea of creating public schools?

A. They feared that educating the working classes would make them less docile and accepting of their position in life and more likely to rise up and overthrow the nobles.

B. They disliked the idea of paying taxes to support public schools and resented the king and Schlabrendorff for forcing this expense on them.

C. They appreciated Schlabrendorff's brilliance in concocting an idea that would both make the peasantry more compliant and simultaneously produce more workers for the spinning factories.

D. They liked the idea because it would make the peasantry more complacent and accepting of their fate, which would help keep the aristocracy safe in their prosperity.

25. According to the passage, what was the purpose of using truant officers to keep children in school?

A. to ensure that all children received the full education that was their right, even if their parents wished instead to keep them working at home

B. to take away the authority of parents and replace it with state power over children and citizens

C. to assist parents in making sure that their children attended school as required by catching and punishing children who failed to attend

D. to indoctrinate children and their parents with political messages designed to help the aristocracy

26. According to the passage, what did nineteenth-century educational theorists believe regarding the future of education?

A. The function of state-run schools is to instill obedience, patriotism, and docility in the working classes; wealthy children whose parents can afford to pay can have a more liberal education provided by private tutors.

B. The most important subject for children to learn is religion, which is why schools should be run by the Church and should include all aspects of worship and theology.

C. Most people cannot adequately educate their children on their own, but the state has an interest in an educated citizenry, so it is the government's job to provide public education and see that people send their children to school.

D. People learn best in an environment that respects their individuality, affords them freedom, and incorporates a variety of aspects of learning, such as physical movement, manual skills, and independent exploration.

Questions 27 - 32 refer to the following passage:

The stored communication portion of the Electronic Communications Privacy Act (ECPA) creates statutory privacy rights for customers of and subscribers to computer network service providers. In a broad sense, ECPA "fills in the gaps" left by the uncertain application of Fourth Amendment protections to cyberspace. To understand these gaps, consider the legal protections we have in our homes. The Fourth Amendment clearly protects our homes in the physical world: Absent special circumstances, the government must first obtain a warrant before it searches there. When we use a computer network such as the Internet, however, we do not have a physical "home." Instead, we typically have a network account consisting of a block of computer storage that is owned by a network service provider, such as America Online. If law-enforcement investigators want to obtain the contents of a network account or information about its use, they do not need to go to the user to get that information. Instead, the government can obtain the information directly from the provider.

Although the Fourth Amendment generally requires the government to obtain a warrant to search a home, it does not require the government to obtain a warrant to obtain the stored contents of a network account. Instead, the Fourth Amendment generally permits the government to issue a subpoena to a network provider that orders the provider to divulge the contents of an account. ECPA addresses this imbalance by offering network account holders a range of statutory privacy rights against access to stored account information held by network service providers.

Because ECPA is an unusually complicated statute, it is helpful when approaching the statute to understand the intent of its drafters. The structure of ECPA reflects a series of classifications that indicate the drafters' judgments about what kinds of information implicate greater or lesser privacy interests. For example, the drafters saw greater privacy interests in stored emails than in subscriber account information. Similarly, the drafters believed that computing services available "to the public" required more strict regulation than services not available to the public. (Perhaps this judgment reflects the view that providers available to the public are not likely to have close relationships with their customers, and therefore might have less incentive to protect their customers' privacy.) To protect the array of privacy interests identified by its drafters, ECPA offers varying degrees of legal protection, depending on the perceived importance of the privacy interest involved. Some information can be obtained from providers with a mere subpoena; other information requires a special court order; and still other information requires a search warrant. In general, the greater the privacy interest, the greater the privacy protection.

27. The primary purpose of the passage is to

   A.   qualify and explain the purpose of ECPA

   B.   argue that the Fourth Amendment alone is not enough protection in our age of technology

   C.   exalt the brilliance of the drafters of the ECPA

   D.   describe the difficulty of obtaining a search warrant for information in cyberspace

28. Using inferences from the passage, the author would be most likely to describe the attitudes of the public network service providers referenced in line 42 as

   A.   ignoble

   B.   impious

   C.   pompous

   D.   indifferent

29. The author argues that the ECPA is an important reinterpretation of our right to privacy because

   A.   subpoenas are extremely easy to obtain

   B.   public network service providers have very little incentive to protect their customers' rights, especially if the providers can make a profit

   C.   the greater the need for privacy, the more protections the ECPA tends to provide

   D.   as our personal information becomes more likely to be stored in a nonphysical realm, the Fourth Amendment alone has a decreasing power to protect it

30. According to the author, the Fourth Amendment had what kind of effect on cyberspace privacy rights before the ECPA?

A. momentous

B. ambiguous

C. incendiary

D. progressive

31. The author most likely mentions that "our homes [are] in the physical world" (lines 11–12) in order to

A. offer a place where there are gaps to be filled in the Fourth Amendment by the ECPA

B. remind the reader of the difference between a real home and a "cyber" home

C. explain why there is less incentive for government officials to pursue obtaining personal data from computer memory when it is far easier to get a search warrant for a physical home

D. address the contrast between the relative simplicity of protecting a physical object as opposed to the uncertain protection of computer memory

32. The passage provides support for which of the following claims?

A. The drafters of the ECPA were some of the most popular legislators in America.

B. Personal emails are legally considered more private than personal account information.

C. It is considered less important to protect privacy in computing services available "to the public" than in those that are "private."

D. In our modern age, the Fourth Amendment is outdated and could be generally disregarded without effect.

Questions 33 - 38 refer to the following passage:

Russia is the largest of the 15 geopolitical entities that emerged in 1991 from the Soviet Union. Covering more than 17 million square kilometers in Europe and Asia, Russia succeeded the Soviet Union as the largest country in the world. As was the case in the Soviet and tsarist eras, the center of Russia's population and economic activity is the European sector, which occupies about one-quarter of the country's territory. Vast tract s of land in Asian Russia are virtually unoccupied. Although numerous Soviet programs had attempted to populate and exploit resources in Siberia and the Arctic regions of the Russian Republic, the population of Russia's remote areas decreased in the 1990s. Thirty-nine percent of Russia's territory, but only 6% of its population, in 1996 was located east of Lake Baikal, the geographical landmark in south-central Siberia. The territorial extent of the country constitutes a major economic and political problem for Russian governments lacking the far-reaching authoritarian clout of their Soviet predecessors.

In the Soviet political system, which was self-described as a democratic federation of republics, the center of authority for almost all actions of consequence was Moscow, the capital of the Russian Republic. After the breakup of the Soviet Union in 1991, that long standing concentration of power meant that many of the other 14 republics faced independence without any experience at self-governance. For Russia, the end of the Soviet Union meant facing the world without the considerable buffer zone of Soviet republics that had protected and nurtured it in various ways since the 1920s; the change required complete reorganization of what had become a thoroughly corrupt and ineffectual socialist system.

In a history-making year, the regime of President Mikhail Gorbachev of the Soviet Union was mortally injured by an unsuccessful coup in August 1991. After all the constituent republics, including Russia, had voted for independence in the months that followed the coup, Gorbachev announced in December 1991 that the nation would cease to exist. In place of the monolithic union, there remained the Commonwealth of Independent States (CIS), a loose confederation of 11 of the former Soviet republics, which now were independent states with an indefinite mandate of mutual cooperation. By late 1991, the Communist Party of the Soviet Union (CPSU) and the Communist Party of the Russian Republic had been banned in Russia, and Boris Yeltsin, who had been elected president of the Russian Republic in June 1991, had become the leader of the new Russian Federation.

Under those circumstances, Russia has undergone an agonizing process of self-analysis and refocusing of national goals. That process, which seemingly had only begun in the mid-1990s, has been observed and commented upon with more analytic energy than any similar transformation in the history of the world. As information pours out past the ruins of the Iron Curtain, a new, more reliable portrait of Russia emerges, but substantial mystery remains.

33. Which of the following best describes the main idea of the passage?

    A. In its transition to self-governance, Russia, unlike the other 14 republics, has been shaken by controversy, political failure, and stubborn remnants of the corrupt Soviet regime.

    B. Corruption among the Communist leadership was the sole problem in Soviet politics, but in the end it was enough to dissolve the Union.

    C. Russia's strength relies on the full exploitation of its resources, and the Soviet Union's inability to tap into Siberian riches led to its downfall.

    D. Over the past several years, Russia's rapid emergence from a corrupt socialist system has required political transformations on a colossal scale.

34. Which one of the following would Russian politicians probably deem the most detrimental contributor to Russian politics before 1991?

    A. the Russian Federation

    B. Boris Yeltsin

    C. Europe

    D. Communism

35. The phrase "monolithic union" most likely refers to:

    A. a metaphor comparing the Soviet Union to obdurate stone

B. the massiveness and perceived indestructibility of the Soviet Union in late 1991

C. the way that the republics together comprised a single association and acted as a uniform block

D. the Soviet leaders' tradition of demonstrating their power by building huge statues that were displayed around the republics

36. The second paragraph primarily serves to:

    A. explain why the effects of the breakup of the Soviet Union meant that the new republics would need to entirely reconstruct their political systems and attitudes

    B. offer several reasons why the 15 republics were better off in the long term as part of the Soviet Union

    C. describe the short-term goals of most of the republics just after the breakup of the Soviet Union

    D. blame the collapse of the Soviet Union on Communism

37. It can be inferred that most Russian citizens view Siberia as which of the following?

    A. intolerably inhospitable

    B. politically overwhelmed

    C. unfairly exploited

    D. favorably desolate

38. According to the passage, all the following are true of Russia since its emergence from the Soviet Union EXCEPT:

    A. it has had to deal with the loss of control of the satellite republics that constituted its buffer zone

    B. it banned Communist parties from the country

    C. it has attracted the attention of many social scientists, historians, and cultural analysts

D. it has developed into a corruption-free, benevolent political entity

Questions 39 - 42 refer to the following passage:

Melvil Dewey developed and introduced his eponymous Dewey Decimal System for book classification and arrangement in 1876. Prior to that, libraries arranged books in order of when they were acquired. Dewey's system arranged titles into 10 classes, with 10 divisions each, with each division having 10 sections. The first set, 000, includes computer and informational volumes. The 300s group encompasses the social sciences, and the last category, the 900s, identifies history and geography. For mathematics, under the general class of 500, 516 denotes geometry, and 516.3 is specific to analytic geometries.

Though the Dewey Decimal System is still in use by many general libraries, the Library of Congress Classification is preferred by many research and academic libraries. In this system, general works fall under the class A, with yearbooks sub classified as AY and dictionaries under AG.

39. According to the passage, in the Dewey Decimal System, all books are categorized into:

A. One General Class

B. One General Class and one division

C. One general class, one division, and one section

D. One general class, Including AG

40. In the first sentence of the passage, the word "eponymous" most nearly means:

A. A Most important

B. Named after a person

C. Uniquely innovative

D. Logical and simple

41. According to the passage, prior to the Dewey Decimal System books were arranged:

A. randomly

B. By age

C. By Author

D. By date of acquisition

42. Geometery is filed under what number in the Dewey Decimal System?

A. 500

B. 400

C. 300

D. 200

Questions 43 - 47 refer to the following passage:

Camp Wildflower is the perfect, year-round escape for you and your family. We offer a variety of accommodations to fit every preference and budget. For families who wish to enjoy a traditional camping experience, we offer large campsites with level ground for your tent, as well as hookups to access electricity and water. Our Rustic Campsites can accommodate pop-ups, trailers, and most midsize recreational vehicles. For those who prefer to camp indoors and have the budget for a few amenities, we also offer a wide range of cabins, from our Simple Bungalows to our Luxury Cottages. Campers who stay during our off-season months (October through May) will enjoy a 20 percent discount on all accommodations. Call today to plan your family's next favorite vacation!

43. Of the following combinations of accommodations, which does the passage suggest would offer the lowest possible rate at Camp Wildflower?

A. Simple Bungalow in March

B. Simple Bungalow in June

C. Rustic Campsite in September

D. Rustic Campsite in February

44. In which months is camp wildflower closed?

   A. March

   B. February

   C. None

   D. July

45. How does the article suggest that interested parties make contact?

   A. Email

   B. Mail

   C. Telephone

   D. Upon Arrival

46. Camp wildflower is marketed primarily at

   A. Families

   B. Single Men

   C. Large Groups of Women.

   D. Scout Groups

47. What does passage imply is the most expensive form of accommodation?

   A. Luxury Cottage

   B. Rustic Campsite

   C. Simple Bungalow

   D. Wild Camping.

   Question 48 - 52 refer to the following passage:

Chang-Rae Lee's debut and award-winning novel <u>Native Speaker</u> is about Henry Park, a Korean-American individual who struggles to find his place as an immigrant in a suburb of New York City. This novel addresses the notion that as the individuals who know us best, our family, peers, and lovers are the individuals who direct our lives and end up defining us. Henry Park is confronted with this reality in the very beginning of the novel, which begins:

The day my wife left she gave me a list of who I was.

Upon separating from his wife, Park struggles with racial and ethnic identity issues due to his loneliness. Through Parks' work as an undercover operative for a private intelligence agency, the author presents the theme of espionage as metaphor for the internal divide that Park experiences as an immigrant. This dual reality creates two worlds for Park and increases his sense of uncertainty with regard to his place in society. While he constantly feels like an outsider looking in, he also feels like he belongs to neither world.

Chang-Rae Lee is also a first-generation Korean American immigrant. He immigrated to America at the early age of three. Themes of identity, race, and cultural alienation pervade his works. His interests in these themes no doubt stem from his first-hand experience as a kid growing up in a Korean household while going to an American school. Lee is also author of <u>A Gesture Life</u> and <u>Aloft</u>. The protagonists are similar in that they deal with labels placed on them based on race, color, and language. Consequently, all of these characters struggle to belong in America.

Lee's novels address differences within a nation's mix of race, religion, and history, and the necessity of assimilation between cultures. In his works and through his characters, Lee shows us both the difficulties and the subtleties of the immigrant experience in America. He urges us to consider the role of borders and to consider why the idea of opening up one's borders is so frightening. In an ever-changing world in which cultures are becoming more intermingled, the meaning of identity must be constantly redefined, especially when the security of belonging to a place is becoming increasingly elusive. As our world grows smaller with increasing technological advances, these themes in Lee's novels become even more pertinent.

48. Which of the following best describes the purpose of this passage?

A. to inform

B. to entertain

C. to analyze

D. to criticize

49. Why does the author of the passage quote the first line of the novel Native Speaker?

    A. to illustrate one of the themes in the novel

    B. to show how the book is semi-autobiographical

    C. it is the main idea of the novel

    D. to create interest in the novel

50. According to the passage, which of the following is not a main theme of Lee's novels?

    A. Identity

    B. Espionage

    C. Immigration

    D. Culture

51. Based on the passage, why do Lee's novels focus on race and cultural identity?

    A. because Lee's ancestors are Korean

    B. because Lee was born in Korea

    C. because Lee feels these issues are the biggest problem facing America

    D. because Lee immigrated to America at a young age

52. How does the author of the passage feel about the ideas presented in Lee's novels?

    A. certain that all borders will eventually be eliminated so world cultures will commingle and fully assimilate

B. critical regarding the role technology has played in society and how it destroys the immigrant experience

C. excited that immigrants are easily able to redefine and establish themselves in new cultures

D. concerned about the disappearance of cultures in a rapidly expanding and mixed world

Read the set of directions below to answer the following question:

This formula is for people with deficiencies and anaemic conditions. It aids in the body's absorption of vital minerals such as iron, calcium, zinc, potassium, and sulphur. Take the following ingredients:

Parsley root

Comfrey root

Yellow dock

Watercress

Nettles

Kelp

Irish moss

Slowly simmer equal parts of these herbs with four ounces to a half-quart of water. Continue to simmer slowly until the volume of liquid is reduced by half. Strain, reserve the liquid, and cover the herbs with water once more. Then simmer again for 10 minutes. Strain and combine the two liquids. Cook the liquid down until the volume is reduced by half. Add an equal amount of blackstrap molasses. Take one tablespoon four to five times daily, not exceeding four tablespoons in a 24-hour period.

53. What is the main reason for taking this formula?

A. to reduce the absorption of minerals

B. to increase the absorption of minerals

C. to serve as a mineral supplement

D. to get rid of unnecessary minerals

ATI TEAS Science

General Informations: 53 questions (47 Scored)

Timing: 63 Minutes

1. Gas particles are able to collide with each other as they move in random and rapid motion. Gas particles contain a high amount of which type of energy?

   A. kinetic energy

   B. potential energy

   C. total energy

   D. random energy

2. Mathematical models are needed to do which of the following?

   A. help produce data that cannot be collected

   B. make quantitative data more like qualitative data

   C. produce viable conclusions based on observations

   D. establish relationships between variables in an experiment

3. An enzyme is subjected to various temperatures over a 24-hour period. The amount of substrate left in the test tube is monitored and recorded at the end of the 24-hour period. The results of the experiment are below.

Initial Amount of Substrate	Final Amount of Substrate
(15ºC) 100 ppm	(15ºC) 90 ppm
(35ºC) 100 ppm	(35ºC) 50 ppm
(55ºC) 100 ppm	(55ºC) 75 ppm

Which of the following conclusions can be drawn from the data?

A. the enzyme is defective

B. the enzyme is non-functional at 55ºC

C. the enzyme's optimal temperature is 35ºC

D. not enough information to determine optimal temperature

4. What subatomic particle(s) is/are located within the nucleus of an atom?

A. protons only

B. neutrons only

C. protons and electrons

D. neutrons and protons

5. For an experiment to measure the volume of CO_2 that can be exhaled by individuals of varying ages, which of the following would be the most appropriate unit of measurement?

A. Amu

B. Atm

C. liters

D. grams

6. Which of the following is true for both chloroplasts and mitochondria?

A. they are both in animal cells.

B. they have a single membrane and contain only RNA.

C. they have a double membrane and contain maternal DNA.

D. they have an impermeable membrane and contain single stranded DNA.

7. Which of the following is a distinguishing characteristic between eukaryotes and prokaryotes?

A. the presence of DNA.

B. the presence of a nucleus.

C. the presence of proteins.

D. the presence of ribosomes.

8. Due to water's polarity, water is known as which of the following?

A. a base

B. an acid

C. universal solute

D. universal solvent

9. During embryo development which of the following germ layers differentiates to form the muscles?

A. endoderm

B. mesoderm

C. interoderm

D. ectoderm

10. Which of the following is a byproduct produced during photosynthesis?

A. O_2

B. H_2O

C. CO_2

D. $C_5H_{10}O_2$

11. Cheetahs, rainbow trout, and inchworms belong to the same

A. Kingdom

B. Phylum

C. Class

D. Order

12. Two elements have similar chemical properties, physical properties, and number of valence electrons. On the periodic table, where would these two elements be located?

A. in the same row

B. in the same period

C. in the same family

D. in the same orbital

13. Cellular respiration, the process responsible for the production of cellular energy would be performed using which of the following organelles?

A. ribosome

B. nucleolus

C. chloroplast

D. mitochondria

14. The movement of oxygenated blood from the heart to the body is referred to as which of the following?

A. cellular circulation

B. pulmonary circulation

C. systemic circulation

D. ventricular circulation

15. Which of the following organisms exhibits a high fitness?

A. a mule that produces infertile offspring.

B. a turtle species that reproduces in low numbers.

C. a cow that has 100% viability for male offspring.

D. a deer that has 90% viability of all offspring.

16. Water does not evaporate easily due to which of the following chemical properties?

    A. polarity

    B. hydrogen bonding

    C. covalent bonding

    D. ionic bonding

17. According to Linnaeus' classification system, which of the following would be less restrictive than the family of an organism?

    A. order

    B. genus

    C. species

    D. taxon

18. According to Darwin's findings, he proposed that the finches he observed in the Galapagos islands differed due to which of the following?

    A. the presence of humans on each island.

    B. the amount of sunlight available on each island.

    C. the presence of predators on each island.

    D. the differing climates and vegetation on each island.

19. A malfunctioning aorta will result in which of the following?

A. deoxygenated blood would not be transported to the heart.

B. deoxygenated blood would not be transported to the lungs.

C. oxygenated blood would not be transported to the heart's atria.

D. oxygenated blood would not be transported to the body's cells.

20. Which of the following occurs during the S phase of interphase?

A. organelles are replicated

B. DNA is replicated

C. proteins are replicated

D. RNA is degraded

21. Which of the following correctly lists the cellular hierarchy from the simplest to the most complex structure?

A. tissue, cell, organ, organ system, organism

B. cell, tissue, organ, organ system, organism

C. organism, organ system, organ, tissue, cell

D. organ system, organism, organ, tissue, cell

22. If a cell is placed in a hypertonic solution, what will happen to the cell?

A. It does not affect the cell.

B. It will stay the same.

C. It will shrink.

D. It will swell.

23. What is the longest phase of the cell cycle?

A. cytokinesis

B. mitosis

C. metaphase

D. interphase

Questions 24–25 refer to the following table.

Table 1 - B = alleles for brown eyes; g = alleles for green eyes

	B	g
B	BB	Bg
g	Bg	gg

24. Which word describes the allele for green eyes?

    A. dominant

    B. homozygous

    C. heterozygous

    D. recessive

25. What is the possibility that the offspring produced will have brown eyes?

    A. 100%

    B. 75%

    C. 50%

    D. 25%

26. What are groups of cells that perform the same function called?

    A. organs

    B. molecules

    C. tissues

    D. plastids

27. When does the nuclear division of somatic cells take place during cellular reproduction?

A. mitosis

B. interphase

C. cytokinesis

D. meiosis

28. Which group of major parts and organs make up the immune system?

A. lymphatic system, spleen, tonsils, thymus, and bone marrow

B. brain, spinal cord, and nerve cells

C. heart, veins, arteries, and capillaries

D. nose, trachea, bronchial tubes, lungs, alveolus, and diaphragm

29. The rate of a chemical reaction depends on all of the following except:

A. temperature.

B. surface area.

C. presence of catalysts.

D. amount of mass lost.

30. Which of the answer choices provided best defines the following statement?

For a given mass and constant temperature, an inverse relationship exists between the volume and pressure of a gas?

A. Ideal Gas Law

B. Boyle's Law

C. Stefan-Boltzmann Law

D. Charles' Law

31. Prokaryotic and eukaryotic cells are similar in having which of the following?

A. Presence of a nucleus.

B. Protein-studded DNA

C. Integral membrane proteins in the plasma membrane

D. Membrane-bound organelles

32. What is the role of ribosomes?

A. make proteins

B. waste removal

C. transport

D. storage

33. Which of the following is an example of a tissue?

A. mammal

B. hamstring

C. liver

D. xylem

34. The adrenal glands are part of the:

A. endocrine system.

B. emphatic system.

C. respiratory system.

D. immune system.

35. Which of the following is exchanged between two or more atoms that undergo ionic bonding?

A. neutrons

B. transitory electrons

C. electrical charges

D. valence electrons

The next figures and table corresponds to questions 36 – 41

The peaks of mountains often lose sediment due to wind erosion. Figure 1 shows mountain peak compositions, mountain heights, in meters (m), and the net change in meters (m), in mean peak height (MPH) from 1910 to 1970 along a section of the Rocky Mountains. A net negative change in MPH indicates a net loss of sediment and a net positive change in MPH indicates a gain of sediment.

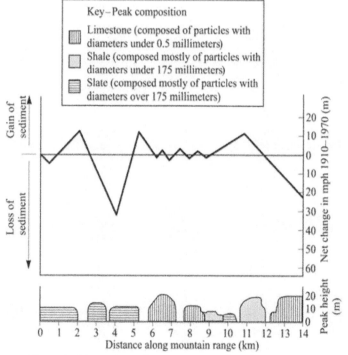

Figure 1 - Mountain peak compositions of Rocky Mountains

Table 1- Shows the approximate percentage of a year that horizontal sections of a mountain are exposed to wind.

Table 1	
Peak section height (m)	Approximate percentage of the year that peak section is exposed to wind
0.0–0.5	1.1
0.5–1.0	3.1
1.0–1.5	7.2
1.5–2.0	10.5
2.0–2.5	14.2
2.5–3.0	19.4
3.0–3.5	23.7
3.5–4.0	29.3
4.0–4.5	37.4
4.5–5.0	42.3
5.0–5.5	48.0
Note: Heights are measured from mean (average) sea level.	

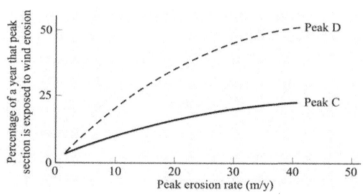

Figure 2 - Shows Peak C and D erosion rates, in m/y, as they relate to percentage of a year that mountain peak section is exposed to wind.

36. According to Figure 1, at a distance of 9 km along the mountain range, peaks of what composition are present, if any?

A. Peaks of slate

B. Peaks of shale

C. Peaks of limestone

D. No peaks are present

37. According to the information in Figure 1, which of the following properties was used to distinguish the various materials that compose the peaks in the study area?

A. Particle size

B. Particle clarity

C. Particle color

D. Cannot be determined from the information given.

38. Based on the information listed in Table 1, a peak section with a height of 5.25 m would be exposed to wind approximately what percentage of a year?

A. 22%

B. 39%

C. 48%

D. 100%

39. According to Figures 1 and 2, the difference between Peak C and Peak D erosion rates could best be explained as a difference in the:

A. heights of the two peaks.

B. force of the winds on the two peaks.

C. composition of the two peaks.

D. annual snowfall on the two peaks.

40. According to Table 1, which of the following figures best represents the relationship between the height of a peak section and the percentage of a year that peak section is exposed to wind erosion?

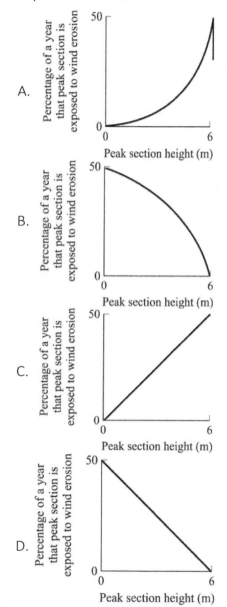

A.

B.

C.

D.

41. According to information in the passage, wind erosion often results in:

    A. an increase in the percentage of a mountain peak that is exposed to snow.

    B. a reduction in the overall sediment of mountain peaks.

    C. a higher number of slate and shale deposits on mountain peaks.

    D. a lower number of record snowfalls each year.

42. Which of the following is an example of deductive reasoning?

    A. Only 21% of a town's population have expressed a desire to ban all cars. Therefore, the new proposition banning cars in the state is not likely to pass.

    B. People who brush their teeth regularly have fewer instances of heart disease. Therefore, good dentistry can prevent heart attacks.

    C. All soccer players who play professionally can kick well. Therefore, any future soccer player who is recruited to play professionally will be able to kick well.

    D. All secretaries are good typists. Cynthia is a secretary. Therefore, Cynthia is a good typist.

43. Which of the following is a possible cause of herniation of discs?

    A. hepatitis

    B. whiplash

    C. plantar fasciitis

    D. ulcer

44. An unknown element is found to contain 45 protons and an atomic mass of 64, what is its atomic number?

    A. It cannot be determined.

    B. 19

C. 45

D. 64

45. Which of the following is a characteristic of the autonomic nervous system?

A. It regulates the voluntary control of body movements through the skeletal muscles.

B. It is the part of the nervous system consisting of the brain and spinal cord.

C. It regulates involuntary activity in the heart, stomach, lungs, and intestines.

D. It is thought to be the center of intelligence.

46. During photosynthesis, which two compounds are combined to create the output of glucose and oxygen?

A. Carbon dioxide and water.

B. Carbon dioxide and bicarbonate.

C. Bicarbonate and water.

D. Carbon dioxide and multiple alkaline substances

Questions 47 & 48 are based on the following diagram:

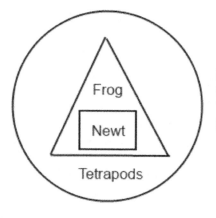

47. Which of the following is true about the frog?

A. It is a member of the salamandridae family.

B. It is a type of amphibian.

C. It is a non-vertebrate.

D. It is closer to most tetrapods than to most newts

48. Which statement can be inferred about amphibians?

A. All amphibians are salamandridae, but not all salamandridae are amphibians.

B. Some amphibians are vertebrates, but not all amphibians are vertebrates.

C. Some salamandridae are amphibians, but not all amphibians are tetrapods.

D. All amphibians are vertebrates, but not all vertebrates are amphibians.

49. What type of bond between the complementary bases of DNA stabilizes the double helix structure?

A. covalent

B. ionic

C. hydrogen

D. Nuclear

50. When a person reaches out and touches a hot pan, the _____ system is triggered and activates the _____ system to move the hand away. Fill in the blanks.

A. skeletal, muscular

B. muscular, nervous

C. nervous, endocrine

D. nervous, muscular

51. Why does the human eye perceive a red colored dress as the color red?

A. The molecules of the dress do not absorb red light wavelengths.

B. The molecules of the dress absorb green and blue light wavelengths.

C. A red dress will primarily absorb red light wavelengths.

D. A red dress will not absorb light wavelengths from non-red colors.

52. In a lab experiment designed to test the rate at which plants grow under artificial light, the kind of light used is which type of variable?

    A. dependent

    B. independent

    C. random

    D. responding

53. Which organ system is primarily responsible for regulating metabolism, mood, and growth?

    A. respiratory system

    B. digestive system

    C. endocrine system

    D. lymphatic system

Answers

ATI TEAS English Language and Usage

1. **Correct answer: B**

Since the "Fair" is mentioned before the comma, there is no need to repeat the word after the comma. B. correctly uses the past tense verb, "originated," and the modifier "which".

2. **Correct answer: A**

"When" can only refer to time. Since a specific year is mentioned just prior to the usage of this word, we can determine that it is being used correctly in this sentence. "After which" does not make sense with the word "originated" that appears in this sentence. "As" means "because" in this context, and also does not make sense in the sentence.

3. **Correct answer: D**

Since the paragraph mentions the festival takes place "each year," we need a verb to reflect that meaning. "Took" is past tense. "Had taken" is past perfect tense, and "did take place" implies an event that occurred in the past but does not continue into the present.

4. **Correct answer: C**

Since "stunning" and "beautiful" are so similar in meaning, this pairing can be considered redundant. Avoid redundancy on the ATI TEAS English Test! A simple "beautiful" is sufficient to express the intended meaning. The words "yet" and "however" both imply a contrast, but these words are similar, not contrasting.

5. **Correct answer: D**

The verb tenses here must agree and both be in past tense. D. Correctly uses the past tense "began" and "completed". The past perfect "had" would only be used to refer to an event even further back in the past than a simple past tense event. "Was began" is not correct. In C., the usage of two past perfect verbs creates confusion: which event occurred first? The correct construction should use two simple past tense verbs or one past tense verb and one past perfect verb.

6. Correct answer: B

A colon is used to introduce a definition or explanation. A semicolon is used to separate two independent clauses. Since the clause after the comma is dependent (not a complete sentence), the semicolon is incorrect here.

7. Correct answer: A

The past tense verb "exited" is parallel with the other past tense verb "was reserved" that appears later in the sentence. The other verbs are not parallel and are in future or present tense.

8. Correct answer: C

The correct idiom is "not only...but also." It is not correct to have "not only...but" in an ATI TEAS English sentence, nor is it correct to have "not...but also." C. creates a sentence with the correct idiom.

9. Correct answer: C

This paragraph focuses on the construction of the Plaza de Toros and the Spanish Royal Family. Note how three of the sentences provide additional information on the Plaza de Toros, while one sentence introduces unnecessary information about the Seville Festival.

10. Correct answer: D

The word "and" implies two similar ideas, but the ideas in these two clauses contrast. The phrase "even though" is the best transition phrase for this sentence. The other options create illogical meanings. Only D. creates a clear contrasting meaning.

11. Correct answer: A

The past perfect "had been completed" correctly refers to an event that occurred even before another past tense event, so it is correctly used in this sentence. The other tenses are incorrect.

12. Correct answer: B

Two independent clauses cannot be separated by a comma. This is called a run-on sentence, or a comma splice. B. corrects the issue by replacing the comma with a semicolon. Simply moving the position of the comma is not enough to correct the run-on, nor is replacing the comma with a dash.

13. Correct answer: C

On the ATI TEAS English Test, many sentences will begin with a modifying phrase and a comma. The subject after the comma must be the person or thing doing the action of the modifying phrase. Here it is the architect, Anival Gonzalez, who is "choosing to redo them in brick," so she must come immediately after the comma. D. incorrectly implies the architect took the years 1914-1915 to decide to replace the grandstands, rather than carry out the actual work.

14. Correct answer: C

The pronoun "they" has no clear antecedent in the sentence. For example, is it the armchairs or the builders who were placed in front of theater boxes? Choice D. cannot be correct because the sentence would then read: "and it were placed in front of the theater boxes."

15. Correct answer: A

This sentence nicely brings the passage back to its original theme: the popular, tourist-filled festival. The other choices provide additional historical or tourist information that do not provide a satisfactory conclusion.

16. Correct answer: B

Assuming that they are right next to each other, as they are here, no punctuation is necessary between the subject of a sentence and the main verb. *The different kinds of prairie wildflowers* is our noun phrase (technically, the subject is *kinds*, and *of prairie wildflowers* is a prepositional phrase, but this doesn't make a difference here), and the main verb is *are*.

17. Correct answer: D

This section of the passage is in the present tense, and the subject phrase is *grasses and herbaceous wildflowers*, so the correct form for the main verb is *dominate* (present-tense plural).

18. Correct answer: D

Coneflowers, and how many types there are, are not mentioned anywhere else in this paragraph or the entire passage. The passage is about prairies, not specific types of flowers. Therefore, this sentence would distract from the main idea.

19. Correct answer: A

The entire passage so far has been about the diverse flora found on prairies. The reader would expect that the assertion that prairies are interesting and colorful would have something to do with biodiversity.

20. Correct answer: A

This choice correctly results in an independent clause followed by a dependent clause, with the two clauses separated by a comma.

21. Correct answer: B

Old railroads are the rarest of the four environments offered as choices, and so this choice best establishes that black soil prairies are difficult to find today.

22. Correct answer: C

The implication of the sentence in the context of the paragraph is that it is regrettable that the original prairies have been destroyed. Therefore, *Unfortunately* is the appropriate introductory word.

23. Correct answer: D

The main idea of the paragraph concerns the depletion of gravel prairies, and so a guess that some of these prairies are probably new seems out of place.

24. Correct answer: A

Since the noun *they* performs both the verb *are* and the verb *contain*, no comma is necessary after *degraded*. Furthermore, the information presented in this choice is the most relevant to the paragraph. (In this question, the right and wrong answers are determined by a combination of grammatical and stylistic factors—the test does not do this often, but it does happen, so watch out for it!)

25. Correct answer: C

The antecedent of the pronoun *they* is the noun phrase *gravel and dolomite prairies*. Therefore, sentence 4 should come right after a sentence that makes this apparent. It should also not come between sentences 3 and 5, as sentence 5 is clearly supposed to immediately follow sentence 3. And it makes sense that sentence 4 should be next to sentence 2, as both concern the physical characteristics of gravel and dolomite prairies. Of the choices, only C (which places sentence 4 between sentences 2 and 3) resolves all of these issues.

26. Correct answer: B

This choice correctly separates two independent clauses into two separate sentences by use of a period.

27. Correct answer: D

This choice correctly uses *that* (with no comma) to attach a grammatically correct essential/limiting clause to the pronoun *those*.

28. Correct answer: B

The subject noun *species* is plural here (although the singular form is identical), and so the plural verb *are* is necessary.

ATI TEAS Math

1. Correct answer: D

The purpose of this question is to understand the process of using geometry to find degree values of angles. Since l and m are parallel lines, the respective angles on both lines will have equivalent degree values. This means that a and w, b and x, and so on will be the same degree amount. A straight line is 180 degrees, so you know that angle d is 180–67=113 degrees; and therefore angle z, which has the same value, is also 113 degrees.

2. Correct answer: B

Let's begin by observing the larger angle. ∠ABC is cut into two 10-degree angles by BD–→–. This means that angles ∠ABD and ∠CBD equal 10 degrees. Next, we are told that BE–→ bisects ∠CBD, which creates two 5-degree angles. ∠ABE consists of ∠ABD, which is 10 degrees, and ∠DBE, which is 5 degrees. We need to add the two angles together to solve the problem.

∠ABE=∠ABD+∠DBE

∠ABE=10°+5°

∠ABE=15°

3. Correct answer: B

The perimeter of the pentagonal track is one third of a mile; one mile is equal to 5,280 feet, so the perimeter is

13 × 5,280=1,760 feet.

Each side of the pentagon has length one fifth of its perimeter, or

15 × 1,760=352 feet.

Jessica runs three and one half sides, or

312 × 352=1,232 feet.

This makes 1,200 feet the closest, and correct, choice.

4. Correct answer: D

Benny runs at a rate of eight miles an hour for ten minutes, or 1060=16 hours. The distance he runs is equal to his rate multiplied by his time, so, setting =8, t=16 in this formula:

d=rt

d=8 × 16=43 miles.

One mile comprises 5,280 feet, so this is equal to

43 × 5,280=7,040 feet.

Since each side of the track measures 264 feet, this means that Benny runs

7,040÷264=2623 side lengths.

This means Benny runs around the track for 25 side lengths, which is 5 complete times, back to Point A; he then runs one more complete side length to Point B; and, finally, he runs 23 of a side length, finishing closest to Point C.

5. Correct answer: A

Let x equal the measure of angle DPB. Because the measure of angle APC is eighty-one degrees larger than the measure of DPB, we can represent this angle's measure as x + 81. Also, because the measure of angle CPD is equal to the measure of angle DPB, we can represent the measure of CPD as x.

Since APB is a straight line, the sum of the measures of angles DPB, APC, and CPD must all equal 180; therefore, we can write the following equation to find x:

x + (x + 81) + x = 180

Simplify by collecting the x terms.

3x + 81 = 180

Subtract 81 from both sides.

3x = 99

Divide by 3.

x = 33.

This means that the measures of angles DPB and CPD are both equal to 33 degrees. The original question asks us to find the measure of angle CPB, which is equal to the sum of the measures of angles DPB and CPD.

measure of CPB = 33 + 33 = 66.

The answer is 66.

6. **Correct answer: D**

Let x equal the measure of angle ABC, let y equal the measure of the supplement of angle ABC, and let z equal the measure of the complement of angle ABC.

Because x and y are supplements, the sum of their measures must equal 180. In other words, x + y = 180.

We are told that one-half of the measure of the supplement is equal to twice the measure of ABC. We could write this equation as follows:

(1/2) y = 2x.

Because x + y = 180, we can solve for y in terms of x by subtracting x from both sides. In other words, y = 180 − x. Next, we can substitute this value into the equation (1/2) y = 2x and then solve for x.

(1/2) (180-x) = 2x.

Multiply both sides by 2 to get rid of the fraction.

(180 − x) = 4x.

Add x to both sides.

180 = 5x.

Divide both sides by 5.

x = 36.

The measure of angle ABC is 36 degrees. However, the original question asks us to find the measure of the complement of ABC, which we denoted previously as z. Because the sum of the measure of an angle and the measure of its complement equals 90, we can write the following equation:

x + z = 90.

Now, we can substitute 36 as the value of x and then solve for z.

36 + z = 90.

Subtract 36 from both sides.

z = 54.

The answer is 54.

7. **Correct answer: D**

Refer to the following diagram while reading the explanation:

We know that angle b has to be equal to its vertical angle (the angle directly "across" the intersection). Therefore, it is 20°.

Furthermore, given the properties of parallel lines, we know that the supplementary angle to a must be 40°. Based on the rule for supplements, we know that a + 40° = 180°. Solving for a, we get a = 140°.

Therefore, a + b = 140° + 20° = 160°

8. **Correct answer: C**

Intersecting lines create two pairs of vertical angles which are congruent. Therefore, we can deduce that y = measure of angle AED.

Furthermore, intersecting lines create adjacent angles that are supplementary (sum to 180 degrees). Therefore, we can deduce that x + y + z + (measure of angle AED) = 360.

Substituting the first equation into the second equation, we get

x + (measure of angle AED) + z + (measure of angle AED) = 360

2(measure of angle AED) + x + z = 360

2(measure of angle AED) = 360 − (x + z)

Divide by two and get:

measure of angle AED = 180 − 1/2(x + z).

9. Correct answer: D

The answer to this problem is 12. This can be drawn as shown below (intersections marked in red).

We can also be sure that this is the maximal case because it is the largest answer selection. Were it not given as a multiple choice question, however, we could still be sure this was the largest. This is because no line can intersect a circle in more than 2 points. Keeping this in mind, we look at the construction of our initial shape. The square has 4 lines, and then each diagonal is an additional 2. We have thus drawn in 6 lines. The maximum number of intersections is therefore going to be twice this, or 12.

10. Correct answer: A

By properties of parallel lines, A+B = 180°, B = 45°, C = A = 135°, so 2 × |B-C| = 2 × |45-135| = 180.

11. Correct answer: D

Since we know opposite angles are equal, it follows that angle ∠AFE=10° and ∠BGE=50°.

Imagine a parallel line passing through point E. The imaginary line would make opposite angles with ∠AFE & ∠BGE, the sum of which would equal ∠FEG. Therefore, ∠FEG=60°.

cos (60) =0.5=EGEF→EF=EG0.5=20

12. Correct answer: C

When the measure of an angle is added to the measure of its supplement, the result is always 180 degrees. Put differently, two angles are said to be supplementary if the sum of their measures is 180 degrees. For example, two angles whose measures are 50 degrees and 130 degrees are supplementary, because the sum of 50 and 130 degrees is 180 degrees.

The answer is (10x+140)°.

13. Correct answer: D

When two parallel lines are intersected by another line, the sum of the measures of the interior angles on the same side of the line is 180°. Therefore, the sum of the angle that is labelled as 100° and angle y is 180°. As a result, angle y is 80°.

Another property of two parallel lines that are intersected by a third line is that the corresponding angles are congruent. So, the measurement of angle x is equal to the measurement of angle y, which is 80°.

14. Correct answer: D

Let A represent the measure, in degrees, of angle A. By definition, the sum of the measures of A and its complement is 90 degrees. We can write the following equation to determine an expression for the measure of the complement of angle A.

A + measure of complement of A = 90

Subtract A from both sides.

measure of complement of A = 90 − A

Similarly, because the sum of the measures of angle A and its supplement is 180 degrees, we can represent the measure of the supplement of A as 180 − A.

The problem states that the measure of the supplement of A is 40 degrees larger than twice the measure of the complement of A. We can write this as 2(90-A) + 40.

Next, we must set the two expressions 180 − A and 2(90 − A) + 40 equal to one another and solve for A:

180 − A = 2(90 − A) + 40

Distribute the 2:

180 - A = 180 − 2A + 40

Add 2A to both sides:

180 + A = 180 + 40

Subtract 180 from both sides:

A = 40

Therefore, the measure of angle A is 40 degrees.

The question asks us to find the sum of the measures of the supplement and complement of A. The measure of the supplement of A is 180 − A = 180 − 40 = 140 degrees. Similarly, the measure of the complement of A is 90 − 40 = 50 degrees.

The sum of these two is 140 + 50 = 190 degrees.

15. Correct answer: C

Solve for a by adding 2 to each side to get 8a = 24. Divide by 8 to find a = 3. Plug a = 3 into the second equation to find 4(3) − 1 = 12 − 1 = 11.

Alternatively, you could save yourself some time by noticing that 8a − 2 is 2(4a − 1). If 2(4a −1) = 22, divide by 2 to get 4a − 1 = 11.

16. Correct answer: A

Twenty percent of the sweaters in the store are white, so there are 200 × 0.2 = 40 white sweaters. There are 200 − 40 = 160 sweaters remaining. Of the remaining sweaters, 160 × 0.4 = 64 are brown. That means that 160 − 64 = 96 are blue. There are 96 − 40 = 56 more blue sweaters than white sweaters.

17. Correct answers: B and D

Use the Average Pie to find that Jill's mean of 3.75 for 8 evaluations gives her a current total of 3.75 × 8 = 30 points. Use the Average Pie to find that if she needs an average of 4.0 for 12 scores, she needs 4.0 × 12 = 48 total points. Jill still needs 48 − 30 = 18 points. Her four remaining scores must total 18 or greater. Only answers B. and D. have a total of at least 18.

18. Correct answer: A

Your best bet is to plug in values for all the angles, keeping in mind that those inside the triangle must add up to 180°, the ones along BC must add up to 180, the ones along CD must add up to 180°, and the ones at A must add up to 90°. Then add up the marked angles.

19. Correct answer: D

Use the Group formula: Total = Group1 + Group2 − Both + Neither. In this problem the total is 2,400. The question also states that 1,200 students (half of the total) take calculus, so that is Group1; one-third of that group (400) take both calculus and English. Because every student takes calculus or English or both, the Neither group is zero. Solve for the number of students who take English by plugging these numbers into the group formula: 2400 = 1200 + Group2 − 400. The number of students who take English is 1,600, or choice D.

20. Correct answer: B

Plug in the answers starting with choice C. Eventually you find B is the correct option.

21. Correct answer: D

$5x + 3 = 7x - 1$

now collect like terms

$3 + 1 = 7x - 5x$

$4 = 2x$

$4/2 = x$

$2 = x$

22. Correct answer: C

$5x + 2(x + 7) = 14x - 7$

$5x + 2x + 14 = 14x - 7$

$7x + 14 = 14x - 7$

$7x - 14x = -14 - 7$

$-7x = -21$

x = 3

23. Correct answer: B

Find the answer by initially solving for t.

- 8 = 2t

t = - 4

24. Correct answer: C

5(z + 1) = 3(z + 2) + 11.   z =?

5z + 5 = 3z + 6 + 11

5z + 5 = 3z + 17

5z = 3z + 17 − 5

5z − 3z = 12

2z = 12

z = 6

25. Correct answer: D

The price increased from $20 to $25 ($5) so the question is 5 is what percent of 20. Or, 5/20 = x/100; 500/20 = 25%

26. Correct answer: C

The book drops by 5 Dollars. 5 Dollars as a percentage of the total of 25 dollars is 5/25 = 20 percent.

27. Correct answer: D

The first time, Brian answered 150 questions correctly and the second time he answered 30% more correctly, so,

150 + (30/100 × 150); 30% of 150 = 45, or (30 × 150)/100

so 150 + 45 = 195

28. Correct answer: B

Let us call this number x:

This number is increased by 2: x + 2

Then, it is multiplied by 3: 3(x + 2)

The result is 24: 3(x + 2) = 24 ... Solving this linear equation, we obtain the value of the number:

x + 2 = 24 / 3

x + 2 = 8

x = 8 − 2

x = 6

29. Correct answer: B

My age: x

My brother is 3 years older than me: x + 3

My father is 3 less than 2 times my age: 2x − 3

My father's age divided by 5 is equal to my brother's age divided by 3: (2x − 3) / 5 = (x + 3) / 3

By cross multiplication:

5(x + 3) = 3(2x − 3)

5x + 15 = 6x − 9

x = 24

My father's age: 2.24 − 3= 48 − 3 = 45

30. Correct answer: C

There are two fractions containing x and the denominators are different. First, let us find a common denominator to simplify the expression.

The least common multiplier of 4 and 7 is 28.

Then,

$7(x - 2) / 28 - 4(3x + 5) / 28 = - 3x\ 28 / 28$ ... Since both sides are written on the denominator 28 now, we can eliminate them:

$7(x - 2) - 4(3x + 5) = - 84$

$7x - 14 - 12x - 20 = - 84$

$- 5x = - 84 + 14 + 20$

$- 5x = - 50$

$x = 50/5$

$x = 10$

31. Correct answer: B

To find x:

$1 / (1 + 1 / (1 - 1/x)) = 4$

This means that $(1 + 1 / (1 - 1/x))$ is equal to 1/4. Then,

$1 + 1 / (1 - 1/x) = 1/4$

$1 / (1 - 1/x) = 1/4 - 1$

$1 / (1 - 1/x) = - 3/4$

This means that $1 - 1/x = - 4/3$. Then,

$1 - 1/x = - 4/3$

$1 + 4/3 = 1/x$

$1/x = 7/3$

So, $x = 3/7$.

32. Correct answer: A

If A and B are complementary,

A+B=90 .... Equation 1

The measure of angle B is three times the measure of angle A

B=3A..............Equation 2

Substituting the value of B from equation 2 in equation 1, we get

A+3A=90

4A=90 and hence A=22.5

Putting this value of A in either of the equations and solving for B, we get

B=67.5

Hence, A=22.5and B=67.5

33. Correct answer: D

Correct Answer is D. 68% equals 0.68

34. Correct answer: B

The difference between each value is 2,4,8, Blank.

If this pattern is followed and the blank space is 16, then the next value would be 32.

18 plus 16 is 34. (option B) and then you can confirm that 34 plus 32 (the logical next value for the difference, does in fact equal 66).

35. Correct answer: C

36. Correct answer: D

3(x-4) =18

Divide by 3 to get

x-4=6

then add 4 to find: x=10

ATI TEAS Reading

1. Correct answer: D.

Manning's work exemplifies how biography can be a powerful tool for a historian of science, who can use the genre to explore the effects of politics, economics, and emotions on the direction of scientific development.

This passage is mainly about the effectiveness of biography as a genre for exploring the history of science and the importance of analyzing scientific discoveries from a historical perspective. The business about Black Apollo is just an example the author uses to illustrate his point. So Choice A. is wrong because the passage's main point isn't the importance of Ernest Everett Just. Choice B. is a point the author makes in the last paragraph, but it's not the entire passage's main point. Choice C. appears in the second paragraph, but once again, it doesn't cover the whole passage. Choice D. looks like the right answer; it sums up the overarching theme of the passage.

2. Correct answer: A.

illuminate the effects of social forces on scientists in a way that scientists themselves are unlikely to do

According to the author, "One of the central principles of the history of science, indeed a central reason for the discipline, is to show that science is a product of social forces." That makes Choice A. look like a very good answer. Choice B. isn't exactly right. The author says people can learn scientific theories by reading the work of the scientists themselves. The drawback is that the picture given by scientists is incomplete because it ignores historical context. Choice C. is also imprecise. Historians of science do write biographies, but biographies are just one way to accomplish their main goal of revealing the social forces behind scientific discovery. Choice D. is wrong because the author never suggests that historians of science want to influence scientific research. Choice A. is right.

3. Correct answer: C.

to explain why biography is both a popular historical genre and a powerful medium for explaining the significance of scientific discoveries

The second paragraph contains a discussion of biography as a historical genre and lists its many advantages. Choice A. isn't at all the main point. It just barely appears in the paragraph. Choice B. is wrong; the author does believe biography is a good historical form for the historian of science. Choice C. looks like a good answer. Choice D. is incorrect; the author says that biographies are very good for teaching children. Choice C. is right.

4.   Correct answer: A.

One of the best ways to come to an understanding of the realities of race relations and scientific development in the 20th century is to read an in-depth account of the life of one of the people who lived and worked in that world.

Choice A. looks pretty good; this is in fact what the author has been saying about the history of science. Choice B. is wrong. The author doesn't think historians should glorify their subjects and notes that Manning doesn't glorify Just. Choice C. is also wrong. The author doesn't imply that a scientific history should downplay science simply because it's "history." Choice D. isn't right. The author explicitly says that Just wasn't the most significant scientist of his time. Choice A. is the best answer.

5.   Correct answer: D.

Just's daily experiences illuminate the conditions characterized by both scientific research and racial relations during his lifetime.

Here's what the passage says: "A comprehensive appreciation of the conditions that Just faced in his daily work offers a powerful lens through which to examine the development of science and racial boundaries in America." Choice D. looks like the answer that matches best with this statement. The other answers are all true, but they're also incidental, facts that add up to a bigger picture but by themselves aren't enough to create a significant history.

6.   Correct answer: D.

the straightforward organization of a biography, which follows the course of the subject's life

A biography is a story of a person's life; the format can't change that much. The author says, "Biographies simply tell a story." The phrase "simplicity of form" doesn't refer to language, so Choice A. is wrong, nor does it mean page design, so Choice B. is wrong. It doesn't mean simple writing style, so Choice C. is wrong. All the author means is that biographies have a standard format, which is fairly consistent from book to book; that makes Choice D. correct.

7.   Correct answer: C.

SLS and SLES are detergents that are commonly used in personal care products because they are effective and safe, despite unsubstantiated rumors to the contrary.

This passage introduces the reader to a couple of detergents commonly used in numerous household products. It describes how they work and mentions a few hazards associated with them. The reason the author mentions those hazards in the second paragraph is to get the facts in ahead of the risks that are solely based on rumor, because her point in the last paragraph is that many of the things people fear about SLS and SLES aren't based on fact. She obviously thinks SLS and SLES are safe as they're commonly used and believes that approval by the FDA and other scientific organizations is sufficient proof of this safety.

Choice A. is a possible answer, but it ignores the discussion of Internet detractors, so it doesn't cover the entire passage. Look for something with a more global application. Choice B. is wrong. The presence of "despite" suggests that the author thinks incorporating SLS or SLES into personal care products is irresponsible or dangerous, which isn't justified by the passage. Choice C. looks like a better answer than Choice A. because it incorporates more of the passage's information. Choice D. is wrong because this passage isn't about the Internet rumors but about counteracting them. Choice C. is the best answer.

8.   Correct answer: B.

shampoo, toothpaste, bathroom cleaners, and engine degreasers

You have to read carefully to answer this one. Don't assume any product contains the substances unless the passage tells you so. If you prefer, you can underline or circle substances that the author mentions in the passage in the answer choices — that makes it easier to see the ones that appear in the text. Choice A. is wrong because the author never mentions mouthwash, sunscreen, or hair dye. Choice B. looks good. They're all mentioned in the passage. Choice C. is wrong because the passage doesn't mention engine lubricants. Choice D. is wrong because moisturizer and baby wipes don't appear. Choice B. is correct.

9. Correct answer: D.

refute claims that SLS and SLES are dangerous

The author says that the rumors about SLS and SLES are absurd and unsubstantiated and "the FDA has approved the use of SLS and SLES in a number of personal care products." That means she's using FDA approval as evidence of the substances' safety. Choice A. looks like a possible answer, though it doesn't mention the author's suggestion that the FDA approval implies safety, so it misses the reason why the author brings up the FDA. Choice B. is wrong because even though the author thinks that the FDA has the best interests of consumers in mind, that isn't the reason why the author mentions the FDA. The purpose of mentioning the FDA is to provide evidence debunking the Internet myths. Choice C. doesn't work because the author isn't in fact suggesting that FDA approval of putting SLS and SLES in personal care products means that manufacturers don't have to test these products for safety. Choice D. works the best because the author mentions the FDA to achieve the larger goal of debunking the Internet rumors.

10. Correct answer: D.

burning eyes, burned skin after long exposure, and diarrhea if ingested in large quantities

Read the passage carefully. The answers to this question appear in the second paragraph, not in the third paragraph, which lists risks that haven't been proven. Skim the answer choices to cross off anything that appears in the third paragraph. Choice D. is the right answer. Every other choice contains ailments that Internet rumors have associated with SLS and SLES but that haven't been substantiated.

11. Correct answer: D.

a description of SLS and SLES and their uses; known risks of SLS and SLES; criticisms aimed at SLS and SLES by detractors on the Internet; evidence that SLS and SLES are safe and the rumors unfounded

Look for an answer that could function as an accurate ordering of all paragraphs in the passage. Choice A. isn't quite right because it leaves off the subject of the first paragraph. Choice B. is wrong. The passage doesn't contain any anecdotal accounts of SLS injuries. Choice C. doesn't work because the first paragraph doesn't describe the chemical composition of SLS and SLES. Choice D. is the best answer because it follows the structure of the passage closely.

12. Correct answer: D.

to explain why some people fear SLS and SLES and to list the diseases that Internet rumors have linked to the substances

The third paragraph discusses the Internet rumors that hold SLS and SLES responsible for a host of ailments without providing proof. The author obviously wants to discredit these rumors; that's what the last sentence is all about. She's not criticizing, so Choice A. is out. She's not describing the substances — that's in the first paragraph — so Choice B. is out. She doesn't believe these risks are real, so she's not warning anyone of anything, and Choice C. is out. She makes no proposals of alternate substances, so Choice D is the best answer here.

13. Correct answer: A.

It is unreasonable for people to be afraid of substances that have been deemed safe by the FDA and several other major organizations, and that have a long history of safe use, simply on the basis of unsubstantiated rumors.

Choice A. looks like a good possibility. The author does seem to think it's silly to believe rumors about substances that people have been using safely for years. Choice B. doesn't quite work. The author does trust the FDA but makes no mention of its sources of funding or mission. Choice C. is wrong. While the author clearly thinks that some Internet information isn't trustworthy, the passage doesn't provide sufficient information for you to infer how she feels about information available about other health topics. For example, she could easily think that the Internet supplies good information on heart disease. Choice D. doesn't work. The author does think SLS and SLES are cheap and effective surfactants and emulsifiers, but she doesn't think that they're unsafe to use in products that contact human skin. Choice A. is the best answer.

14. Correct answer: D.

the amount of time that has passed since the eyewitness experienced the event

Answer this question by eliminating answers that Passage A indicates have been researched to discover their effect on the accuracy of eyewitness testimony. The third paragraph comes right out and tells you that race, gender, and age have been studied, so Choices A and B are ruled out. The second paragraph states that "much research" has been done on the effects of witnesses who are asked misleading questions. A misleading question is a type of question, so you can infer that the effect of the question type on eyewitness accounts has been studied and cross out Choice C. You can reasonably assume that the amount of time that passes between an event and an eyewitness's account of that event would affect the accuracy of the testimony, but the question doesn't ask for your reasonable assumption. Because Passage A doesn't mention any studies conducted to see how time affects eyewitness testimony, Choice D. offers the exception. Remember to answer questions based solely on information in the passage, regardless of any outside or personal knowledge you may have on the subject matter.

15. Correct answer: B.

Eyewitness testimony is often flawed because it is influenced by a variety of factors.

The best answer incorporates a point suggested by both passages. Eliminate answers that can be supported by only one of the passages. Passage A makes the statement that there's no difference between the accuracy of male and female testimony, but Passage B doesn't discuss the role of gender, so Choice D. is supported by only one passage and can't be right. Although both passages mention that eyewitness testimony is affected by a number of variables, only Passage B discusses the importance of determining an error rate. Neither passage discusses how memory improves or declines over time, so Choice C. is out of contention. That leaves Choices A. and B. Choice A. doesn't seem likely. The first line of Passage A states that "there are many factors that may account for mistaken eyewitness identification" and then goes on to describe the research of these factors, which implies that mistaken eyewitness identification occurs frequently enough to warrant significant study. Passage B stresses the science of memory and human cognitive abilities and states that they're "not perfect." In the third paragraph, the author of Passage B points out that establishing an error rate involves an awareness of the many factors that affect eyewitness accounts. Neither passage suggests that eyewitness testimony is "highly" accurate, but both imply that accounts may be flawed by the influence of several factors or variables. Because it's a better answer than Choice A., Choice B. is correct.

16. Correct answer: A.

How the lighting in a particular event affects the reliability of eyewitness identification is a variable that warrants a good amount of study.

Your job is to eliminate reasonable implications of Passage A. The passage tells you that one's race can affect how well one recognizes someone's face, so it implies that one's race may adversely affect the reliability of an identification. Cross out Choice B. The passage justifies the statement in Choice C. It categorizes the factors as system variables and estimator variables. So Choice C. is wrong. The passage states that the majority of research has gone into studying system variables, and the makeup of a lineup is a system variable. So you can reasonably infer Choice D. from the statements in Passage A. The passage tells you that the way questions are worded is a system variable, and the judicial system has control over system variables. Therefore, the author of Passage A must think that the judicial system has control over whether a witness is asked misleading questions. Choice A. must be the answer. Passage A states that lighting can affect an eyewitness identification, but because lighting is an estimator variable over which the judicial system has little control, it's unlikely to receive much research. The passage states that system variables receive the majority of study. The best answer is Choice A.

17. Correct answer: D

To understand how memory and human cognitive abilities are affected by a variety of different factors

Both passages discuss memory and how it's affected by different factors; what differs is the factors they discuss. Passage A covers variables that include the age, race, and gender of eyewitnesses and the wording of the questions they're asked. Passage B emphasizes the complexity of memory and cognitive abilities. Rule out choices that pertain to one passage but not the other. Choice A. is a concern of Passage B but isn't mentioned in Passage A, so it's wrong. Choice C is important to Passage A but not to Passage B. Choice B. isn't a goal of either passage. Passage B does indeed mention episodic memory, aside from defining the term, the passage doesn't show how the concept contributes to judicial proceedings. By process of elimination, the best answer is Choice D. Both passages deal with the complex factors that affect cognitive ability and memory as they relate to the accuracy of eyewitness testimony.

18. Correct answer: D.

Both passages concern improving eyewitness accuracy, but Passage A focuses on controlling variables and Passage B concentrates on understanding the science behind human recollection.

You can eliminate some answers quickly because they aren't true. Choice A. is wrong because Passage B doesn't discuss witness questioning and therefore doesn't dismiss its importance. Choice B. isn't right because how the judicial system controls certain variables is a concern of Passage A, not Passage B. because both passages deal with how research can improve eyewitness accuracy: through research of system variables for Passage A and the establishment of an error rate in Passage B. Choice C. may be tempting because Passage A mentions the effect of race on eyewitness identification, but the way the question is worded implies that Passage B does indeed discuss race, at least to some degree, which is inaccurate. Choice D. is the only option that appropriately defines a noticeable difference between the content of the two passages. The primary focus of Passage A is the variables that affect the accuracy of eyewitness identification. Passage B is more concerned with the workings of the human mind and how this knowledge can be used to establish an error rate for witness testimony. Choice D. is best.

19. Correct answer: D.

Lighting issues and the length of time someone witnessed an event are examples of system variables.

This question asks you for the statement that isn't supported by either passage. Eliminate answers that appear in either of the two passages. Choice A.is a premise of both passages;

they both state that human memory doesn't get it right every time. Passage B says that eyewitness memory should make "guilty people seem more likely to be guilty," and Choice C. seems to paraphrase that statement. Passage B's first paragraph states that cognitive abilities are incredible and supports that statement with the assertion that visual, auditory, olfactory, tactile, and taste information synchronizes with past information to bring that information into the present, so the statement in Choice B. is supported by Passage B. If you thought Choice D. was supported by Passage A, you confused system variables with estimator variables. Lighting issues and the length of time someone witnessed an event are actually examples of estimator variables. Choice D. is the answer that neither passage supports.

20. Correct answer: C.

the philosophical origins of public schools in 18th century Germany and the transformation in educational thinking in the 19th century.

This passage is about the origins of public education and the changes that occurred in educational philosophy in the first century of public schools; the whole thing is set in Germany. Choice A. doesn't cover the whole passage; the political message seems to apply only to the first half. Choice B. also focuses on just the first half and so isn't the passage's primary point. The final paragraph doesn't focus on exploitation at all. Choice C. conveys the passage's overarching theme. Choice D. is wrong because the passage doesn't get into modern educational practices. Choice C. is correct.

21. Correct answer: C.

They were indifferent to the well-being and needs of their workers, caring only to maximize production and profits no matter what it cost their employees.

The author tells you that textile mill owners exploited their workers badly enough to incite revolts and that they embraced the concept of schools in the hopes that it would make the workers more docile. Choice A. is quite wrong. The first schools weren't created to help the students so much as to help the nobles. Choice B. could well be true, but the passage doesn't discuss it. Remember, all correct answers must not stray too far from the text. Choice C. fits well with what the passage says about the owners. It does appear that they were indifferent to the well-being of their workers. Choice D. isn't quite right. The passage doesn't specifically tell you that they were all aristocrats. Although some of them may have believed their authority was divinely ordained, you can't assume that was true of them all, nor is there any reason for you to assume that they cared about nurturing their workers. Choice C. is the best answer.

22. Correct answer: B.

Eighteenth-century schools were concerned primarily with teaching working-class children to accept their fate and love their ruler; 19th-century schools began to focus on developing the full human potential of students.

The educational difference between the two centuries was philosophical. Schools in the 1700s were meant for workers and intended to instill patriotism and gratitude toward the government into their students, but schools in the 1800s aspired to develop children to their full potential. Choice A. isn't right because 18th-century schools had nothing to do with efficient textile mills. Choice B. looks like a very good answer. Choice C. doesn't work because 18th-century schools were for the children of workers, not the aristocracy, and in the 19th century, no one had to spin anymore. Choice D. is tricky because it's very close to being correct, but the passage doesn't tell you that 19th-century schools aspired to create free-thinking students in general (though academic freedom was prized for advanced students), so it's wrong. Choice B. is the right answer.

23. Correct answer: A.

riots and other forms of violence against the owners of textile factories by peasants unhappy at their treatment.

Look at the sentence after the one that mentions increasing levels of unrest. It says that the rulers wanted "to channel the energy of restless peasants into something that would be less dangerous to the throne than riots." So "unrest" must mean riots and other violent uprisings by workers who disliked their lot in life. That would be Choice A. None of the other answers work. Choice A. is correct.

24. Correct answer: D.

They liked the idea because it would make the peasantry more complacent and accepting of their fate, which would help keep the aristocracy safe in their prosperity.

According to the passage: "Aristocrats liked this idea. They liked the thought of schools making peasants more docile and patriotic, and they appreciated the way state-run schools would teach children of lower social classes to accept their position in life." Choice A. is wrong because the schools were intended to do just the opposite; educating workers was supposed to make them more docile, not more violent. Choice B. doesn't work because the passage never mentions aristocratic resentment of taxes. Choice C. may be a true statement, but the passage doesn't directly come out and say it. You know nothing of the aristocratic opinions of Schlabrendorff himself. Choice D. is the most suitable answer to this question.

25. Correct answer: B.

to take away the authority of parents and replace it with state power over children and citizens.

The truant officers were meant to take away parental authority over children and replace it with state control. Choice B. is the most accurate answer. The truant officers weren't there to make sure every child was educated, so Choice A. is wrong. They didn't help or indoctrinate parents or children, nor did they recruit boys into the army, which nixes Choices C. and D. Choice B. is best.

26. Correct answer: D.

People learn best in an environment that respects their individuality, affords them freedom, and incorporates a variety of aspects of learning, such as physical movement, manual skills, and independent exploration.

Nineteenth-century educational theorists believed in nurturing innate abilities and using holistic techniques. That's not Choice A. In fact, Choice A. is just the opposite of what experts thought in the 1800s. Choice B. is wrong because nothing in the passage mentions religion. Choice C. isn't right. The passage never suggests that the state has an interest in an educated citizenry, just an interest in a docile and patriotic one, and that wasn't the prevailing view in the 19th century anyway. Choice D. looks like a perfect answer to this question. That makes Choice D. correct.

27. **Correct answer: A.**

The purpose of the passage is to discuss ECP

A. and why it was enacted.

B. This is an issue that is addressed in the passage, but it is not the major issue of the passage.

C. The brilliance of the drafters cannot be said to have been exalted. Instead, the ECPA is said to be confusing and unusually complicated.

D. This statement is not made by the passage.

28. **Correct answer: D.**

Public network service providers are said to be indifferent to the rights of their users because the providers are so tenuously connected to the users.

A. This word is not an accurate description.

B. The service providers do not completely ignore the rights of their users; they are just disinclined to jump through legal hoops to protect those rights.

C. This word is not an accurate description.

D. Correct

29. **Correct answer: D.**

The author describes how the added importance and growth of cyberspace has created legal issues regarding privacy that are not covered by the Fourth Amendment. In order to protect the spirit of the Constitution, ECPA was drafted to outline the rights of Internet users.

A. This statement was not made in the passage. It was merely said that they are easier to gain than search warrants.

B. The passage does not say that service providers protect no rights, just that they do not protect the rights of privacy zealously.

C. This statement is not really supported by the passage; the ECPA protects rights where they deserve to be protected, not where there is a "need for privacy."

30. Correct answer: B.

It was hard to tell what the Fourth Amendment would and would not allow in cyberspace.

A. The opposite was stated.

(C–D) These words do not describe the effects of the Fourth Amendment.

31. Correct answer: D.

The purpose was to contrast that which the Fourth Amendment was designed to protect with that which it is currently being used to protect, namely, computers on the Internet.

A. This statement is partially true, but this is not a place where the gaps would be filled in.

B. There is no mention of cyber homes in the passage.

C. This is not the case.

32. Correct answer: B.

This is stated explicitly

A. This point is not stated or implied by the pas-sage.

C. The opposite is stated to be true.

D. This statement is not true. The Fourth Amendment still applies to our homes.

33. Correct answer: D.

The passage relates the facts surrounding the dissolution of the U.S.S.R, and Russia's reemergence onto the global scene. It goes on to tell how Russia has had to change in order to adapt to the new system of government.

A. This description was true of the other governments also.

B. It was never stated that this was the only thing wrong with Russian politics.

C. It was not stated that the inability to tap into Siberian resources hurt the Soviet Union in any way.

34. **Correct answer: D.**

A. The Russian Federation came into existence after 1991.

B. According to the passage, Yeltsin came onto the scene after 1991.

C. Europe did not break up the Soviet Union. The Soviet Union was destroyed in an internal coup.

35. **Correct answer: C.**

The "monolithic union" refers to the unified states under the Soviet Union.

A. The word monolithic is used to describe "unwieldy" and "large" instead of "stone."

B. This could be correct if the date preceded 1991, but afterward there was no sense of indestructibility.

D. This point is not mentioned in the passage.

36. **Correct answer: A.**

This passage explains the implications of the breakup of the Soviet Union.

B. The passage makes no such claim.

C. There is no explanation of the short-term goals of the smaller republics.

D. This point was hinted at by the paragraph, but the purpose of the paragraph is to explain how the states would need to reorganize, not to cast blame.

37. Correct answer: A.

This view was shown by their preference to avoid living in Siberia.

    B. This statement is not true. There is thought to be almost a vacuum of power in the region since the fall of the Soviet Union.

    C. This inference is not accurate.

    D. This is a contradiction in terms. Favorably desolate?

38. Correct answer: D.

Nothing is said about Russia currently being benevolent or corruption free.

    A. The passage makes this point

    B. The passage makes this point.

    C. The passage makes this point

39. Correct answer: C

One general class, one division, and one section.

This question is asking for a detail stated in the passage. The Dewey Decimal System is outlined in the first paragraph, which states that titles are arranged "into 10 classes, with 10 divisions each, with each division having 10 sections." This matches answer choice (C). Choices (A) and (B) each omit at least one part, and choice (D) would be found in the Library of Congress Classification.

40. Correct answer: B

Named after a person

The question is asking for the meaning of a word as used in the passage. Research the first sentence for context clues. This sentence introduces Melvil Dewey and the system that carries his name. Answer choice (B) clearly relates to the meaning of the sentence. There is no suggestion that the new system was the most important one or uniquely innovative (it could have been based on a previous system), making (A) and (C) incorrect. Nothing in the passage indicates that the Dewey Decimal System is logical and simple to use, as in (D).

41. Correct Answer: D

by Date of Acquisition

This is stated in the passage.

42. Correct answer: A

500

This is stated in the passage

43. Correct answer: D

Rustic Campsite in February

The question asks for an inference about the least expensive accommodations. Research the passage for information about rates. The next-to-last sentence notes that all accommodations are less expensive during the off season, so you can infer that choice (A) is less expensive than (B) and that choice (D) is less expensive than (C). Eliminate (B) and (C). Now determine which costs less, the Simple Bungalow or the Rustic Campsite. The passage introduces the cabins by saying they are appropriate for those with "the budget for a few amenities." (Amenities are comforts or conveniences.) This statement suggests that the indoor options are more expensive than the preceding outdoor options. Thus, you can infer that a Rustic Campsite rents for a lower rate than a Simple Bungalow, and choice (D) is correct.

44. Correct answer: C

None

None although there is a closed season, the passage indicates the park is open all year.

45. Correct answer: C.

Telephone

This is stated in the passage.

46. Correct answer: A.

Families

This is implied in the passage.

47. Correct answer: A.

Luxury Cottage

This is implied in the passage, although not explicitly stated.

48. Correct answer: C

The passage was written to analyze the works by Chang-Rae Lee and the themes presented in his most famous novels.

49. Correct answer: A

The author of this passage uses the first line of the novel to provide an example of one of the themes of the novel.

50. Correct answer: B

Espionage is part of the plot of the novel Native Speaker, but it is not a theme that recurs in Lee's works.

51. Correct answer: D

The passage states that Lee's interests in cultural identity and race emerge from his own experiences with these issues as a young immigrant to America.

52. Correct answer: D

The tone of the last paragraph suggests concern over the preservation of cultural identities in an increasingly mixed and expanding world.

53. Correct answer: B

The passage indicates that the formula increases or boosts the absorption of minerals in the body.

ATI TEAS Science

1. Correct answer: A

Gas particles are in random, rapid motion because they have high amounts of kinetic energy. Kinetic energy is the energy of motion and this leads to gas particle's ability to sustain rapid movement. Conversely, a solid would have the lowest amount of kinetic energy of all the states of matter but would have more potential energy. Energy is stored in chemical bonds and a solid has chemical bonds that are strong, keeping it a solid, whereas a gas has no bonds and no stored energy. The total energy of any state of matter is constant. What varies is the amount of potential and kinetic energy present. So, if the kinetic energy is high in a state of matter, then the potential energy must be low and vice versa.

2. Correct answer: D

Mathematical models are essential in drawing quantitative conclusions based on both quantitative and qualitative data. Mathematical models are also the underlying foundations of technology, without which would make everyday life more challenging. Mathematical models can help to disprove a hypothesis or confirm a hypothesis and can also be used to infer further data outside of the collected data. Mathematical models can be used for predictive purposes, as long as the parameters of the input data are well defined.

3. Correct answer: D

Though the data shows that at 35°C more of the substrate is consumed, signaling an active rate of photosynthesis. However, the increments in temperature are wide and the optimal temperature for the enzyme may not be modeled in the experiment. For example, the optimal temperature for the enzyme may actually be closer to 40°C. A follow-up experiment would need to be conducted using temperatures near the 35°C mark but with smaller increments to isolate the exact optimal temperature.

4. Correct answer: D

The three subatomic particles of an atom are: protons, neutrons, and electrons. The nucleus of an atom contains the weight of the atom and is made up of both protons and neutrons.

Electrons orbit around the nucleus in orbitals or in the electron cloud.

5.   Correct answer: C

CO_2 Is a gas, and to measure the amount exhaled, the best method would be to record the volume in litres, as the other units given are not units of measurement for volume.

6.   Correct answer: C

The chloroplast is important for photosynthesis in plants and the mitochondria is essential for cellular respiration in both plants and animals. Both are organelles that have a double membrane and have their own DNA. The DNA in these organelles is maternal DNA, that is only inherited by the mother of the organism. DNA in all forms is double stranded and neither the mitochondria nor the chloroplast contain any forms of RNA.

7.   Correct answer: B

A prokaryote does not have a nucleus, whereas a eukaryote has a nucleus. This is one of the most common distinguishing factors between these two types of organisms. Prokaryotes are able to perform many of the same molecular functions that a eukaryote is able to do like: cellular respiration, DNA replication, and protein synthesis. These processes are often less complicated and done quicker in the prokaryotic cell.

8.   Correct answer: D

Water is said to be polar, which means that there are opposite charges (+ and -) in the water molecule. This allows water to attract to other polar and ionic compounds and pull the compounds apart, therefore dissolving them. A solvent is a compound that is able to dissolve other compounds. A solute is the compound that gets dissolved. Water is not dissolved, but instead water is the compound that dissolves other compounds, therefore water is a solvent. As a note: water is unable to dissolve oils and fats because these compounds are non-polar and do not have charges that water can attract to and pull apart.

9.   Correct answer: B

The three primary germ layers of the embryo include: the ectoderm, endoderm, and mesoderm. The interoderm is not an actual term in biology. The endoderm forms the gastrointestinal tract, the lungs, the pharynx and parts of the urinary system. The ectoderm forms the skin (or epidermis) and related structures like hair and nails, as well as the brain and spinal cord. It is the mesoderm that differentiates during embryonic development to form connective tissues like cartilage, bone, and muscle.

10. Correct answer: A

During photosynthesis, water and carbon dioxide are used in conjunction with light to make oxygen and glucose. The formula for glucose is $C_6H_{12}O_6$, not the $C_5H_{10}O_2$ listed as an answer option. The only byproduct of photosynthesis in the answer options is oxygen or O_2.

11. Correct answer: A

All three animals belong to the same kingdom of Animalia, but are too different to be classed in the same phylum. Cheetahs and rainbow trout are in the Chordata phylum, while inchworms are in Arthropoda phylum.

12. Correct answer: C

In the same family, elements with similar chemical and physical properties are located in the same column on the periodic table. Columns on the periodic table are called families or groups. The rows of a periodic table cut across different families and no general statement can be made about the similarities of elements within a row. A row is also called a period. Elements with similar characteristics would have similar valence shells (the outer most orbital) or outer electrons, but may not have the exact same inner orbital shells.

13. Correct answer: D

Cellular respiration is the process where sugar, in the form of glucose, is broken down by extract in energy from the covalent bonds. The steps of cellular respiration include: glycolysis, Krebs cycle, and the Electron Transport Chain. During this process energy from the glucose molecule is temporarily stored in NADH and $FADH_2$. These are referred to as energy-carrying molecules that transport energy to the Electron Transport Chain located in the mitochondrial inner membrane where the energy is converted into ATP. The main organelle responsible for cellular respiration is the mitochondria.

14. Correct answer: C

The circulatory system involves the movement of blood from the heart to the lungs to absorb oxygen and the movement of blood from the heart to the body's cells. The latter circulation is referred to as systemic circulation and the former is pulmonary circulation.

15. Correct answer: D

Fitness in biological terms refers to an organism's ability to produce viable offspring that are also able to reproduce in later generations. Organisms that have a low fitness can either be infertile or produce offspring that die before reaching reproducing age. Those organisms with a high fitness are considered to be better adapted to the environment.

16. Correct answer: B

Hydrogen bonding is a strong type of intermolecular force that prevents water molecules from evaporating. Water does evaporate when there is enough heat to break the hydrogen bonds. In comparison to other liquid compounds water is not as volatile and does not evaporate very easily due to these strong bonds between water molecules. Water is an example of covalent bonding (bonding between non-metal elements), however this alone does not account for water's inability to evaporate easily.

17. Correct answer: A

In Linnaeus' classification system organisms are grouped/classified according to their kingdom, then the phylum, class, order, family, genus, and species. The less restrictive groupings would be the Kingdom and Phylum as many organisms may fit under the same grouping in these categories, as organisms are assigned to families, genus, and species, the classifications become more and more specific. An order is less restrictive (more inclusive) than the family category.

18. Correct answer: D

The finches though similar enough to be categorized as finches, did differ in their color patterns, head size/shape and beak size/shape. Darwin proposed that this change was due to the finches adapting to their natural habitat. The climate on each of the Galapagos islands differed and as a result the vegetation and habitat differed among the islands. According to Darwin's theory of natural selection, organisms adapt to their environment and this adapting process will influence the physical appearance of an organism.

19. Correct answer: D

The aorta is responsible for pumping oxygenated blood from the heart to the upper and lower extremities. If the aorta is not functioning correctly and is unable to pump oxygenated blood, this would most likely result in the death of cells throughout the body, as cells need oxygen to perform cellular respiration to generate energy within the cell.

20. Correct answer: B

Interphase is part of the cell cycle and is responsible for getting the cell prepared to divide. During the S phase of interphase, DNA is replicated inside of the nucleus with the help of DNA Polymerase.

The cell must replicate its DNA prior to undergoing cell division (either mitosis or meiosis). When the cell divides, each cell receives an equal amount of DNA. The other phases of interphase include G1 and G2, which are characterized by the replication of the organelles and other components of the cell.

21. Correct answer: B

The cellular hierarchy starts with the cell, the simplest structure, and progresses to organisms, the most complex structures.

22. Correct answer: C

A hypertonic solution is a solution with a higher particle concentration than in the cell, and consequently lower water content than in the cell. Water moves from the cell to the solution, causing the cell to experience water loss and shrink.

23. Correct answer: D

Interphase is the period when the DNA is replicated (or when the chromosomes are replicated) and is the longest part of the cell cycle.

24. Correct answer: D

Recessive alleles are represented by lower case letters, while dominant alleles are represented by upper case letters.

25. Correct answer: B

Dominant genes are always expressed when both alleles are dominant (BB) or when one is dominant and one is recessive (Bg). In this case, 3/4 or 75% will have brown eyes.

26. Correct answer: C

Groups of cells that perform the same function are called tissues.

27. Correct answer: A

The nuclear division of somatic cells takes place during mitosis.

28. Correct answer: A

The immune system consists of the lymphatic system, spleen, tonsils, thymus and bone marrow.

29. Correct answer: D

The rate at which a chemical reaction occurs does not depend on the amount of mass lost, since the law of conservation of mass (or matter) states that in a chemical reaction there is no loss of mass.

30. Correct answer: B

Boyle's law states that for a constant mass and temperature, pressure and volume are related inversely to one another: PV = c, where c = constant.

31. Correct answer: C

Both prokaryotes and eukaryotes interact with the extracellular environment and use membrane-bound or membrane-associated proteins to achieve this. They both use diffusion and active transport to move materials in and out of their cells. Prokaryotes have very few proteins associated with their DNA, whereas eukaryotes' DNA is richly studded with proteins.

Both types of living things can have flagella, although with different structural characteristics in the two groups. The most important differences between prokaryotes and eukaryotes are the lack of a nucleus and membrane-bound organelles in prokaryotes.

32. Correct answer: A

A ribosome is a structure of eukaryotic cells that makes proteins.

33. Correct answer: D

A xylem is an example of a tissue. A liver is an organ, a mammal is a type of organism, and a hamstring is a muscle.

34. Correct answer: A

The adrenal glands are part of the endocrine system. They sit on the kidneys and produce hormones that regulate salt and water balance and influence blood pressure and heart rate.

35. Correct answer: D

An ionic bond forms when one atom donates an electron from its outer shell, called a valence electron, to another atom to form two oppositely charged atoms.

36. Correct answer: B

Figure 1 provides information on the compositions of mountain peaks. At a distance of 9 km along the mountain range, the peak composition is shown in the key as shale. This supports answer choice B.

37. Correct answer: A

To determine the correct answer, you must look at the key in Figure 1, which shows the different composition of the mountain peaks. It defines limestone as "particles with diameters under 0.5 mm," shale as "composed mostly of particles with diameters under 175 mm," and slate as, "composed mostly of particles with diameters over 175 mm."

The only difference between the different compositions is the size of the particle, answer choice A.

38. Correct answer: C

As the peak section heights in Table 1 increase, the percentage of the year that peak section is exposed to wind also increases. The highest percentage shown is 48%.

39. Correct answer: A

Figure 2 shows that Peak D is exposed to wind erosion for a greater percentage of the year than Peak C. Table 1 suggests that the percentage of the peak exposed to wind is directly proportional to peak section height. Therefore, because Peak D is exposed to the wind for longer than Peak C is, Peak D must be taller than Peak C. This information best supports answer choice A.

40. Correct answer: C

Table 1 shows that as the peak section height increases by equal increments, the percentage of the year that peak section is exposed to wind also increases by approximately the same amount. Therefore, the slope of the graph is positive and the graph is a straight line as shown in answer choice C.

41. Correct answer: C

The passage starters that the peaks of mountains have a higher number of deposits.

42. Correct answer: D

Deductive reasoning starts with basic premises that are assumed to be correct, and draws a specific logical conclusion. It often follows the logic: A ➞ B, C ➞ A, therefore C ➞ B. (C) might be tempting, but is an example of inductive reasoning. (A) and (B) are logically flawed.

43. Correct answer: B

Disc herniation occurs when the inner core of a disc in the spine leaks out through the outer portion of the disc. This type of spinal injury is usually caused by an injury to the back and/or spine. Whiplash suffered from a minor impact could potentially cause a herniated disc.

44. Correct answer: C

Atomic number is the number of protons.

45. Correct answer: C

The autonomic nervous system controls voluntary actions, while the autonomic nervous system functions primarily below the level of consciousness, to control functions such as digestion, heart rate, respiratory rate, perspiration, salivation, swallowing, and breathing. The central nervous system consists of the spinal cord and brain.

46. Correct answer: A

During photosynthesis, water and carbon dioxide are absorbed by the plant and converted to glucose and oxygen.

47. Correct answer: B

Since the frog is inside the triangle, and the key indicates the triangle represents amphibians, it is logical to conclude that the frog is a type of amphibian.

48. Correct answer: D

While all the amphibians are located inside the "circle" of vertebrates, there is nothing to indicate that ALL vertebrates are amphibians.

49. Correct answer: C

Hydrogen bonds form between the bases to stabilize the double helix structure of DNA.

50. Correct answer: D

The nervous system triggers the muscular system to move the hand away. The nervous system is responsible for communication between the different body systems. In the example provided, the nervous system activates first and sends a signal to the muscles to move in order to avoid damaging the body. The muscular system is responsible for movement, the skeletal system provides structure to the body, and the endocrine system is responsible for regulating hormones within the body.

51. Correct answer: A

When light hits an object, the object absorbs some of the light and reflects the rest of it. The wavelengths that are reflected determine how our eye perceives the color. We see a red dress as "red" because those wavelengths are reflected and not absorbed.

52. Correct answer: B

In an experiment, an "independent variable" is a factor controlled by the scientists. A "dependent variable" represents the output or effect. Since the light is controlled by the experimenters, it is an independent variable.

53. Correct answer: C

The endocrine system is the collection of glands that regulate metabolism, growth and development, tissue function, sexual function, reproduction, sleep and mood, among other things. Also 'Regulating' is a big hint in this problem.

Grading your ATI TEAS

ATI TEAS GRADING

The ATI TEAS exam uses a complex a grading system in which the questions are given a variety of point values. This grading system is known as equating. You will not be able to know which of the questions will receive more weight, so test-takers are advised to complete the test while maintaining a mindset that each question has the same value.

The TEAS score report will also detail the percentage of questions there was answered correctly, for each sub-section. The report includes suggested areas that could likely benefit from additional studying.

When you're grading your practice test, calculate a total percentage and then check against your nursing school's requirements. All schools require different percentages to get in, so it will vary each time. However, I would advise that most are in the 60-70% area.

Final Advice for ATI TEAS

ATI TEAS Reading Tips

The ATI TEAS Reading section is 64 minutes long and contains 53 questions. The questions are often preceded by a long or short passage.

It is easier to first read the questions and then read the document. This will give you an understanding of what the passage requires your attention to be centered on.

Questions beginning with "logically conclude" would always seem obvious to you. Don't be inclined to make conclusions about the document that you understand yourself — try to stick to the truth in the document.

You should be able to determine the difference between perception and reality in other questions. If you are not used to such questions, it can be tricky to understand the distinction between fact (the grass is green) and perception (the grass is beautiful).

Know multiple types of writing, including convincing and insightful types of writing.

Seek to improve the speed at which you read and your ability to interpret beforehand. You want to make sure you can finish the section before the time comes.

Handle your time! Ensure that you're trying to speed up through the questions and don't spend too long per question. Practice reading a variety of document your home with teas and guess how long you have to spend on each question.

Please take note of how a question is worded. The wording in the question itself typically gives you useful clues to find the right answer.

ATI TEAS Math Tips

36 questions will be answered in 54 minutes in the ATI TEAS Math segment. The problems include arithmetic, algebra, calculation and data.

You could be a little rusty if you haven't practiced math in recent times. Take some time to review some mathematical calculations needed for the TEAS mathematics section.

Be mindful of what in the examination hall you can and can't do. The ATI TEAS can be taken with a 4 function calculator, this will on screen in the computerized test and a 4 function calculator if you take the test on paper. Be sure you have a real calculator, not your phone or screen, to practice in a realistic manner.

Study the four fundamental features, including fractions, ratios and percentages (addition, subtraction, multiplication and division).

Make sure that you know how percent, decimals and fractions are converted.

Be sure you are able to add, subtract and divide fractions.

Make sure that you are up to speed with arithmetic rules.

ATI TEAS Science Tips

The ATI TEAS Science section is 63 minutes long with 53 questions. It is one of the most difficult sections and has questions mainly on human anatomy, but also on scientific reasoning, and life and physical sciences.

The TEAS Science section differs from the rest of the sections because it requires a great deal of prior knowledge. Therefore, this section may require extra preparation. Hence in this book I have included much more detail in the science chapter. Factor this into your study time!

Overall, you will be expected to have basic knowledge of various processes involved in chemistry, physics, biology and the natural world.

Make sure you know some quick facts about population growth and decline, and birth and fertility rates.

Most questions will focus on the body's systems, anatomy, and physiology.

Brush up on your knowledge of the periodic table! If you are anything like me, you probably blocked that word from your memory.

Pay special attention—you will be asked not only factual questions but also scientific reasoning questions. They might present you with an experiment, and ask for different interpretations and explanations.

ATI TEAS English and Language Usage Tips

The ATI TEAS English and Language Usage section is 28 minutes long and contains 28 questions. Expect questions on grammar, spelling and sentence structure.

In this section, certain questions will take longer to answer than others. For example, it might be quicker to resolve simple spelling mistakes, and take you longer to assemble proper grammar for a passage.

Review grammar rules! Make sure you know the names of the various grammar terms, and what they mean (i.e. subject-verb rules, pronoun- antecedent rules etc.)

Be able to identify different parts of speech (possessives, pronouns, adjectives, etc.)

Context clues are your friend in this section. If you are not sure about the meaning of the word, use context clues and process of elimination.

Understand word structure! Learn the meaning of common prefixes and suffixes.

Know the rules of punctuation.

Bottom line, don't assume that you don't need to prepare for this section. A lot of it you haven't met since school.

Good Luck!

So that's it! You've done the practice test; I hope it went well. I wish you the best of luck in your future endeavors and hope that you make it to the school that you want! Your job now is to keep practicing and preparing, use my advice for test preparation, and may I take this opportunity to wish you good luck!

Made in the USA
Monee, IL
01 March 2021